INVENTING THE NATION

General Editor: Keith Robbins

Already published in the Inventing the Nation series:

India and Pakistan	Ian Talbot
Russia	Vera Tolz
Italy	Nicholas Doumanis

Titles in preparation include:

China	Henrietta Harrison
Ireland	R.V. Comerford
Germany	Stefan Berger
France	Timothy Baycroft
The United States of America	Richard Carwardine

Italy

Nicholas Doumanis

Department of History
University of Sydney

A member of the Hodder Headline Group
LONDON
Co-published in the United States of America by
Oxford University Press Inc., London

First published in Great Britain in 2001 by
Arnold, a member of the Hodder Headline Group,
338 Euston Road, London NW1 3BH

http://www.arnoldpublishers.com

Co-published in the United States of America by
Oxford University Press Inc.,
198 Madison Avenue, New York, NY10016

British Library Cataloguing in Publication Data
A catalogue record for this book is available from the British Library

Library of Congress Cataloging-in-Publication Data
A catalog record for this book is available from the Library of Congress

ISBN 0 340 691603 (hb)
ISBN 0 340 691611 (pb)

Production Editor: James Rabson
Production Controller: Martin Kerans
Cover Design: Terry Griffiths

Typeset in 10 on 12 pt Sabon by Cambrian Typesetters, Frimley, Surrey
Printed and bound in Great Britain by MPG Books Ltd, Bodmin, Cornwall

This book is dedicated to Helen,
with all my love

Contents

General Editor's Preface

The contemporary world is both repelled and attracted by the existence of the nation. Talk of globalisation sometimes presumes that the nation will fade away as organisations and individuals build for themselves new networks which by-pass the commonalities and loyalties expressed in the idea of the nation. Nationalism, too, whenever it is that various writers have supposed it to have 'risen', has been held to have been an unmitigated disaster, at least when it has been accompanied, as it not infrequently has been, by virulent xenophobia and intolerance. In the twentieth century there were significant attempts to restrain or circumvent the influence of nationalism by creating international or supranational structures and agencies.

On the other hand, it is apparent that the nation has not in fact faded away and, despite the surge of new nations, or at least new states, in the second half of that century, there remain across the contemporary world communities which feel themselves to be nations, or are in the process of becoming nations, and who see in the attainment of statehood a legitimate, desirable and beneficial goal. In other contexts, too, old nations reaffirm themselves as necessary carriers of individuality and distinctiveness in a world threatened by homogeneity. It is asserted that the nation remains the essential building block in the structure of the contemporary world. Nationalism need not be vicious. Nations can and do speak peace unto nations.

It becomes clear, however, reading references of 'narrow nationalism' on the one hand or 'national liberation' on the other, that how particular nations come to exist or be defined remains obscure and contentious. This series revisits these issues in the light of extensive debates about national identity which have been conducted over recent decades by historians, anthropologists, political scientists and sociologists in particular. To speak of 'Inventing the Nation' picks up one of the interpretations which has gained favour, or at least excited interest. Influential writers have seen 'invention' taking place in Europe in the 'springtime of the nations' at the dawn of 'modern' history, though their explanations have varied. Others, however, have regarded 'invention' with some suspicion and identify a medieval if not primordial 'nation'. Problems of definition and location clearly abound.

The history of Italy has a special place in such a context. Its 'unification' seemed to many nineteenth-century observers to be a shining example for all Europe to emulate. If one was swept along by Mazzini one could envisage a future in which all liberated nations would live together in beneficent harmony. Italy's 'special mission' had implications far beyond the boundaries of the peninsula. Was it not remarkable that the eight separate states of 1815, most of them more or less subjected to Austrian influence, turned into the single Kingdom of Italy? Here apparently was a story of unvarnished progress. Mr. Gladstone, then a Conservative, went to Naples in the autumn of 1850, saw liberals in prison and returned to write revolutionary pamphlets against the Neapolitan regime. He formed a moral and passionate conviction that justice for Italians demanded a united Italy and therefore the overthrow of kings, dukes, the Austrian Emperor and the Pope. Later, the English historian G..M. Trevelyan was captivated by 'the story of Italian freedom'. He devoted himself to the life a Garibaldi, a man far above base racial pride. Italy's struggle, for Trevelyan, was 'a part of the imperishable and international poetry of the European races'. Even as the volumes were published, however, (1907–11) he was already wondering whether the Risorgimento had proceeded too rapidly. Italy was still divided between the prosperous and industrializing North and the impoverished agrarian south. The civil service was incompetent or corrupt, or both. The remark of the Piedmontese statesman D'Azeglio – 'We have made Italy – now we must make Italians' – had enduring force in the twentieth century. The making of 'united Italy' might be one thing, the creation of an 'Italian nation' another. In addition, the appearance of Fascism added another complication to this simple success story. The extent to which it inherited, distorted or destroyed the nineteenth-century legacy has remained controversial, a controversy whose political implications go beyond the realms of academic history. So, in exploring the 'story of Italian freedom' Dr. Doumanis is dealing with a subject which is not a 'done deed' but one which, as he shows, has even given rise, on occasion, to internal tensions which some have supposed might yet lead to 'The Unmaking of Italian Unity'.

Keith Robbins
Vice-Chancellor
University of Wales, Lampeter

Acknowledgements

I should particularly like to thank the Australian Research Council for allowing me to finish this book and to continue working on other projects that have nothing to do with Italy. To the Department of History at the University of Sydney, which provided an ideal environment in which to write, and my former colleagues at the University of Newcastle, particularly David Lemmings, Claire Walker, Chris Dixon, Hilary Carey and Wayne Reynolds, I extend my warmest thanks. I am especially grateful for Richard Bosworth's generous support over the years. Other people I would like to thank are Christopher Wheeler, Vanessa Mitchell, Keith Robbins, Richard Waterhouse and Milan Voykovic.

Introduction

Most historians agree that the nation is a relatively recent invention. The contemporary world consists of a collection of nations-states, none of which existed before the eighteenth century, and most of which came into being within the last fifty years. Nowadays, and despite the triumphal march of globalization, society continues to regard the nation as the political, economic and cultural unit that holds primary significance. How the nation came to acquire such deep cultural resonance and became so entrenched in modern everyday life is one of the most exciting, yet difficult, matters being debated among historians, cultural theorists and social scientists today.

For historians especially, difficulty arises from the mere fact that the nation is a subjective construct, that it came to mean different things to different cultures, classes and generations, and that each story of nation formation, without exception, has followed a distinctive historical path. A simple formula for nation building therefore does not exist. Instead the historian is presented with a series of compelling historical patterns that require explanation: the first appearance of the nation in the Americas and Europe in the eighteenth century, its spread through Europe in the nineteenth century, and its success as the world's fundamental political form in the twentieth. That historians have only recently sought to explicate the rise of the nation within the broader context of historical change is mainly attributable to the fact that they, along with most people, have held the assumption that nations were essential or natural. From the nineteenth century, academic historians made it their business to create and uphold a national narrative that celebrated the birth of the nation state, such as 1789 for France, 1860 for Italy and 1870 for Germany. Indeed, they did more, scrutinizing antiquity and even mythology to find the origins of 'the French' and 'the Germans'. The presumption was that the French, the Italians and the Germans had always been, and that the early histories of these peoples serve as a prelude to the French Revolution, the Italian Risorgimento or the Unification of Germany. All earlier history came to be read as if it anticipated the coming of the nation. Although scholars would become more aware of the fallaciousness of teleological history, whereby the past is seen to unfold inevitably towards a given end-point, they were nevertheless reluctant to abandon the implicit understanding that humanity was destined to organize itself into a collection of nations. It is not coincidental that historians only began to look seriously at the nation as a mutable, historical, and therefore finite construct in the 1980s, when global market trends began to expose the diminished power of the nation-state, and when the end of the nation was first being mooted. At the same time, scholars became increasingly appreciative of global developments that accounted for the triumph of the nation in the first place – that it was the rise of capital-ism and broad-based developments in state formation which provided the context for the invention of the nation, and which, in the end, may well account for its demise.

This study seeks to locate Italy within this broad continuum, to explain its mere existence and its construction within the general context of nation formation. Doing so helps to expunge any familiar but fanciful notions that Italy or any other nation has an innate essence that transcends history. Apart from investigating the invention of 'the nation', historians can also legitimately pursue the task of explaining particular nations. Given that each nation is the product of creative construction and is culturally unique, so each provides a particular case study that sustains or problematizes our thinking on the nation in history. Italy is presented here as such a case study, one that in many ways conforms to broader international patterns, partic-ularly within Europe. Thus Italy was formally created at much the same time as many other European nations, and in the decades preceding the First World War the Italian state did much the same as its German, British and French counterparts in consciously seeking to inculcate the citizenry with a national identity. But in many ways, the case of Italy is idiosyncratic, or *sui generis*. Among its salient features is the absence of the strident mass nationalism of the sort nowadays associated with Eastern Europe and the Balkans, and which exists more latently within other Western nations. Italians are notable for their weak or moderate sense of nationalism, a fact that was underscored by the extremism of Italian nationalism promoted by the Fascists, who, whilst in power, attempted at great cost and with misspent energy to construct a popular national culture for the very reason that none existed. Italy is one of the few places in contemporary Europe where prominent journalists and intellectuals have the temerity to question the substance of their nation, and where flagrantly secessionist parties can attract a significant national following.

In terms of nation formation, Italy offers an intriguing pathway. Despite its apparent fragility, nationhood has proved to be a resilient construct, capable of surviving malign, corrupt and incompetent political regimes through nearly all of its existence, and of outlasting two world wars and the seismic changes to world order prompted by the end of the Cold War. Thus although particularist loyalties and attachments to the Catholic Church tend to remain more important to individuals than national identities, since the 1870s there has been no significant attempt to break the country up. It is doubtful that the supporters of the Northern League (*Lega Nord*), which since 1996 has demanded the independence of north and much of central Italy, are really interested in creating a break-away nation. Much more powerful secessionist pressures can be found within the United Kingdom.

Yet the mere fact that Italians wear their nationalism lightly, if at all, has usually been deemed by scholars (as well as Italian political leaders and Italian nationalists) as a failing. When it comes to the history of nation-building, Italy is usually dismissed by historians and social scientists as an anachronistic bulwark resisting the tide of modernity, as a country in which people have always been eccentrically immune to the allures of nationhood. Italy only features in synoptic studies of nationalism in order to provide that rare case where the otherwise triumphal march of the nation faltered in the mire of traditional parochialism. To this way of thinking, Italians are positioned in the dustbin of history, accorded similar disrespect by many sociologists and anthropologists, who until quite recently have seen Italian mistrust of authority as cultural backwardness. Yet by the end of the twentieth century, what with the nationalist-inspired bloodbath in the Balkans and cultural adjustments demanded by European unification, such value judgements had come to seem inappropriate. Italy now appears in a new light as a country prepared better than most to cope with a future in which, as politicians and pundits often prophesy, there will be greater emphasis on globalization and regionalism.

The student of Italian nation formation thus needs to guard against many value-laden assumptions about its historical trajectory, as well as against unfair and inappropriate comparisons with supposedly model nations. Historians have tended, whether consciously or not, to judge a particular national historical experience against a successful paradigm, normally that provided by Britain, France or the United States. Past historians of Italy, comparing its political, economic and social progress to that of such 'ideal' models of national development, have found Italy unimpressive. Yet in seeking to explain why Italy failed to be more like Britain or France, much that is edifying about its particular pathway through the modern age is ignored.[1] Nowadays, historians of Italy try to avoid the distorting effects of ideal paradigms – effects which the present reputation of Italy rebuffs, and paradigms which the histories of Britain and France do not sustain. Now that Italy ranks among the world elite economic powers, perhaps it is time to revise long-established historical narratives.

To outsiders, particularly those of us from countries with (seemingly) well-functioning political systems and social services, so much about Italy appears difficult to fathom. It is a place where governments collapse and are

---

[1] John A. Davis, 'Remapping Italy's Path to the Twentieth Century', *Journal of Modern History*, 66 (1994).

reconstituted in rapid succession, yet where one party effectively dominated national politics from the end of the Second World War to 1992. The northern and southern halves of the peninsula appear in social, cultural and economic terms to be two very different countries, much as the nation's international image is contested by Milanese fashion and Florentine art on the one hand, and Sicilian and Neapolitan organized crime on the other. To the wider world Italy appears to have a sharply distinctive national culture, yet internally it is so culturally diverse that 'the Italies' might be a more appropriate name for the country.

This study of Italian nation formation was written with the express purpose of making this most peculiar of nation-building experiences more explicable, particularly to an undergraduate readership. It is not a history of Italy, at least not in the conventional sense. Fine general texts have been written in recent years by Roger Absalom, Martin Clark, and Christopher Duggan, each of which, admittedly, have nation formation as a unifying theme, but which must also deal with much more.[2] This book focuses entirely on nation formation, and has very little to say on many important issues of historical significance, such as the country's economic history, the 'Southern Question' and the Italian Communist Party, except where these topics shed light on the history of nation building. My hope is to explain the origins, creation and development of Italy as a national form so that students might better understand Italy and the nation respectively as historical phenomena, rather than as constants in an ever-changing world.

How does one trace the formation of nations? Of late historians have developed a deeper appreciation of the fact that nations have not been the product of linear, self-conscious processes, and that, quite often, the development of the nation does not follow the pattern envisaged by its so-called 'founding fathers'. In the case of Italy, many of those regarded as founders actually abhorred the very idea of an 'Italian' nation until political unification was in full swing. The current consensus among historians of Italy is that the early nineteenth-century nationalist movement had less to do with the making of an Italian nation than did social unrest, rising crime and the declining political authority of the old regime. The vision of the nationalists was hijacked by political elites who, very late in the day, espoused national unity as an expedient way round a dangerous social and political impasse. Italy was therefore not created by idealists such as Giuseppe Mazzini, who saw the nation as the means of political emancipation and social improvement, but by pragmatists who came to recognize national unity as a means of maintaining their power. Indeed, in the making of nations generally, historians have found functional playing a

---

[2] Roger Absalom, *Italy since 1800: A Nation in the Balance?* (London, Longman, 1995); Martin Clark, *Modern Italy, 1871–1995* (London, Longman, 1996); Christopher Duggan, *A Concise History of Italy* (Cambridge, Cambridge University Press, 1994).

more decisive part than intentional factors. In recent historiography, attention has focussed on the development of social mindsets that made it possible to conceive of, or believe in, something as abstract as the nation, and beyond that, on the objective economic and demographic circumstances which generated such mindsets.

The making of the Italian nation must therefore embrace a variety of contributing factors, some of which come into play at particular moments and are irrelevant in others, and many of which have a telling impact but are not quite obvious, such as the expanding trade in books and other printed material. This text will focus on the dominant vectors of nation building, setting the stage in Chapter 1 by considering the relevance of the 800 years preceding the French Revolution, particularly the influence of inter-state politics, state formation and capitalism. These global processes both actively involved and passively affected the Italian states, and were instrumental in forcing them to modernize government structures and practices. Moreover, political and economic decline over this period made Italian elites acutely aware of their collective predicament, and thus helped promote a belief in a collective identity. Besides this, there was the production or transformation of the cultural capital, for example the development of a standardized Italian language and a literary canon, that was essential to the later construction of a national culture.

Crucially, one must keep in mind that in no way did any of the above pre- or proto-national developments actually determine the coming of the nation. One can certainly find references over the centuries to 'Italy' as a cultural and geographic unit, as when the Emperor Augustus celebrated the unity of Italy ('tota Italia'), and even references to Italian patriotism, as for example in the utterances of the early seventeenth-century Duke of Savoy, Carlo Emanuele I, who attempted to rally the Italians against Spanish domination. Regardless of such occasional citations from the sources, there was no Italian nation lying dormant.

Significantly, nationhood in Italy begins life as a foreign import. By the late eighteenth century, European states had expanded their activities to such a degree, and were making so many demands on ordinary subjects, that rulers had to assume a direct interest in the condition of the subject population. As outlined in Chapter 2, the solution propounded by the French Revolution was the nation-state, in which, among other things, sovereignty was transferred from the monarch to 'the people'. Moreover, the new state system functioned on rational principles and was comparatively efficient. France imposed its government systems on the Italians, giving them, between 1796 and 1814, a foretaste of nationhood. But the French were motivated by their own national interests, and depended on their administrative systems to squeeze as much revenue from their imperial territories as possible. The Italians therefore came to associate French reform, including the nation-state, with tyranny and extortion.

Chapter 3 considers the aftermath of the so-called *epoca francese*, when Europe's old regimes were restored and yet retained most of the efficient administrative, fiscal and military structures bequeathed by Revolutionary and Napoleonic France. Nationalism persisted among young wealthy and middle-class Europeans as an underground, radical resistance to the *ancien régime*. For Italy, this phase is crucial for two reasons. Firstly, an indigenous nationalist movement had appeared by the 1830s, led by Giuseppe Mazzini. Although Mazzini's followers and fellow-travellers could not dislodge the *ancien régime*, they did succeed in planting the idea of national unity in elite social circles. Secondly, Italian unity appeared increasingly attractive because of a widespread desire to free the peninsula of Austrian domination, and, more significant, because most Italian states were wilting under the strain of deepening debt, poverty, and uncontrollable banditry. The revolution of 1848 provided a temporary release of pent-up political and social tensions, after which Italian elites were determined to find a solution to the general crisis of political authority and Austrian domination. As will be discussed in Chapter 4, national unity was their main goal, though it was never clear what form a united Italy would take. The lead was assumed by Piedmont–Sardinia, the most powerful Italian state, and the most modern in political and administrative terms. Chapter 4 details the course of events that led to the unification of Italy in 1860, whereby the Piedmontese political elite, largely because of foreign assistance and good fortune, quite unexpectedly found themselves in control of most of what is now Italy. The 'Risorgimento' affirms the importance of events, as opposed to long-term structural developments, in explaining why and in what particular form nations emerge.

Although it had not been planned by the Piedmontese, nor by Tuscan and other political elites, Italy as a single nation-state was nevertheless retained as the only guarantee of independence and as a solution to the long-term crisis in political authority. The next major hurdle was the legitimation of the new nation in the eyes of its subject population. The new political order believed Italy's cultural heterogeneity and disposition for political particularism had to be overcome if the new nation was to be consolidated. Indeed, Italians had to be made where very few existed. Chapter 5 considers some of the principal ways in which the state and non-state agencies sought to fashion a national culture and a national identity, which all Italians were meant to adopt as their own. The Savoy monarchy was positioned as the symbolic centrepiece of the new national culture, while scholars set about constructing a national foundation myth embodying national values. However, these attempts to forge a new identity generally fell flat for a number of reasons. Crucially, the Italian state was anathematized by the papacy, which continued to exert a profound and pervasive influence. A sterile secular *italianità* simply could not compete with Catholicism. Moreover, the state also promulgated a national culture based on empire-building and military values, yet Italy's military capacities were such that it could barely achieve even its most modest foreign policy aims. Italians were promised a new Roman Empire and were instead saddled with 'Italietta'. Chapter 6 deals with societal disillusionment with the Italian state, and how the latter became the target of a reactionary form of nationalism. Indeed, by the end of the nineteenth century, nationalism was effectively appropriated by radical right-wing critics, especially the *nazionalisti*, who argued that Italy's salvation lay in the formation of an authoritarian regime that was wholeheartedly dedicated to imperial expansion. Nationalism, somewhat ironically, became an anti-state ideology.

Chapter 7 discusses the Fascist regime, the incarnation of these anti-state nationalist desires. Liberal Italy's last attempt to find imperial glory through participation in the Great War came to nothing, by which time extremist nationalism had found a mass following. Soon after their assumption of power, the Fascists committed themselves to the construction of a radically nationalist society and the imposition of an exclusively Fascist rendition of *italianità*. They would go much further than any Italian regime in seeking to socialize the population, exploiting the modern media, inventing new mass rituals and commemorative practices and, to its detriment, committing the nation to reckless imperial adventures. The Second World War not only destroyed Fascism as a political force but made Italians warier than ever of nationalism and nationalist politics.

Italy nevertheless survived the war, partly due to the efforts of resistance movements that oversaw national reconstruction and the establishment of the republic. The final chapter considers the extent to which the political order that grew out of the wartime resistance sought to reconstitute Italian nationalism as an anti-Fascist ideology, and how that attempt largely failed. Much of it had to do with the inability of the post-war political order, dominated by the conservative Christian Democrats, to establish its moral authority. Riddled by corruption, encumbered with wasteful practices, and culpable of malign neglect of societal welfare, the political order eventually crashed in 1992, after which authority was contested by parties explicitly advocating 'national' revival (*Forza Italia*), and one major party that would eventually call for northern secession (*Lega Nord*). Regardless of the state's defects and its inability to fashion a dominant or hegemonic national ideology, the second half of the twentieth century in fact witnessed the most effective phase yet in mass socialization. The nation-state, by means of national economic policies, development and welfare programmes, was the vehicle through which capitalism was revived in Western Europe after the Second World War. Italy's standing in the eyes of both its citizenry and the wider world was radically improved in the post-war decades by the nation's stunning economic performance. Moreover, the concomitants of rapid economic modernization – urbanization, mass education, secularization, consumerism and mass communications – each played an indisputable role in making Italy relevant to each and every citizen. By the end of the twentieth century, nationhood had been achieved without the mobilizing agency of nationalist ideology.

My text proceeds on the assumption that Italy is a nation, albeit a distinctive one whose development bears little resemblance to, say, British or American experience. While seeking to elucidate its particular path, I present it as a case study that tells us something about how nations are formed. I resist trying to define what is to be Italian, except in the broadest and sketchiest way. Any attempt to render a precise description runs the risk of essentialism, which counters the consensus among scholars in the field that national identity is historical, mutable and contestable. As with every other nation, Italy is constantly in the making.

|1|

The nation's prehistory: state formation and Italian culture, c.1000–1796

Italy certainly existed long before the advent of modernity. Since ancient times, *Italia* has endured both as a geographical designation and as a cultural ascription applied to the peoples of the peninsula. Extant historical sources provide more than enough evidence that there has almost always been an *Italia*, but nationalist historians and other myth-makers have insisted, as they have everywhere in Europe and beyond, on the corollary that national consciousness or national spirit must also be ancient. Although belief in the primordiality of being say German, Romanian or Russian continues to retain great meaning among the patriotically minded today, most scholars decisively reject primordialism as being a contrivance of nation building. Scholars concern themselves rather with the extent to which pre-modern developments came to influence the character of the nation. While most appear to claim the nation is fundamentally modern, there is a significant minority view that earlier ethnic or cultural formations played a decisive role in determining the shape of nation-states and national movements.[1]

Whatever the merits of the ethnic origins approach, it is not particularly helpful in understanding the making of Italy. The Italians had never formed a distinctive ethnic group: they definitely did not constitute 'a people' on the eve of national unification in 1860. The cultures inhabiting the peninsula had little in common, no common language or commonly held symbols or myths celebrating common lineage. When the Italian nation-state was established in 1860, the new political order was well aware that the task of creating a nation of Italians, of creating an ethnic identity, was before them. This is not to say, however, that Italian identity had been a meaningless concept prior to the Risorgimento. Since the early Middle Ages being Italian

---

[1] E.g. Anthony Smith, *The Ethnic Origins of Nations* (Cambridge, Polity, 1986).

was sometimes a useful label of self-identification for statesmen, merchants and artists dealing with the outside world, for it was in the wider world that firm ideas about Italians could be found. It was outsiders who ascribed an ethnic identity to the Italians, much as Italians could cluster foreigners into tidy ethnic categories such as *tedeschi* (the Germans) and *greci* (the Greeks). Moreover, Italians would often discriminate between themselves as a collective and foreigners who dwelled outside the peninsula or beyond the Alps. At least since the time of Dante, this vague sense of 'us' and 'them' was implicit in the long-term quest by cultured elites from Lombardy, and even from as far south as Sicily, to construct and maintain a common Italian language. Yet among that exceedingly small number of people who thought of themselves as Italian, rarely did that identity define them as individuals. It was not until the time of Mazzini in the nineteenth century that we begin to encounter individuals claiming to be Italian above all else, and even then such self-confessed nationalists constituted a tiny minority.

Nevertheless, it is clear that *italianità* constituted a form of 'cultural capital' that predated the Risorgimento in that it had long been employed by Italian elites to locate themselves in the wider world. The purpose of this chapter is to assess the significance of cultural capital and other features of Italy's deeper past that may help us understand why early nineteenth-century radicals risked their lives for 'Italia'. Why Italy and not something else? Why did Napoleon Bonaparte create a satellite state called Italy and not say 'Padania'? The choice of 'Italy' was something too obvious for people like Napoleon and Mazzini to justify, yet the reason why the study of nations and nationalism has burgeoned in recent times relates to the fact that such unspoken assumptions and beliefs have finally been subjected to critical scrutiny, and because they have been belatedly placed in their historical context.

An equally edifying undertaking would be to explain why a 'nation' rather than something else? On this score too, the wider context is crucial. The Italian nation appeared in an age when many other nations also emerged, which reminds us that, in state formation as in other ways, Italy was a product of broader European trends. From the late Middle Ages, the Italian states found themselves increasingly vulnerable to foreign domination, particularly by imperial powers that were capable of marshalling much greater military and economic resources. Italy's diminishing standing in relation to the continent's major territorial states had the effect of sharpening Italian self-awareness, as well as fuelling reform movements that sought to revive the fortunes of the Italian states. As it happened, protracted reform failed even to make the Italian states viable, and it was a growing sense of precariousness that, by the middle of the nineteenth century, convinced a significant proportion of Italian elites that some form of unification was necessary. If one were to identify the single most important process in the making of an Italian nation, it had to be state formation.

Prehistories, national histories

At this point it would be useful to clarify the relationship between the modern nation and the *longue durée*, particularly as nations have tended to present themselves as primordial, that is, as having always been. Primordialism has been a feature of nationalist thought since the earliest formulations of the idea of the nation, according to which nationality was cast as a natural essence that united countless generations of a particular ethnic group through time, reaching back to, or perhaps beyond, antiquity. As Benedict Anderson has pointed out, nations invented histories that envisaged societies to be moving in 'simultaneity' through 'calendrical' time, whose changing fortunes were marked along the way by historical events.[2] In the case of the Old World nations especially, however, the nation's timeline has no beginning or endpoint, much as conveyed in Italian nationalism during the first half of the twentieth century. Thus fervent nationalists such as Mussolini looked back to Imperial Rome as a golden phase in Italy's national history. The Romans and modern Italians were assumed to be the same people, spiritually and genetically. Moreover, the search for Italy's origins meant looking back into deepest antiquity, even before Romulus, Remus and the She Wolf, where history recedes into myth. Thus Mussolini's Italy, Dante's Italy, Caesar's Italy and Coriolanus's Italy are separated by time but constitute the same Italy.

Nothing attests to the monumentality of the nation more than the idea of its immortality, which remains an intrinsic feature of many nationalist ideologies and national cultures. Of course serious scholars would not accord that quality to nations nowadays, but an enduring legacy of primordialism has been the assumption that the nation is a given, a natural sociological, political and cultural unit. This is suggested by the mere fact that historians and social scientists have only recently bothered to examine the nation critically and as an historical phenomenon. Save for a few honorable exceptions, until the early 1980s historians rarely thought it necessary to explain why the nation triumphed, despite the fact that nations to this day remain the primary unit of reference for historical investigation. To be sure, historians have paid a great deal of attention to the origins of particular nations, indeed the establishment of history as an academic discipline in its own right in the nineteenth century was driven largely by the need to construct and even fabricate a *curriculum vitae* for each nation. Yet with each case the road to nationhood or national unity was framed as if it were inevitable, meaning the triumph of the nation was a given.

It is difficult to underestimate the importance of time and the past in explaining the appeal of nationalism. The presentation of the nation as

---

[2] Benedict Anderson, *Imagined Communities: Reflections on the Origins and Spread of Nationalism*, 2nd edition (London, Verso, 1991), Chapters 2 and 11.

monumental and immortal made it more amenable to mass consumption, for one is more liable to venerate something that is grander than the self, something that could be held in awe. Yet to make the nation knowable it must also be made to appear familiar. In many cases where national elites consciously sought to enlist mass allegiance, traditional folk cultures and ordinary peasants were celebrated as quintessential aspects of national culture. Another strategy was to present the nation's long history in a fashion that was readily imaginable, particularly through the employment of life-cycle metaphors that could make something as abstract as national history seem vivid and tangible. Thus most Serbs, regardless of whether they have read any history textbooks or not, believe Kosovo was where their nation was 'born', hence popular Serb support for the recent war in Kosovo was predicated on the desire to keep their collective birthplace from the clutches of apparently recent intruders. In many cases the contradiction of having a nation that is both timeless and yet having a birthday is solved by claiming a 'rebirth'.[3] The term Risorgimento applies to the movement whereby Italy was reunified, while also indicating that the Italian nation was resurrected or reawakened from its slumber. A further way in which the nation is made familiar at the broadest social level is through the popularization of an epitomized historical narrative, one that is poignant yet digestible. Thus most Britons take as given that their country has a 'great' history, with, not long ago, an empire on which the sun never set, yet they are not much interested in the details. The English know theirs is a long history sign-posted by monarchs such as Henry VIII, Elizabeth I and Victoria, and consequential battles such as 1066 and the Battle of Britain. Even those uninterested in history possess at least a cursory understanding or impression of British or English history, enough to affirm their sense of British-ness or English-ness as opposed to being something else. Even in such a threadbare form, historical consciousness is an essential underpinning of national identity.

The appeal of the monumentality and timelessness of the nation is to be found at all levels, and even the finest scholars are sometimes susceptible. The great French historian Fernand Braudel at times succumbed, but was prepared to admit to his vulnerability, whereas whole generations of historians before him, scholars who helped established history as an academic discipline, were quite spellbound by nationalism and were rarely conscious of their complicity in the apotheosis of the nation.[4] As mentioned earlier, academic history was initially conceived in the nineteenth century to construct narratives that simultaneously monumentalized the nation and rendered it familiar. The years following the unification of Italy saw a great

---

[3] Anderson, *Imagined Communities*, pp. 195–6.
[4] Fernand Braudel, *The Identity of France*, Vol. 1, *History and Environment* (London, Fontana, 1986), p. 15.

number of historians, working within and outside universities, dedicate themselves to the creation of a unifying national narrative that demon-strated how the new nation was the culmination of centuries of historical development. None of these historians, including the leading figure in late nineteenth- century Italian historiography, Pasquale Villari, found this quest inimical to critical research. On the contrary, Villari and his colleagues believed that the national narrative would become transparent as the body of scholarship was accumulated. Villari's contemporaries and successors were self-conscious of their nation-building role, and were instrumental in perpetuating the assumption that national history ran along a determined path. In the case of Italy, readers of history were encouraged to believe that Dante, Machiavelli, Galileo and all other significant Italians of the past were anticipating the Italian nation. Such ideas were perpetuated by acade-mic historians who trained generations of teachers to preach to children about Italy's past and its destiny as one continuous thread.

For nationalists who had been weaned on ideas of an immortal Italy, questioning the antiquity of the Italian nation was anathema, but critical scholarship in the present age requires a completely secular approach and the total abstention from teleological assumptions. This does not necessarily mean that the pre-modern world is irrelevant. After all, the very fact that by the twentieth century the nation had become the dominant feature of world politics, means that historical factors must have been in place to facilitate this. The French Marxist philosopher Etienne Balibar has usefully described such background developments as the nation's 'prehistory', by which he means the objective structural developments and historical conditions that made it possible for something like the nation to come into being, yet which did not make its realization at all inevitable.[5] Anderson cites the importance of the advent of capitalism and the introduction of print technology from the sixteenth century, which allowed for the mass production and wide circula-tion and consumption of printed material in vernacular languages.[6] This innovation influenced readers, or social elites that could afford books and read them, to imagine themselves as part of a cultural formation. By 1500, most Italian authors were writing in the vernacular, but there was much debate over what kind of Italian should be used or should serve as a stan-dard throughout the peninsula. This *questione della lingua* (Language Question) was not resolved until the nineteenth century, though Florentine Tuscan, owing to the prestige accorded to it by Dante, Petrarch and Boccaccio, was widely accepted as the basis of a prospective standard Italian. The mere existence of the *questione della lingua* presupposed that Italy was widely regarded as a cultural unit, but it did not necessarily augur the

---

[5] Etienne Balibar, 'The Nation Form: History and Ideology', in G. Eley and R. G. Suny (eds), *Becoming National: A Reader* (New York, Oxford University Press, 1996), pp. 133–4.
[6] Anderson, *Imagined Communities*, Chapter. 3.

coming of the Italian nation-state. Only when the French Revolution made the nation an appealing alternative to the *ancien régime* was the cultural formation known as Italy among the first nations to be touted.

The role of state formation

Another key 'prehistoric' development that set the stage for the nation was the rise of the modern state, which began with the unravelling of the feudal system in the late Middle Ages. It was a process driven by mounting inter-state rivalries and the increasing costs of waging war, which compelled each European power to expand and refine its capacity to mobilize material and human resources. Put crudely, maintaining large armies, keeping them in the field as long as possible, and equipping them with the best technology, required a state system that wielded greater and much more comprehensive powers than ever before. From the fourteenth century the history of state formation was characterized by centralization, as monarchs asserted their sovereignty over their kingdoms at the expense of the nobility, the bishops and other centrifugal forces. From the sixteenth century the machinery of government becomes progressively modernized through the creation of government ministries, of bureaucracies managing the day-to-day functions of state administration, and paid agents enforcing laws and collecting taxes. In other words, the modern state is realized through the development of government structures that are capable of imposing authority or sovereignty over the whole realm, in which the state maintains a monopoly of violence and justice. Another relevant feature of state formation in Europe is the concomitant development of capitalism. By the eighteenth and nineteenth centuries, the more successful states were those that were able to promote and harness the wealth generated by domestic markets and foreign trade. State policy could promote private economic interests and thereby increase its revenue sources by protecting local markets with tariffs, or providing military assistance to merchants venturing into overseas territories where trading access was inhibited by other states. Recurrent revenue was one reason why medium-sized territorial states such as England and France were capable of bullying much larger states.

What relevance has the rise of the modern state to developments in Italy? At first sight it might seem there is none. In the late Middle Ages the larger Italian states were among the most powerful and were certainly the most wealthy in Christendom, but the destiny of Europe, both in terms of power relations and in terms of the type of state systems that would prevail, was to be decided outside Italy. The decline of the Italian states was in large part attributable to their failure to centralize state authority and develop modern administrative structures, though some belatedly tried to do so from the late seventeenth century. Another reason for decline was their inability to escape the yoke of foreign domination. In the Spanish-dominated south, centrifugal power was if anything strengthened. From the late sixteenth century Italy fades and becomes a backwater in European affairs, a land which greater powers fought over and divided. Yet the long history of European state formation is relevant on a number of counts, the first of which is the goading effect that foreign domination had on the Italian states to reform their internal power and administrative structures, in the forlorn hope that they might be able to re-assert their independence. Further motivation came from Italy's diminishing economic fortunes in relation to dynamic Atlantic seaborne powers, such as England and Holland, which were capturing markets once dominated by Italians, and whose economic penetration of the peninsula itself underscored a growing local sense of inferiority. The cruellest legacy of economic decline, the intractable problem of pauperization – a millstone that Italy was not able to throw-off until well into the twentieth century – also provided impetus to change. State modernization was urged by those concerned with social decay, but more often it was driven by the fear of social revolution, or of a complete breakdown in law and order. Through the eighteenth century, intellectuals led a push to have Italy 'rejoin' Europe, to become a constituent part of its cultural, political and economic life. Reforming outdated state systems was an essential part of this project. Emulating 'Europe' was widely regarded as the route to redemption.

The *longue durée* is also useful because it offers insights into why centralization was unusually difficult to attain within the Italian states, and indeed why most Italians continued to find it hard to relate to the Italian nation after 1860. It is hard to underestimate the enduring power of particularism in Italian history, not only in terms of the exceptional strength of municipal identities, but also the doggedness with which local interest groups defended their powers, rights and privileges vis-à-vis the state. The source of this exceptionally resilient form of particularism dates back to Roman times, when the empire functioned as a vast network of cities, and where administrative responsibilities were delegated to local oligarchies. Following the collapse of the Roman Empire, urban life and government continued to flourish in Italy while the rest of Christendom slid into feudalism and ruralization. Feudalism did penetrate rural Italy but it did not become the dominant mode of production. Despite the disruptive effects of invasions at various stages by Germanic tribes, Byzantines and Muslims, urban life persisted and trade remained its life-blood. The towns retained strong municipal traditions which they consciously associated with their Roman heritage, and which they stoutly defended against all later attempts by powerful outsiders or ambitious popes seeking to impose their sovereignty. With the revival of trade in the Mediterranean towards the end of the first millennium, many towns throughout Italy had become rich trading centres, including Amalfi, Salerno, Naples, Venice, Genoa and Pisa. In the mid eleventh century, many northern towns or 'communes' formed alliances in order to maintain their independence, and they were generally quite successful. In 1176, for example, the Lombard League routed the powerful Emperor Frederick Barbarossa at the Battle of Legnano. Commune independence was also secured by playing-off the two major powers in the region: the Holy Roman Empire and the papacy.

From the end of the twelfth century, however, Italian towns were absorbed into larger regional states or city-states. Along with the king-doms of Naples and Sicily, the dominating states were the republics of Venice and Florence, the Duchy of Milan, and the Papal States. Venice and Florence especially had emerged as significant powers on the international stage, even though their territorial base was minuscule compared with that of the major monarchies of Christendom. The Venetians and Genoans had been formidable enough between the twelfth and early fifteenth centuries to bully the Byzantine Empire into making humiliating territorial and trad-ing concessions. Indeed, as late as the fifteenth century, major Italian city-states such as Florence and Venice were capable of mobilizing greater resources and larger troop numbers than much larger territorial states, such as France, Spain and England. Italian cities were the wealthiest in western Christendom, and were by far the most culturally sophisticated and densely populated. At the same time, sovereignty within these city-states remained fragmented. Other urban centres within these territorial states retained a considerable degree of autonomy, having preserved their local institutions, traditions and identities. Nor was it necessarily the case that the laws and power structure of a given city applied to its rural envi-rons. Simply put, within Italian states one did not find uniform adminis-tration, laws and institutions. Venice, for example, was totally averse to integrating the patrician elites of other urban centres, such as Padua and Verona, into its political dominion, and these centres of the Terraferma never had cause to identify with Venice. In essence, Venice and the Terraferma functioned as a series of centres. Respect of the laws and priv-ileges of these localities had, for a long time, been one of the strengths of the Venetian state. Some states were united only in the person of the monarch. Thus the Kingdom of Naples was based on a complex series of relationships between the monarchy and feudal magnates who wielded immense power in their localities.

From late antiquity to the Renaissance period, fragmented sovereignty had been a key ingredient of Italy's vitality, but by the sixteenth century the mastery of Europe was being contested by states in which sovereignty was being increasingly consolidated under powerful monarchies. The French invasion of 1494 has traditionally been regarded as the beginning of the end of Italian independence, after which Spain and France vied for domination in the peninsula. Scholars once assumed that the eclipse of the Italian city-states was inevitable once the larger territorial powers had disengaged themselves from their own drawn-out conflicts – France from the Hundred

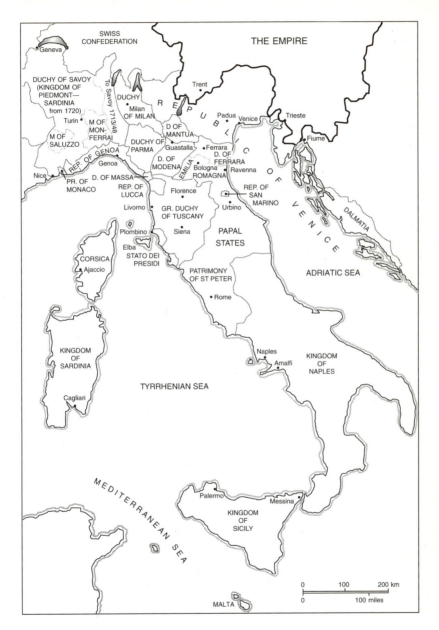

1 Italy, 1559–1796
After C. Duggan, *A Concise History of Italy* (CUP, 1994)

Years War, for instance, and Castile from its conquest of the Iberian peninsula. Yet at the beginning of the sixteenth century, the major Italian states could still muster enough men, military technology and logistical resources to match any invading force. The significant new factor was the willingness of Italian states to make alliances with foreign powers and deploy them against their Italian rivals. The precedent had been set in 1494, when Charles VIII of France was drawn into Italian politics by Ludovico Sforza of Milan, who used the French in a dispute with the Kingdom of Naples, after which the French presence was exploited by both the Venetians and the Papacy. More significant still were the changes experienced within the French and Spanish states as their struggle for influence in Italy mounted. Within a short period of time, these large territorial states were capable of fielding armies of a size not seen since the time of the Roman Empire. From 1492 to 1532, the number of soldiers actively serving the Spanish monarch rose from 20 000 to 100 000, the costs of which were largely borne by Spain's wealthy Italian and Dutch territorial acquisitions. In short, at the beginning of the sixteenth century the large territorial states were beginning to muster much greater resources than any single Italian state could ever hope to match. And as the cultural and economic heart of Europe, Italy was a natural focus of attention for powers seeking to master Christendom.

The rise of large and centralized territorial states seriously threatened the independence of the Italian states in the sixteenth century, but it was towards the end of that period that the physiognomy of Italy began to alter substantially. Commercial life lost much of its vitality, partly because northern European manufacturers managed to undercut their Italian counterparts with cheaper, albeit lower-quality, goods. Long-distance trade was captured by Atlantic seaborne powers (first Portugal and Spain, and then England, Holland and France), as the centre of gravity in terms of world trade had shifted from the Mediterranean to the Atlantic. For so long the centre of trade and finance, Italy was now relegated to the economic periphery. Other factors that accounted for Italy's decline included the devastation caused by incessant warfare in the early seventeenth century, and plague that ravaged much of the peninsula through the 1620s. Italy had entered its dark ages: centuries of foreign domination, economic backwardness, deepening poverty, rising social disorder and social polarization. Italians certainly continued to play a major role in European high culture: Italian names dominated branches of the arts, yet high culture often flowers in times of abject decline, and by the eighteenth century, when privileged Europeans would visit Italy as part of the so-called Grand Tour, they came in large part to see antiquities and decadence.

Nothing made political elites more aware of the decline of the Italian states than foreign political mastery of Italy. Little could be done to dislodge the series of suzerains that directly and indirectly dominated the peninsula; initially Spain and then Austria, while France always played an influential part in determining Italy's fortunes. Most degrading was the way in which the country was apportioned by the major powers in peace settlements. The Spanish, Polish and Austrian 'wars of succession' of the first half of the eighteenth century were each settled with parts of Italy being distributed as spoils or compensation. Only Piedmont and Venice remained independent, but their ability to pursue an independent foreign policy was extremely limited, although Piedmont found some scope by playing-off France with Austria.

Italy's subordination was made all the more humiliating by memories of better times, when the Italian states were at the centre of European affairs and wielded considerable power. Yet these memories also had a positive role to play. History served as a measure of Italy's potential and worth, and by the end of the seventeenth century, intellectuals and the more astute dynasts were increasingly driven by the desire to revive Italy, to once again see it become a part, not a pawn, of Europe. The Enlightenment had a profound impact in this regard. Historians counted among a growing host of intellectuals, including scientists and philologists, who from the end of the seventeenth century were captivated by European advances in learning, and who were frustrated by the reactionary, anti-intellectual culture that had prevailed in Italy since the Counter-Reformation, maintained by papal authority. The new culture of free and critical thinking made Italy's backwardness appear all the more transparent, and much intellectual energy was channeled into considering how the country might be reformed. For intellectuals, who by the mid-eighteenth century were to be found in universities, clustered in learned associations, and identified with periodicals such as the Milanese *Il Caffé*, the imperative was to have Italy rejoin Europe's cultural, political and economic mainstream.

Administrative and economic reform offered the direct route to renewal, and it was Europe's more dynamic powers that showed the way. What Britain, France and Holland had in common was centralized authority, bureaucratic administrative structures, and policies actively promoting domestic economic interests. It was this 'Europe' that eighteenth-century Italian reformers sought to emulate, and it was Piedmont or the Duchy of Savoy that made the greatest strides. War provided the stimulus for Piedmontese state formation in more ways than one. Chastened by the War of Spanish Succession (1701–13), the Savoyards sought to become major players in European inter-state affairs by extending their power at home. In 1717 Vittorio Amadeo II launched a cadastral survey, a systematic demarcation and valuation of land for the purpose of establishing a broadly based taxation system, as well as to facilitate the appropriation of properties usurped from the duchy by the nobility, and other properties to which title could not be established. Inevitable resistance from the Church and the nobility was overcome by a resolute prince who took inspiration from Louis XIV, the archetypal absolutist monarch of the age. Vittorio Amadeo also created a more efficient state bureaucracy and rationalized the legal system. These reforms were consolidated by Vittorio Amadeo's successor, Carlo Emanuele III (1730–73).

Most Italian states enjoyed some success in reforming their administrative structures, but without exception all efforts were impeded by entrenched interests, namely by the nobility and ecclesiastical authorities, who stood to lose a great deal of power and wealth. European states generally were preoccupied with the rationalization of administrative and judicial structures, but such reform was particularly difficult in Italy because of the antiquity and the particularly fragmented nature of those structures. In some Italian states privileged groups were able to exploit the confusion resulting from overlapping judicial and administrative jurisdictions and a whole range of other anomalies to defend their privileges against sovereign usurpation. Their tenacity served as a significant constraint on state reform, as did the fact that not all rulers were committed to reform. The king of Naples and the pope, in particular, shared the nobility's attitude to safeguarding tradition and privilege. The nobility was, however, receptive to economic reforms that shored up their position, particularly the sale of ecclesiastical land and other measures promoting commercial agriculture. Most states made a conscious effort to implement current ideas that allowed for the functioning of a free market, which involved removing all impediments such as tariffs and dissolving the guilds, whose practices made manufactured goods too expensive and therefore uncompetitive. By selling expropriated ecclesiastical properties and common land, and removing restrictions on imports, the Italian states hastened the modernization of their economies. However, modernization did not necessarily lead to real economic growth, while the social ramifications were so adverse as to threaten the very existence of the states. Common people who had long depended on common land and Church welfare for sustenance found that such basic rights were being removed as part of the process of modernization. The effect was the exacerbation of social inequality and mass poverty.

By the 1790s, the Italian states had made some progress towards rejoining Europe through economic and administrative reform, but the quest had barely started. Economic reforms had only marginally improved Italy's trading position, the Italian states were still dominated politically by foreign powers, and the nobility remained a powerful and obstructive force. Worse still, the pauperizing effects of economic modernization had destabilized the social order to the point where elites lived in constant fear of revolution. Their fears were justified, though revolution, when it did come, was imposed from above. In 1796 Italy did join Europe, in a manner of speaking, when French armies invaded the peninsula for strategic reasons and in order to spread their revolution. Among other things, the French removed many of the constraints to state modernization and even imposed a rudimentary form of nationhood on the Italians, which will be the subject of the next chapter.

Recognizing and recording Italy

For a moment it would be useful to consider reasons as to why *italianità* acquired some purchase among cultural elites during these Italian dark ages, and how the development of *italianità* as cultural capital made it possible to imagine Italy. As will be discussed in a later chapter, the French regarded themselves as having invaded 'Italy', and proceeded to create a state, and then a kingdom, to which they gave this name. As far as the wider world was concerned, the patchwork of states along the peninsula was familiar as 'Italy' and had always been referred to as such. As with the modern Greeks in the late eighteenth and nineteenth century, it made sense to the Italians to 're-awaken' with an identity with which Europeans were already familiar, and which in any case linked them with a long and glorious history. For cosmopolitan intellectuals of the eighteenth century, being Italian was part of finding a place within Europe.

Through the seventeenth and eighteenth centuries, Europe's familiarity with Italy was sustained by the continuing export of high culture, and there was one cultural form that gave veritable meaning to the term 'Italian culture'. Opera, which was first performed in Florence in 1600, depended on a whole range of artistic and scholastic specialities that could readily be found in Italy. Its unique combination of music and theatre appealed to Italian ruling elites, and it was their patronage which allowed it to develop as the peninsula's most distinctive contribution to European culture. Opera became popular among the courts of Europe, which enthusiastically sought to imitate the new musical form but too often resorted to calling upon Italians to do it for them. European courts also continued to take an avid interest in Italian fine art and architecture – Russia's imperial capital, St Petersburg, was a product of Italian architectural expertise – but it was musical expertise and innovation which sustained Italy's elite place in Western high culture. The seventeenth century saw the emergence not only of opera but of the *concerto grosso*, the *cantata* and the *oratorio*. This was the age of Farinelli (Carlo Broschi, 1705–82), the internationally acclaimed soprano castrato, and Antonio Vivaldi (1678–1741), exponent of purely instrumental concerts. Cultured Europeans sought to learn the Italian language because of their passion for opera and other musical exports. Indeed, the passion for *italianità* was never more explicit than in the way Italian musical terms entered the vocabularies of foreign languages. The word *pianoforte* was adopted in its shortened form, piano, by the English, German and French in the late eighteenth century, as was the term 'violin' and the acclamation *bravo*. Other words which signified the association of Italy with high art included fresco, virtuoso, picturesque (*pittoresco*) and *improvvisatore*.

This is not to say that *italianità* was simply imposed on the Italians by more powerful outsiders. For centuries the peninsula's political and cultural elites had adhered to an 'us and them' binary opposition of Italians and foreigners. Geography obviously set the parameters, which meant the status of Sicily and Sardinia was always ambiguous, but among the cultured elites there was always the sense that the peninsula formed a cultural unit. We have already noted that the *questione della lingua* referred to a broad agreement in principle that Italy should have a standardized language. It was in the seventeenth and eighteenth centuries, however, that one can detect a more conscious effort to develop an Italian culture, and hence an Italian identity, which was fostered partly by foreign domination and partly by the desire of scientists, philosophers and intellectuals generally to join the European cultural mainstream. As with the 'prehistories' of many other European nations, Italy's nation-building project was preceded by a long phase of scholarly activity in which histories were written, dictionaries were produced, grammar was standardized, and literary anthologies were assembled. In direct and indirect ways, these activities were essential for producing a standardized conception of Italy, even if they did not necessarily translate to national independence or unification. The seventeenth and eighteenth centuries nevertheless provided a great deal of the raw material that nationalists of the nineteenth century could use to invent the nation.

The seventeenth century, or in Italian terminology, the *seicento*, has traditionally been regarded as the nadir of Italian history. Thinkers from the Enlightenment onwards regarded it as a time of purgatory and one in which few positive contributions to Italy's development were made. This sense of the *seicento* was epitomized by trial of Galileo Galilei, when the spirit of learning was crushed by the censorious, anti-intellectual and backward-looking Counter-Reformation Church. Recent scholars have drastically qualified this black image, but there is little doubt that Italian intellectuals towards the end of the *seicento* were deeply conscious of their distance from the world of Descartes and Newton, and that Italy's backwardness was directly attributed to the Papacy and its Inquisition. Intellectual achievement in Europe's centre bred a sense of inferiority, but also a thirst for renewal that could be achieved by bringing together Italy's pool of talent. In 1690, for example, the *Accademia dell'Arcadia* was established in Rome, and soon developed cells through much of Italy. It specifically sought to promote awareness of literary trends throughout Italy, mainly in poetry. The *Arcadia* attracted a sizeable membership, which by 1728 had risen to 2619, healthily balanced between clergy and laymen.

The *Arcadia* was criticized, however, by one of its founding members, the distinguished jurist Gian Vincenzo Gravina, who argued it lacked serious purpose and was not equipped to resuscitate Italy from its comatose intellectual condition. An alternative and more purposeful body was planned by the Modenese librarian Ludovico Antonio Muratori, who proposed a formally organized 'Republic of Letters' which would embrace other branches of learning, including science. Muratori believed that there were enough talented minds to compete against other countries, but what Italy lacked was organization. Although his 'republic' never materialized, the idea aroused interest in Naples and the Duchy of Savoy, where it led to educational reform, while in Venice, Muratori's example inspired the launch of the *Giornale de' Letterati d'Italia*, another venture that was consciously dedicated to the revival of Italian cultural life. The journal, which was the most authoritative and innovative of its time, survived for thirty years (1710–40). Other less successful movements emerged, such as the *Accademia Sanpaolina* in Piedmont, in which members were particularly interested in discussing questions regarding Italian language and history, while another Piedmontese organization with similar interests, the *Accademia Filopatria*, was established in 1782. Some organizations effectively promoted a sense of *italianità* by bemoaning the impoverished state of Italian culture, as did the most famous eighteenth-century intellectual mouthpiece, the critical periodical *Il Caffè*. Between 1764 and 1766, the *Milanese Accademia dei Pugni* (Milanese Academy of the Fisticuffs), which was heavily influenced by the French Enlightenment, used *Il Caffè* to deal with a whole range of political, philosophical and philological subjects. Among its stridently discussed subjects was the poor quality of Italian literature and the inadequacies of the Italian language.

Another important development of the seventeenth and eighteenth centuries was the production of an increasing number of texts which referred to, or presupposed, an Italian collectivity. In the early seventeenth century patriotic sentiment was exemplified by the lyric poetry of Fulvio Testi of Ferrara, whose famous *Pianto d'Italia* (The Lament of Italy) attributes the homeland's decline to Spanish hegemony. A similar kind of patriotism can be found in the works of Alessandro Tassoni, who in 1614–15 produced the polemical 'Fillippiche contro Spagne', expressing anti-foreign sentiments in satirical verse. From the early eighteenth century, patriotism was found in more scholarly ventures that sought to rediscover an Italian past. Muratori dedicated much of his extremely active life to the writing and compiling of sources on Italian history. With the financial support of a group of Lombard noblemen, and in collaboration with major scholars from Bologna, Venice, Siena, Florence and elsewhere, he produced the *Rerum italicarum scriptores*, a massive collection of primary sources covering Italian history from 500 AD to 1500. Through this multi-volume volume work, Muratori hoped to demonstrate the glories of Italian history by focusing on the Middle Ages rather than antiquity. His *Antiquitates italicae medii aevi* and its summarized version in Italian, *Dissertazioni sopra le antichità italiane* (1738–43), looked at a variety of aspects of medieval social, cultural and institutional life in order to prove that there was a continuous thread linking Italians ancient, medieval and contemporary. Additionally, Muratori drew from the *Rerum italicarum scriptores* to compose the

Annali d'Italia, a twelve-volume chronicle that covered the same period of history as the *Rerum*.

While Muratori consciously promoted *italianità* through his exaltation of the medieval period, others did so inadvertently by simply promoting the study of history. The great Neapolitan philosopher Giambattista Vico, for example, who betrayed little, if any, Italian patriotism, nevertheless increased awareness of Italian history through his study of the Etruscans in *De antiquissima italorum sapienta ex linguae originibus eruenda* (1710). In it he argued that Italian culture predated the Romans, and by shifting focus to the Etruscans, the peninsula's ancient history could be imagined as Italian and not just Roman. Vico inspired a great deal of interest in Etruscan archaeology and history, and in 1726 an Etruscan academy was formed in Cortona, to which scholars were drawn from all over Italy. Until the French invasion of 1796, the academy produced regularly published dissertations, but its members were also known for demonstrating what could be described as Italian chauvinism. Much like Vico, members argued that Italian civilization and ingenuity was developed independently of the Greeks, to whom it was believed too much credit had been apportioned in the past. Their effort to prove by scholastic means that *italianità* was not in any way derivative attested to its growing symbolic significance in academic circles.

Through the eighteenth century, a mounting corpus of works dealt with Italy as an historical subject. These included *Riflessioni sopra lo stato d'Italia dopo la pace di Utrecht*, which was produced in the 1760s by Carlo Denina, and Gerolamo Tiraboschi's *Storia della letteratura italiana*, which was published between 1772 and 1782 in nine volumes, and had the effect of convincing the reading public that there was an Italian literary canon. Italian language was a major issue in this period. Throughout the country there were calls to improve Italian and promote its usage, particularly in written form. It was more or less agreed that Tuscan should remain the cornerstone of the language, but there was significant dispute over how much French influence, which was particularly strong in Piedmont and Parma, should be permitted. In 1612 the Accademia della Crusca had launched what was widely considered to be the most authoritative guide to literary Tuscan, the *Vocabolario degli Accademici della Crusca*, but later editions, such as that of 1729–38, failed to resolve the problem of standardization. There was much debate over the inclusion of archaic Florentine words. In *Saggio sopra la lingua italiana* (1785), Melchiorre Cesarotti recommended solving the vocabulary problem by proposing a national council which would oversee the production of a national dictionary. This Florentine-based council was to include representatives from all over the country, who would deliberate and decide upon such matters as the incorporation into the language of regional terms, as well as 'gallicisms' where no Italian equivalent for modern concepts could be found. As nothing came of Cesarotti's proposal, the long-running debate over language continued, but debate on the *questione della lingua* reflected the ever-increasing importance accorded to standardization and the broader desire for Italian cultural renewal. Each Italian state on its own was too small to form a self-sufficient cultural unit, and a fragmented cultural scene prevented the Italians from having a stronger political presence on the wider stage. This much was commonly accepted by Italian intellectuals, hence their interest in standardizing the language.

Conclusion

By most accounts the nation is recognized as a modern phenomenon, even if longevity has been claimed for it in the interest of legitimacy. 'Useable pasts' are constructed by creatively fashioning a history of the nation that showed it following a particular, linear path since time immemorial. In many cases, some nations were able to draw upon traditional culture and earlier ethnic bonds to construct a modern nation, as has often been the case in Eastern Europe. The Italians, however, did not have recourse to core ethnic traditions; unlike the Russians there was no popular conception of 'Mother Italy', or anything comparable to the German notion of the 'volk'. The only popular cultural feature common to all Italians was Catholicism, but whereas the Poles, the Irish and Croatians could utilize Catholicism as a mark of distinction, the absence of substantial 'others' in Italy precluded Catholicism as a source of *italianità*. Indeed, the Catholic Church came to regard Italian nationalism as a mortal threat and, as will be shown in later chapters, would campaign actively against the Italian nation.

There was no ethnic basis for Italy, but its nation-builders could nevertheless draw on an embarrassingly rich repository of cultural achievement in the high arts, accumulated over centuries and widely recognized as distinctly Italian. The Italian language could boast an impressively large canon of literature in a variety of genres, and there was a continuous production of various forms of art, such as opera, architecture and fashion that ensured that Italy retained a place in Europe's consciousness. Certainly, at home Italian identity did not carry much weight at all outside elite circles, and even within these circles it could not compete with local identities. Nonetheless, Italy's prehistory remains crucial for our purposes. Long-term developments in state formation, in the arts and most branches of learning provided the soil out of which an Italian nation could emerge in the nineteenth century.

|2|

Nationhood imposed: the impact of Revolutionary France, 1796–1814

Towards the end of the eighteenth century, Italy's reform movements were faltering. Obstructionist privileged groups and unsympathetic princes frustrated the reformists, many of whom were also disturbed by the social misery and inequalities that economic reform was visibly perpetuating throughout the country. Of course, the nature of Italy's problems was not at all unique, as many continental states were grappling with vexed questions relating to political and economic modernization. It was the French Revolution, however, which suddenly promulgated radical solutions that had wide-ranging ramifications for the rest of the continent. The tumult in Paris in 1789 led to the creation of a Constituent Assembly, a parliament that theoretically reflected the will of the French people, which asserted its legitimacy on that basis, and which therefore was able to appropriate political power from the monarchy and the *ancien régime*. The French people or 'nation', not the king, was deigned the sovereign authority, and to consolidate the new order, the monarchy was abolished and the reigning king, Louis XVI, was later executed. The causes of this revolution have been hotly contested by historians, but few would dispute the fact that it was induced by intractable economic difficulties that precipitated a legitimation crisis. The solution put forward in 1789 was a nation-state. Hitherto the nation had been an idea contemplated by philosophers such as Jean-Jacques Rousseau and Johan Gottfried Herder, who argued that humanity's emancipation required recognition of cultural or 'national' differences within humanity. By adopting the nation as an alternative to the old order, France's revolutionaries put the general thrust of state formation on a wholly new course.

What is significant about the French Revolution is not merely the fact that it launched Europe's first nation, but that the Revolution sought to impose its very radical solution to state reform on the rest of Europe. The

Revolution spread nationhood and republicanism as part of a civilizing mission, and perceived its struggle with those classes and states that resisted it as one between the past and the present, between progress and backwardness, darkness and light. Of course, French motives were not quite as pure as that, particularly when Napoleon Bonaparte, as 'First Consul' and then emperor, transformed the Revolution's mission into one of imposing his nation's dominance over Europe. Suffice it to say that Italy was enveloped by the changes sweeping the whole of the continent, and among the ideas now confronting the Italian public was that of the nation. The Revolution imposed itself on the Italians through a series of invasions and occupations between 1796 and 1814, and through its ideological mission, which found a receptive, albeit limited, audience in the Italian cities that formed the seedbed of an indigenous national movement.

To appreciate Italy's historical path to nationhood, therefore, one needs to keep abreast of what was happening elsewhere, as the Italian states were being swept into a current that they could not withstand. At the same time, one must keep in mind that what has often been referred to by historians as the 'Age of Revolution' (*c.* 1789–1815) was still very much a 'prehistorical' phase for Italy in terms of nation formation. For France's mission encountered resistance at all social levels, and those converted to its cause never really constituted what one could call a national movement. In merely planting the seeds of nationhood, the French Revolution in no sense made inevitable the later emergence of the Italian national movements in the 1830s and 1840s, let alone the creation of an Italian nation in 1860. The impression that the entire period from the French Revolution to 1860 experienced a drive towards nationhood, that it was all part of the 'Age of the Risorgimento', was grafted onto that period by latter-day historians.

Yet the mere fact that the idea of the Italian nation had been planted makes the revolutionary period an important one for our purposes. Even more important was the profound impact that the French had on so many related factors, particularly on the peninsula's social and cultural evolution, and on state formation. The French imposed reforms that swept away centuries of traditions and privileges, for they had the power to overcome nearly all forms of resistance. Though they were forced to withdraw finally in 1814, their legacy on state government in Italy was lasting. But French reforms exacerbated social inequalities and swelled the ranks of the desperately poor. Indeed the 'Age of the Risorgimento' that followed would be dominated by the growing threat of social revolution and the increasing sense of insecurity among Italian elites. In desperation and with considerable reluctance, many of these elites came to support the cause of Italian unity in the hope that the social order might be preserved. In other words, the French Revolution continued in a more efficient manner the implementation of reforms that came at the expense of social equity. It centralized power within the Italian states but made them ever more vulnerable to revolution. Italian nationalism was to emerge in a period in which reform and instability went hand in hand.

The French Revolution and the Italies

By the outbreak of revolution in France, the impetus for political reform in Italy had slowed to the point where much of the earlier optimism regarding the potential for reform had dissipated. Indeed, as early as the mid-1770s there were signs that intellectuals were doubting the wisdom of relying on princes to carry out the reform process. In some cases, the centralization of power had bolstered the autocratic powers of the dynast, as was the case in Habsburg Lombardy, where state modernization also included the introduction of censorship and a police force. At the same time, economic modernization did not necessarily lead to the desired effect of economic growth, as exemplified in the Grand Duchy of Tuscany under Leopold I (1765–90). Yet in states where reform was carried out with far less urgency or not at all, the consequences were equally disturbing. Naples and Papal States, which introduced reform measures belatedly and in a piecemeal fashion, continued to suffer serious financial deterioration. Other states that adhered vigilantly to the status quo and sought to shield society from the more threatening influences of the Enlightenment suffered the same fate.

Given that eighteenth-century reform movements produced such disappointing outcomes, many intellectuals began to look to more radical solutions. Some had begun to focus upon questions of social inequality and how best one might secure the welfare of humanity as a whole. By the end of the century, many believed that the obstacles to reform were so great that nothing less than a complete overhaul of the political structure was necessary. Symptomatic of the new mood in Italy was the appearance of radical groups, such as the *Illuminati*, who became influential in Naples and advocated something akin to revolution. It was the French Revolution, however, that revived hope in the possibility of fundamental change and, more usefully, offered a paradigm for change. Italians were certainly receptive to developments in Revolutionary Paris. Reading clubs, masonic lodges and university students talked incessantly of the possible consequences of the French Revolution for Italy. Initially, state authorities did little to curb the activities of enthusiasts, largely because the more perfidious elements were functioning in secret. As the Revolution became more radical through the first half of the 1790s, so too did Italy's so-called secret societies, which spent much of their time plotting revolutions at home. Membership of these clandestine groups reflected a generational change among the ranks of Italians seeking change to the status quo. The typical Italian revolutionary was young, normally under the age of 35, and had either an upper- or middle-class background. Among the revolutionaries were professionals, military officers, students, clergymen, and others whose personal ambitions were stifled in one way or another by the old order. Among their ranks were also men who had participated in the French Revolution directly, and who later sought to spread revolutionary fervour back home. The most famous of these was Filippo Buonarroti, who advanced to considerable prominence within France and who would advocate revolution for the whole of Italy.

In reality, the secret societies of this period were not particularly threatening, although an insurrectionary plot was uncovered in Bologna in 1794 and many of these revolutionary cells were actively supported by France. The ascendancy of the Jacobins in France, which brought on the most radical phase of the Revolution (1793–95), was accompanied by the spread of Jacobinism in Italy, but the '*giacobini*' never formed a united movement and were too weak to wreak real havoc. For Italy's political elites, however, the mere existence of the *giacobini* was unsettling. The execution of King Louis XVI and the violent attacks on the Church and the nobility in France rang alarm bells among the elites of Europe, to the point where any of the Revolution's influences at home, however innocuous, were determinedly eradicated. The *giacobini* were good propagandists for the Revolution, and however small and divided they might have been, they were deemed by Italy's *ancien régime* as the vanguard of a most dangerous and degenerate force. Jacobinism was enough to frighten reformers of an earlier generation, including Pietro Verri. Perhaps what concerned Italy's rulers more than the *giacobini* was the fact that throughout much of Europe the news of Revolution incited a series of massive social revolts, and that revolutionaries such as the *giacobini* were eager to exploit social upheaval to secure their political aims. Many parts of Italy were engulfed in peasant rebellions that were motivated by traditional grievances yet which could conceivably be translated into something that was much more politically charged. That the *giacobini* appeared to have done little to capitalize on these social forces was immaterial.

Neither the scale of social unrest nor the *giacobini* were capable of destabilizing the status quo, yet the impetus for reform came to a halt within the prevailing atmosphere of political reaction. Fortune favoured the defenders of the old order, but only temporarily. Revolutionary France was forced to defend itself against hostile powers, including Austria, which threatened France from its Italian base. In the spring of 1796, a French force led by an ambitious Corsican named Napoleon Bonaparte, crossed the Alps and drove the Austrians out of Italy. He then proceeded to secure the north for the Revolution. Not content to merely occupy this strategically important zone, Napoleon proceeded to implement reforms that sought to reconstitute Italy in France's image. Backed by his powerful army, Napoleon redrew the political map of the Italian peninsula and instituted political reforms that swept away centuries of privileges, laws and customs. He also imposed something that none of the Italian states had ever contemplated: nationhood.

The defeat of Austria in two battles in April and May in 1796 left Napoleon in control of most of northern Italy. By this point the French Revolution had moved into a conservative phase, with the Jacobins being replaced by the so-called Directory, a more moderate regime, which was keen to stamp out Jacobin radicalism throughout French-occupied territories. Moreover, French foreign policy was guided far more by strategic interests than it was by any desire to disseminate progressive Revolutionary values. Napoleon himself privileged strategy over ideology, and in his efforts to secure Italy for France created a series of new republics in the north that eventually combined as the Cisalpine Republic. He recognized that locals sympathetic to the Revolution, known as 'the patriots' or *patrioti*, could play a useful role in consolidating this new political order, and enlisted their support. These *patrioti* included the *giacobini* as well as political moderates, all of them receptive to French propaganda which promised to spread the Revolution's egalitarian principles among its liberated peoples. Even before Napoleon could manage to impose his authority over Milan, local *patrioti* had already created a Lombard army, adopted an Italian tricolour and attempted to set up a republic (the Republic of Alba). The *patrioti* remained devoted to the principles of Revolution throughout the three-year French occupation or 'the triennio' (1796–99). Among these principles was democracy, a theme featured in a number of newspapers that appeared in 1797, including the *Giornale democratico* in Brescia, the *Democratico imparziale* and then the *Genio democratico* in Bologna, the weekly magazine *Il Democratico* in Florence, and the Genoese *Frustator*, which appeared in March 1798.

Early French deeds in Milan did much to encourage such optimism. The initial spirit of emancipation was exemplified by an essay competition launched in September 1796, which required participants to consider the form of government which best suited Italy. The sixty-odd entrants were somewhat divided over whether Italy should be a federation, or a united, centralized state in accordance with the current French model. The winner of the contest, Melchiorre Gioia of Piacenza called for the latter. In this he reflected the views of the majority of entrants, for most sought a system of government that had the power to preserve the modern political reforms which the French presence now promised. The federal option reflected the cultural realities of Italy, but the fragmentation of power that federalism entailed might produce a state that was too weak to push through reforms. In proposing a centralized Italian nation, neither Gioia nor the other entrants were 'nationalists' in that they were not guided by an urge to create Italy. Rather, for them national unity was a means to an end.

Ironically, the idea of a united Italy was to gain more currency as French domination became more oppressive, and as it became clear that the French had subordinated their revolutionary principles to their strategic and economic interests. During the *triennio* the duplicity of French policy in Italy was exposed repeatedly, for while Napoleon spent a great deal of his time refashioning the Italian political landscape, he did not hesitate to forsake Italian interests if they happened to clash with French military ones. The most telling example was the Treaty of Campoformio in October 1797, in which Austria formally relinquished control of Italy to France, but which also saw Napoleon hand Venice over to the Austrians as part of the deal. Centuries of Venetian independence were terminated at a stroke, betrayed by Italy's ostensible liberator. Nor was the Directory willing to brook the activities of Italian Jacobins, especially as radicals such as Buonarroti were hoping to exploit Italy as a base for reviving the fortunes of the Jacobin cause in France. The *giacobini* were progressively excluded from positions of authority, and by 1798 their leaders were actively persecuted and forced out of French-controlled territory. Many had moved to central and southern Italy, but they were pursued as the French proceeded to conquer these territories in 1798 and 1799, creating two more republics in the process.

Duplicitous as French motives might have been, however, the territories under their control were subjected to unprecedented modernization, and there was much that some Italians could find appealing. Thus the French streamlined governmental structures in the same way as had been done in France. Each republic was highly centralized, had a citizen army, and each wrested control of education from the clergy. Each republic was organized into departments – the Cisalpine Republic had 20 such. Each republic was given a moderate constitution, and a legislature that was based on a limited franchise. Many of the vestiges of the *ancien régime*, such as feudal privilege and the use of torture for judicial purposes, were swept aside. The practice of castrating young boys before they reached puberty so that they could continue to perform in alto voice was also abolished, while barbaric methods of execution were replaced by more 'civilized' methods, such as the guillotine. Jews were accorded equal rights. The new republic based in Rome was initially popular among the educated laity who could now aspire to administrative positions that had been hitherto restricted to the upper clergy. The French pushed through reforms that were meant to foster economic growth, such as the complete abolition of the guilds and the sale of Church properties to commercial interests. There were suddenly new opportunities for key groups in Italian society, and state reform now made it much easier for political authorities to deal squarely with financial problems.

There was much more to French domination, however, than the modernization of the administration. The fate of Naples is instructive. Sections of Neapolitan society had eagerly awaited the imposition of French reforms in this most politically and socially fragmented kingdom, but no sooner was the Republic of Naples declared in January 1799 than French forces were withdrawn to deal with military matters elsewhere, leaving the new polity exposed to the possibility of a counter-revolution. A fierce revolt broke out in Calabria only a month later, followed by an invasion of the mainland by a counter-revolutionary force from Sicily, led by Cardinal Fabrizio Ruffo. When the insurgents entered Naples on 13 June there was a dreadful massacre of anyone that had been associated with the regime. Ruffo's force contained a whole range of disenchanted groups that did not necessarily harbour any love for the Bourbon monarchy that had been deposed by the French, and held confused and contradictory aims. Yet it appears that the 'Sanfedisti' had been driven to desperate revolt by the economic impositions of the new republican order, and that their acute sense of rage found expression in waging a holy struggle against an ungodly regime. The French, having earlier assumed control of a moribund economy replete with massive social problems, simply worsened matters by imposing even more punitive taxes. They also expected Neapolitans to immediately raise and hand over 2 500 000 ducats, and required localities to remunerate French occupying troops in the area.

For most Italians, the *triennio* was remembered for its punitive taxes and French looting. Local state revenues were siphoned by a French state that was constantly at war, while French military and many civilian officials could not resist lining their own pockets and amassing large personal fortunes. Another factor that created great friction between occupiers and occupied was the anti-religious behaviour of the more zealous state officials and *giacobini*. Attacks on the clergy, ecclesiastical property and religious practices traumatized this overwhelming Catholic population, much as aggressive anticlericalism had done in France itself. Hence the two largest rebellions, the Sanfede in Naples and the Viva Maria! rising in Tuscany (also 1799), were religious in character. Italy's ostensible 'liberators' were not regarded as such by the great majority of people, and anti-republican and anti-French feeling was prevalent.

Napoleonic Italy and the modernization of the Italian states

1799 seemed to signal the end of the French Revolution in Italy. Through the spring and summer of that year, popular insurrections swept across the length and breadth of the peninsula, and retribution was taken against *patrioti* and collaborators. The War of the Second Coalition and the arrival of a Russian and Austrian force to the north of Italy in April 1799 forced the French to evacuate. In the meantime, Napoleon, who had been conducting a disastrous campaign in the Near East, abandoned a plague-stricken army in Egypt in order to intercede in the political turmoil convulsing his nation's capital. The Directory, now in its death throes, saw the still popular Napoleon as the one man who could save the regime. Napoleon complied but proceeded to build a dictatorship. Towards the end of 1799, with the levers of power set firmly in his hands, France resumed its offensive against the Second Coalition and returned to Italy. In June 1800 Napoleon defeated the Austrians at the Battle of Marengo in southern Piedmont, following this up with a further defeat at Hohenlinden in January 1801. Italy was formally secured by France through the Peace of Lunéville, which was signed the following month. The Cisalpine Republic was reconstituted as the Italian Republic in 1802, and again re-named the Kingdom of Italy in March 1805. In 1806, Venice was added to the kingdom, followed by the papal cities of Urbino, Macerata and Ancona in 1808, and the Trentino and Alto Adige in 1809. Other territories were annexed to France, such as Piedmont in 1805 and Tuscany in 1807, as well as Umbria, the Republic of Liguria, Parma, and what was left of the Papal States, including Rome, in 1809. In March 1808, the Kingdom of Naples was made a satellite of the empire, and was initially ruled by the emperor's brother, Joseph Bonaparte.

From his return in 1800, through to the second French withdrawal in 1814, Napoleon was determined to remake Italy. This new phase of French domination continued most of the reforms that were barely introduced during the *triennio*, only now these reforms were afforded a much longer period of time to take root. The whole of Italy was again restructured administratively. The Italian territories annexed to France and those grouped into the kingdoms of Italy and Naples were reconstituted and were ruled respectively by Paris, Milan and Naples. Each state was again divided into departments, each of which was divided into districts, which in turn were split into communes or *comuni*. Each tier of government played key administrative and fiscal roles for the state. Given the bewildering complexity of Italy's erstwhile administrative, legal and economic structures, the Napoleonic reforms were profound and, for the most part, lasting. Although the Napoleonic states did not survive the emperor's fall, most of the other reforms were retained.

Indeed, the significance of the Napoleonic period for the peoples of the peninsula was not so much their short experience of nationhood, nor was it the mere fact that a nation called 'Italia' had been created. These years were so oppressive that the French, if anything, had made it impossible for most Italians to love *Italia* or nationhood. Nor was the significance of the *epoca francese* found in the importation of progressive ideas, such as egalitarianism and freedom, values which Napoleon would readily betray. Rather, his most telling impact was in breaking the mould of *ancien régime* Italy. By jettisoning existing systems of government and administrative practices, and by replacing them with more rational and centralized alternatives, Napoleon made it easier for Italians in later times to fashion a nation for themselves.

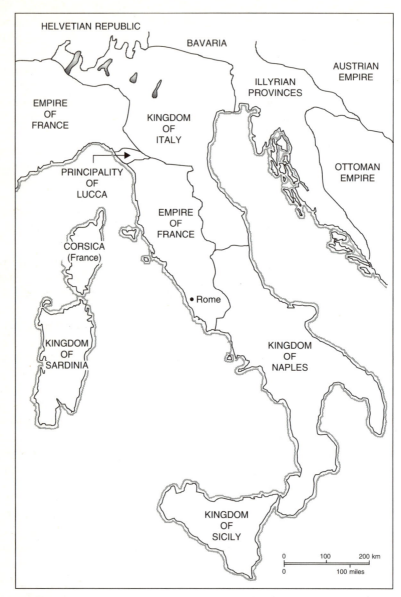

2 Italy in 1810
After Hearder & Whaley, *A Short History of Italy* (CUP, 1966)

Removing traditional and customary methods in favour of more efficient and modern ones was a formidable undertaking, even for Napoleon. Thus from 1806 the regime proceeded to eradicate feudalism throughout the empire, and it was particularly successful in territories where the *ancien régime* had already been weakened, as in Lombardy and Piedmont. Southern Italy was a far more difficult proposition. French rule in 1799 was all too brief and turbulent for more than a superficial implementation of reform, and here the obstacles to change were particularly formidable. A mere 600 families collected 80 per cent of the feudal revenues, and judicial privileges were concentrated in the hands of a mere 90 nobles. Only as powerful an entity as Napoleonic France, with the assistance of zealously committed ministers such as Giuseppe Zurlo and Francesco Ricciardi, could effectively reduce the power of a class that controlled the lives of millions of people. The personal privileges and jurisdictional rights of the nobility were steadily dissolved, and any properties for which they could produce no legal titles were expropriated. Though the landed classes retained immense power in southern Italy, the so-called 'Mezzogiorno', their influence had been significantly curtailed by the state.

Another measure that diminished the power of traditional privilege was the restructuring of state finances. Admittedly, by reforming inefficient and inequitable taxation systems within their empire, the French were primarily hoping to secure enough surplus to pay for their crushingly expensive wars, yet there were also quite positive reasons for wholesale fiscal reform. All European states had been struggling with debt throughout the eighteenth century, and in most cases financial strain had been the underlying cause of social instability and revolution. Fiscal reform accorded with the new spirit of rationalization, as well as being essential to the consolidation of the new order. In the Kingdom of Italy, for example, reforms were planned and orchestrated by its Minister of Finance, Giuseppe Prina, who, through the life of the kingdom, succeeded in overhauling the multiplicity of systems that had existed within Lombardy, Reggio, much of the Veneto, Alto Adige and some Papal departments. In order to impose a uniform land tax, which was the principal source of the state's tax revenue, all these territories were subjected to a wide-ranging cadastral survey. Inevitably the survey faced stiff resistance from landed interests and Prina was not able to complete it. By 1812 about one-third of the kingdom had yet to be surveyed; the anticipated completion date was 1816–17. A modern bureaucracy was developed to manage the variety of direct and indirect taxes that were imposed, and as always, the French model was copied. There were two ministries, treasury and finance, and within these ministries there were departments which dealt with such matters as customs, lotteries, and the census. And among the *comuni*, there were departmental representatives who dealt with duties on the ground and who provided regular reports.

It is difficult to know the extent to which the mental horizons of Italians were altered by such reforms; one can only assume that new dispositions were forged. The centralization of authority and state functions, and the concomitant dissolution of traditional authority, were developments that most Italians were forced to accommodate. Perceptions of authority were adjusted accordingly. That most Italians had to deal with state authorities, that their lives were greatly affected by state legislation, regulations and the decisions of functionaries, no doubt compelled citizens/subjects to think of the state as the essential unit of reference. In the Kingdom of Italy, peasants and landlords alike, from Alto Adige down to the Marches, had their financial affairs regulated by authorities whose offices and records were kept in Milan. The same rules governed the people of the Terraferma as they did the Lombards, Bolognese and Modenese. That these expanded political horizons also produced new cultural identities is unlikely, as it would be premature to describe these new bonds as 'national'. Traditional identities and loyalties continued to command far greater allegiance than any newfangled state organized by Napoleon could muster. The French had significantly rationalized government and standardized administration in Italy, but the cultural ramifications on Italian society varied. The least affected was Naples, where the cadastral survey was produced rather hastily and haphazardly because of the strength of opposition at the communal level. Those most deeply impressed by the values of the new order were no doubt the personnel who functioned within the state system itself. Bureaucrats, accountants, clerks and cashiers, all of whom owed their living to the state, were more likely than most to believe in the legitimacy of the Napoleonic system and its societal role.

Another group that might have developed an emotional attachment to the new order were those who served in the Italian army. Organized essentially to serve the interests of France, an Italian army was nevertheless regarded by the man appointed to administer the Kingdom of Italy, Count Francesco Melzi d'Eril, as an essential requisite for the creation of a fully-fledged state. Four military academies (Bologna, Lodi, Modena, and Pavia) were established in order to create a locally generated officer corps. Promotion was based on merit, a measure which Pietro Teulie, a general, claimed would promote a much stronger emotional bond with Italy. Men between 20 and 25 were eligible for service, from which the state would select a small proportion that appeared most suitable for the rigours of military service. The kingdom provided 6 of the 32 divisions in the *Grande Armée*, including 70 generals. Conscription was introduced as early as August 1802, and through the life of the Italian Republic/Kingdom, a total of 155 000 men were recruited. Italy's standing army rose from 22 779 in 1804 to 40 000 in 1807, and 71 690 in 1812. 27 000 men played a part in Napoleon's invasion of Russia, though only an estimated 1000 managed to return. Each department was required to provide the state with a set quota of recruits: in 1811, of the 6 473 888 inhabitants of the kingdom, 15 000 were designated for the draft. Each of the *comuni*, in turn, was to provide the department with its share of the quota.

Once recruited, the conscripts were distributed between 300 barracks, whose food, shelter and other basic amenities were the responsibility of the local *comuni*. Living conditions were quite harsh, but it is likely that recruits experienced a sense of camaraderie, and the mere fact that they lived away from their homes and among other Italians probably contributed to an identification with Italy. So too did the fact that Italians earned a good reputation on the battlefield. At the same time, the Italian officer corps were known to have developed an antipathy towards French domination, and the Italian army was at the heart of their newfound patriotism.

Overall, through the experience of marching, fighting and living together, of participating in Napoleon's campaigns and in quelling local disturbances, the Italian soldiery probably developed a sense of loyalty to the Italian state, though the depth of that loyalty is hard to fathom. Conscription has normally played a positive role in cultivating national identities, but in the case of Napoleonic Italy one cannot push this line too far, especially as conscription was not at all popular. As in the case of other French reforms, it fostered more resistance than collusion. Recruitment was a massive bureaucratic exercise, the more so since draft dodging was endemic and the recruitment process required the use of force. Conscription was deeply unpopular for several reasons, among them being the fact that peasant families lost an important source of labour. Another was that conscription was widely regarded as nothing less than a child levy. Throughout the empire, conscription had been the main source of friction between the Napoleonic order and communities, and popular resistance often came in the form of open rebellion. Desertion was also a major problem. Between 1806 and 1810, the number of deserters and draft dodgers were estimated at 40 000 men, most of whom had little choice but to survive through brigandage. Mindful of the depth of feeling against conscription in the north, Joseph Bonaparte and his successor in Naples, Joachim Murat, adhered to a less intensive conscription policy.

Although the Napoleonic regimes had reformed the Italian peninsula more effectively and thoroughly than any regimes in the past, one must not exaggerate the extent to which Italian political culture or mentalities had been transformed. After all, the French engendered a great deal more antipathy than admiration. Their intervention in Italian religious affairs was a case in point. While Napoleon was not as hostile to the Church as his Jacobin predecessors, he did force the Pope Pius VII to conclude the Concordat in 1801, which, among other things, forfeited alienated Church property to the State and gave the latter a great deal of power over ecclesiastical matters. One of the most distressing feature of Napoleonic rule was the enforcement of the Concordat, which included the closure of monasteries and the suppression of cultural festivities and celebrations that held a central place in Italian regional cultures. Nothing antagonized the great mass of the population more than the violation of these cultures.

Consent for the Napoleonic political order could only be found among a small minority that had been given a livelihood as functionaries, or those landed interests that were able to capitalize on the sale of Church and other alienated properties. One of the distinguishing characteristics of Napoleonic Europe was the way in which the French sought to secure the allegiance of the propertied classes by absorbing them into the political order. Offices of state in Italy were reserved for men of means, regardless of whether they were nobles or *nouveaux riches*. Princes who had been deposed were generally disconcerted by the extent to which members of the nobility had been absorbed by the new political order. Many of the key figures of the Risorgimento, such as Camillo di Cavour and Massimo d'Azeglio, came from families that had done well under the French. Yet the French could not really count on the loyalty of all of their collaborators, for even this favoured group harboured quite serious grievances. Too many of the key positions in the army, judiciary and upper echelons of the bureaucracy were reserved for French appointees. The logic of such appointments was that outsiders would be less corruptible and more impartial – Italians were often appointed to comparable posts in France, but the symbolic effect of French appointments was to confirm Italy's subordination. More importantly, noblemen who had been co-opted into the new states structures continued to yearn for the return of their cherished privileges and the *ancien régime* generally. Napoleon took away much more than he offered in return: the nobility no longer had a stranglehold over local administrative structures and the courts, and many among them lost property for which they lacked written documentation.

Given the rise in crime against property through the late eighteenth century and the social upheaval experienced during the *triennio*, the French believed they might be able to win the support of propertied Italians through the assiduous maintenance of law and order. In northern Italy especially, the nobility were impressed by the way in which banditry had been stamped out: by 1808, for example, bandit groups that had been operating in Piedmont had been effectively eradicated. Yet it was too high a price to pay for French domination. The Continental Blockade directed by Napoleon at the British severely disrupted trade. The insatiable demands of the Napoleonic war machine meant that propertied Italians were paying far more tax than ever before. More efficient administrative and taxation systems not only meant the French were much more successful than previous regimes in extracting revenue, but it was relatively easy for them to increase taxes and introduce new ones. Indeed all classes chafed under the yoke of Napoleonic rule, especially the lower orders, among whom destitution was rife. Vagabondage was on the rise throughout Italy, to which authorities responded with persecution rather than relief. The imposition of a milling tax in March 1809 saw revolts break out in more than two-thirds of the Italian Kingdom's departments through the following summer months. Italian chagrin was symbolized by the tragic fate of Prina, the Italian Kingdom's resourceful finance minister, who was lynched by a Milanese crowd once the French had finally departed.

Overall, the *epoca francese* was a deeply unhappy experience for most Italians, who consequently rejected nearly all that the French represented. After Napoleon's abdication on 11 April 1814, in the wake of his disastrous campaign in Russia, there was very little support for the maintenance of the satellite kingdoms in Italy. The last Napoleonic monarch of Naples, Murat, tried to muster supporters of the Napoleonic order to fight for a united Italy, but the rallying cries of this Napoleonic satrap fell largely on deaf ears. His army dissolved after being defeated by the Austrians on 2 May 1815, and he was hunted down and executed on 13 October.

Yet the *epoca francese* did have an impact on Italian political life. However much the French had alienated their Italian subjects, the centralized and rationalized government structures that had been introduced were more or less maintained by post-Napoleonic regimes. Princes that had been restored saw little sense in fragmenting state power or dissolving proficient administrative structures. Although the French were extremely unpopular, many middle- and upper-class Italians admired the French model of governance. Thus even those who suffered under Prina's reforms could appreciate the value of an efficient taxation system in a modern state. There was no going back to traditional norms and practices. Through the nineteenth century, Italian politics was dominated by a political class that remained faithful to the Napoleonic policy of a centralization, and whose members included major figures such as Cavour and d'Azeglio of Piedmont and Baron Bettino Ricasoli of Tuscany. Such men were also to be among the founding fathers of the Italian nation-state of 1860.

One of the more negative legacies of the Napoleonic period was cultural elitism. The restoration regimes and the post-Risorgimento state aspired to visions of society that were based on selected Enlightenment values, such as the sanctity of private property and individual liberties, the inviolability of the constitution and the rule of law. Each envisaged a society that would function very much like a city-state or commune, where matters of public importance were discussed openly in the public sphere between men of talent and achievement. It was a liberal political culture, which took a principled stand against privilege and yet sustained a hierarchical conception of society. Thus political power was restricted to those who had a high level of cultural attainment or *civiltà*. Only the propertied, the educated, those who could read Dante or could appreciate opera, could be entrusted with public responsibilities. Throughout the nineteenth century, political elites would seek to absorb the nobility and other men of means, but they also insisted that the rest of the population, because of their lack of *civiltà*, be restricted from access to political power.

Another notable legacy of the *epoca francese* was authoritarianism, for the liberal society that Italy's political elites sought to fashion could only be secured under the aegis of a paternalist state. Napoleon's overhaul of the *ancien regime* had necessitated a measure of ruthlessness, and later Italian state authorities believed that force was necessary if progress was to be achieved. Throughout the nineteenth century, Italy's political elites sought to impose their vision of state and society regardless of the social and cultural realities of this most complex country. That their efforts met with constant resistance merely strengthened their faith in authoritarianism.

Needless to say, the political culture bequeathed by the *epoca francese* had limited social appeal and was stoutly resisted by the Church, which was to remain hostile to Enlightenment and especially liberal values. Indeed resistance was so great that by the end of the nineteenth century Italian elites had made but a superficial cultural impact on society. Their idea of *civiltà* had very little purchase beyond the well educated, who still only constituted a small, albeit expanding, minority. Indeed, what Italy's political elites did succeed in doing was instituting a divide between themselves and the rest of society, thus creating two quite inimical Italies. Generations of Italian social commentators and intellectuals would later identify this great cultural chasm, which was generally construed as a divide between state and society, as the single most important problematic in Italian history after 1860. Not only was the state never able to secure its legitimacy in the minds of the Italian people, but the antagonism of subjects also seriously hampered state attempts to cultivate and nurture an Italian national identity.

The secret societies as forerunners of nationalism

Thus far we have considered how the French Revolution and the Napoleonic period affected the political and social fabric of the peninsula. As well as creating a new political class and a liberal political culture, the Revolutionary period bequeathed another legacy that fed more directly into the making of the Italian nation. That legacy was nationalism. Although the *epoca francese* did not produce a movement that consciously aimed at the creation of a single Italian nation – such movements only really begin to appear in the 1830s – it was the period in which the concept of the nation nevertheless took root. 'Nation' had become an entrenched feature of radical political vocabulary. For French Revolutionaries, the nation was 'the people', and it was the people who were sovereign. In less abstract terms, the nation was the only vehicle that could safeguard and sustain such progressive values as individual liberty, equality before the law and political democracy. The nation was an integral feature of the Revolution's ideological message, hence it was shared with equal enthusiasm by the Revolution's devotees everywhere, including the Italians.

The nation as conceived in the Revolutionary period was essentially a means to an end. In their quest to spread the Revolution, the French took the logical step of creating other nations, such as the Cisalpine, Cispadane and Italian republics. And as the national interests of France, particularly under Napoleon, became a burden on the rest of the empire, it was equally logical for Europe's devotees of Revolutionary values to think of themselves as violated nations. Thus poets such as the great Ugo Foscolo vented their rage against Napoleon because *Italia* had been betrayed. However, such sentiments are not to be confused with the anti-French feelings that were shared at all social levels throughout the occupied territories. For Napoleon's opposition on the left, such as the *giacobini*, the core concern was the betrayal of Revolutionary values. These groups were essentially forced underground, from where they waged a struggle against tyranny, rather than against a foreign nation. Thus the *epoca francese* did not see the emergence of real national movements: conspirators did not conceive their conflict as between nations but as fighting for the integrity of such things as republicanism, equality and nationhood. However, these clandestine movements did become an enduring tradition in Italian and European politics long after the demise of Napoleon, and while they served as vehicles for many radical ideologies, ranging from liberalism to early forms of socialism, the tradition eventually produced real nationalist movements. Among the most important was the national movement that had emerged in Italy by the 1830s. The rest of this chapter will consider the ways in which the early movements of the *epoca francese*, as well as key individuals such as Ugo Foscolo, paved the way for Mazzini and his milieu a generation later.

The initial effect of the French Revolution in Italy was to promote revolution itself. The spectacularly successful precedent set in Paris in 1789 encouraged groups throughout Italy to plot the overthrow of their own state regimes, and by the time of the French invasion in 1796 many such plots had been uncovered and numerous young revolutionaries had been arrested. It also appears that these early *patrioti* were not solely driven by ideological motives in bringing the Revolution to Italy, for these plots related to very long-standing local issues, such as the desire of Bolognese to break from Papal control, or Sicily from Naples. The Revolution fed into centre–periphery antagonisms as much as it did into class conflicts, yet there were also signs in these early years that some revolutionaries were envisaging a complete break with the past. Activists who had actually taken part in the Revolution in France, such as Buonarroti and Enrico Michele L'Aurora of Rome, thought that Italy had to be completely remade in accordance with the French paradigm, and creating a nation was an inevitable corollary. The prospect of a united Italy in the early 1790s was perhaps too fanciful for *patrioti* to take completely seriously, but as the Revolution went through its most radical phase under the Jacobins, and as revolutionary movements in Italy spread more widely, the idea of an Italian nation appeared to gain some currency. By the time the French had arrived in 1796 to introduce nationhood for them, some *patrioti* had already developed quite firm ideas regarding what kind of Italian nation they wanted. This was attested to by the fact that the majority of those who entered the essay competition of September 1796 opted for Italian unity. Needless to say all contestants, including those who preferred a federal solution, were concerned about what form of government would best allow for the retention of democratic life in Italy.

The *patrioti* were also aware they only constituted a tiny minority and were almost totally dependent on the French, hence there was little interest in Italian independence at first. Under French protection, the *patrioti* were initially free to influence public opinion. They set up schools, newspapers, and new clubs and societies through which they sought to educate society and disseminate new ideas. By 1797, however, it was clear that the aspirations of the French and the *patrioti* were inimical, and the more radical among the latter group would develop links with Jacobin conspirators in France as part of their campaign for Italian independence. Among the better known underground groups to emerge in this period was the *Società dei Raggi,* or the 'Society of Rays' (1798), which sought independence as well as the overthrow of the Directory. The French had created the republics in Italy, but the future prospects of these republics now depended on getting rid of the French.

Many among the *patrioti* genuinely believed the Italian masses should play an active role in political life and sought to educate peasants in the virtues of republicanism and secularism. The great majority of Italians, however, saw no virtue in a political order that desecrated religious institutions and imposed massive fiscal burdens. Whatever the differences between the French authorities and the *giacobini,* to the Italian masses they were the same thing, and in 1799, as exemplified by the Sanfede and the Viva Maria! uprisings, the insurgents showed no mercy to the *giacobini.* Thus for liberal and national movements one of the significant legacies of the *triennio* was a reluctance to involve the masses in revolutions and political life generally. The peasants' lack of *civiltà,* their devotion to tradition and deep suspicion of change, made them, if anything, a counter-revolutionary force. Subsequent attempts at revolution would confirm this view.

Once he had betrayed the hopes he aroused in Italy, Napoleon gave the *patrioti* much greater cause to fight for independence. It was not merely the fact that the republics he had initially restored were converted to monarchies, but that he effectively abandoned the idea of the nation as a political community. The secret societies continued their struggles against authoritarian states that seemed to owe more to absolutism than to the French Revolution. The Napoleonic state was so powerful, however, that the secret societies were for the most part inactive. An easily suppressed insurrection in Bologna in July 1802 amounted to the last stand of the *giacobini* and the

Società dei Raggi. Conspiratorial groups continued to exist throughout the Napoleonic period, but they were more secret and obscure than ever. They included the Knights of the Sun, the Adelfi, the Guelfi, the Spilla Nera, the Decisi, the Society for Universal Regeneration, and the most famous sect, the Carbonari, who would have a much greater impact during the ensuing Restoration period. These groups seem to have maintained the ritualistic traditions and hierarchical structures that characterized earlier conspiratorial societies. As far as we can tell, there was considerable communication between the various sects, and there was correspondence with comparable sects in France, and with anti-Napoleonic French officers within the Italian and Neapolitan armies.

Given the secrecy of these groups, it is difficult to know with any certainty the nature of their aims. The Guelfi, for example, seemed to be aiming for an Italy that might emulate Britain. Another northern secret society, the Adelfi, appeared to have been influenced by the *giacobini* and other radical groups, and was radical enough for Buonarroti to join after his return from prison in 1809. Not all accepted the idea of a united Italy or an Italian nation. Some Carbonari, for example, were in favour of the restoration of the Bourbons in Naples. None of the secret societies, however, proved capable of threatening the Napoleonic order in Italy, and most of them heeded the lessons of 1799 and made little attempt to take advantage of the social unrest that plagued the Napoleonic states. Some of them chose instead to appeal to outside assistance, which normally meant looking to Britain. From their base in Sicily, which had never been part of the Napoleonic Empire, the British remained in close contact with the secret societies along the peninsula. Indeed the British system of government attracted a great many of those dejected by the *epoca francese*, and at one point the British commander in Sicily, Lord William Bentinck, entertained, albeit briefly, the promotion of a unified Italian state that would be based on the British model.

While the French succeeded in rendering the secret societies inactive, there were cultural forms of dissent that were much more difficult to police. Resistance was particularly noticeable in the field of language, as the French presence inevitably brought with it a flood of resented 'gallicisms' that quickly entered local usage. The revolution in governance, the new legal, policing and bureaucratic systems, introduced new terms that were inevitably drawn from French or were recently invented by the French. Words such as 'funzionario', 'sotto-ufficiale', 'controllo', 'processo verbale' entered the vocabulary of Italian administration, while others like 'metro' and 'grammo' entered into more common usage. The long-running question over the Italian language was now influenced by the need to fend off this cultural invasion. Regarding the language of bureaucracy, the poet Vincenzo Monti complained of the 'miserable barbaric dialect' introduced into public administration. The reaction was particularly pronounced in territories ruled directly by Paris, where French was indeed being imposed as the national language. Napoleonic satraps and ministers, such as Melzi and Murat, actually believed that Italy should be independent, and in the case of Melzi, an Italian publishing industry was actively promoted. From this period, the capital of the Kingdom of Italy, Milan, began its life as the centre of Italian publishing. The *Società tipografica dei classici italiani* was important in reproducing and publishing classics written in Tuscan, which was but one useful way of propagating the Italian language.

It was difficult for artists, writers and musicians to play the role of dissident, given that their livelihoods normally depended on court patronage, and this was no less true of the *epoca francese*. The great violin virtuoso, Niccolò Paganini, for one, developed his career through the courts of this period, but there were others who decided to take a stand against the French and suffered accordingly. Their example would become a major source of inspiration for latterday patriots, and their works were given pride of place in the canons of national culture. The two greatest literary figures of this period were later honoured as forefathers of the Italian nation, not so much for having provided political programmes but for having evoked passion for *Italianità*. They established Italy as a romantic ideal, an object of love.

The dramatist Vittorio Alfieri (1749–1803) was so important in this regard that Mazzini much later described him as 'the first Italian'. Alfieri was born in 1749 into a Piedmontese noble family, hence he grew up speaking French. His Italian was initially very poor, but as a young man developed a love for Italian and eventually managed to master it. Before the French Revolution he travelled widely and lived for a while in Paris, and though he was a man of the Enlightenment, he was quickly disillusioned by the French Revolution. A famous collection of his writings was entitled 'Misogallo', which constituted an anti-French polemic and in which he exalted the name of Italy. One of his better known plays, the *Bruto minore* (the second Brutus – the first had been dedicated to George Washington), was dedicated to Italy and its liberation. Alfieri's legacy to the Italian national movement was ito infect his audiences with his own passion for Italy. Importantly, his writings also contributed to the formation of a national memory, as his work is replete with allusions to earlier writers going back to Dante, whom he identifies as Italians. Through such allusions, audiences would draw the assumption that they belonged to an Italian historical tradition themselves, and Alfieri showed them the emotions with which such attachment could be expressed.

Alfieri died in 1803 in Florence, the French presence remaining a constant source of distress for him till the very end. An equally important forerunner of Italian nationalism, and a generation younger than Alfieri, was Ugo Foscolo (1778–1827), the son of a Venetian doctor, but born and raised on the Ionian island of Zakynthos or Zante. In Venice he studied classics, developed an intense love for Italian language and literature, and became an ardent opponent of the *ancien régime*. In 1797 he wrote his 'Ode to a Buonaparte Liberatore' (note the Italian spelling) which celebrated the dissemination of the values of freedom and liberty in his beloved Italy. He served for two years in the army of the Italian Republic before becoming Professor of Rhetoric in Pavia in 1806. He nevertheless maintained a critical distance from the Napoleonic order. In 1802 he attended a conference in Lyon on the political future of Italy, where he indirectly criticized Napoleon in his *Orazione a Bonaparte* (now French spelling) by speaking against tyranny. He continued his oblique criticisms through his work. His *Le ultime lettere di Jacopo Ortis*, about a young man's love affair with a noblewoman who nevertheless marries the man to whom she has been betrothed, is set against a backdrop Napoleon's betrayal of Venice in 1797. The turbulence and passion found in this work are widely interpreted as reflecting the age of revolution. Foscolo's allusions to the Italian predicament were often more direct. His *Dei sepolcri* was a thinly disguised criticism of a French law which regulated the size of, and wording on, tombstones. Foscolo regarded this law as an infringement of liberties and centuries-old traditions. His most emblematic action, however, took place after the French had withdrawn and the successor power, Austria, demanded that Foscolo take an oath of allegiance. His refusal forced him to live out the rest of his life in exile. He spent most of those years in England, where he led a miserable existence till his death in 1827. His preference to live in exile rather than suffer the indignity of more foreign rule symbolized a turning point in Italian history. If people were prepared to suffer for Italy, Italy was a possibility.

Foscolo's relationship with the *epoca francese* was ambiguous, much as it was for most progressive Italians who had initially welcomed the transposition of the Revolution to Italy. To their great chagrin, the French brought tyranny and produced an epoch that was oppressive to the great majority of the population. Regarding the history of Italian nationhood, the legacy of the *epoca francese* is equally ambiguous. It is difficult to imagine the establishment of the national idea among the Italians without the period of French rule, yet the mere association between this rule and nationhood made the latter distasteful to most Italians. Even Mazzini believed the *epoca francese* did more to hinder than to help the prospects of national unity, and it was only after decades of many failed attempts to secure Italian independence, specifically the revolution of 1848, that the idea of Italian national unity gained credibility among political elites. The next chapter considers the ways in which the national idea would re-emerge in the post-Napoleonic years, this time through local sources. It was the period in which Italian nationalism made its first appearance.

|3|

The birth of Italian nationalism: political radicalism and state formation, 1814–1847

The collapse of the Napoleonic empire is often accepted by historians as the starting point of Italy's 'Risorgimento', for in the ensuing years, from the beginning of the Restoration period through to the moment of unification almost half a century later, Italy supposedly experienced a process of maturation. Thus whereas in the past unity had been imposed upon Italians by an outsider like Napoleon, it was during the Age of the Risorgimento when that responsibility was gradually assumed by the Italians themselves. It is certainly true that the first real nationalist movements were to appear in the 1830s, that Italian unity became an issue of serious discussion among social elites by the 1840s, and that the pace of Italian unity gathered serious momentum after the revolution of 1848. With the benefit of hindsight, the history of the period 1814 to 1860 can be read as an age in which Italians experienced a national reawakening and decided to make their own history.

In recent times, however, the consensus among historians has been to radically minimize the importance of nationalism in explaining the push for Italian unification. Indeed the label 'Age of Risorgimento' is now deemed a serious misrepresentation for the very reason that nationalism and national unity were hardly the defining issues of that period, and because other processes such as state formation were far more telling in shaping the peninsula's historical path. Before considering the relevance of the period covered in this chapter, it would be useful to discuss basic assumptions regarding the Risorgimento, if only to demonstrate the importance of historical distortion when it comes to the creation of nations. More importantly, by drawing attention to the distortions we can better appreciate the ways in which the 'Risorgimento' period actually *did* contribute to the nation-building process.

Nowadays we speak of the Risorgimento as 'myth'. The use of the term 'myth' in this case can be understood in two ways: in the functional sense of stories that impart values and ideas, and in the literal sense of stories that are substantially fictitious. As with every newly created nation seeking to establish its legitimacy, the Italian state had to cultivate a foundation myth that evoked the values of the new nation. Historians dedicated their working lives to searching out historical facts on which to creatively construct narratives to that effect, yet all the while being convinced that what they were fashioning was scientific and true. Their actual contribution to nation formation was the invention of a national history that had objective credibility and gave modern Italians a belief in their nation's historicity. The myth of the Risorgimento went something as follows. The end of the *epoca francese* ushered in a new spirit of resistance that was exemplified in Ugo Foscolo's decision to endure exile rather than foreign rule. Italians were now prepared to suffer for their freedom, and their chief oppressors, the *ancien régime* and Austria, were eventually overcome as the push for Italian independence gained momentum. The Restoration monarchies suppressed revolutions in 1820–21, 1831 and 1848, yet in hindsight it appeared as if they were stalling the inevitable. Giuseppe Mazzini, Camillo di Cavour, Giuseppe Garibaldi, Massimo D'Azeglio, Carlo Cattaneo and other heroes of the Risorgimento pantheon, driven by their love for Italy and desire for unity and independence, secured Italy's long-expected reunification. Thus the rebirth of the Italian nation in 1860 was deemed to be the conscious design of selfless patriots, achieved against overwhelming odds and accomplished in spectacular fashion. Their commitment and unity of purpose personified the spirit of modern Italy.

This version of the Risorgimento story is typical of national foundation myths in that it cannot bear the scrutiny of critical analysis. Scholars have shown without much difficulty that many 'Founding Fathers' had not been committed to Italian unification at all, that traditional municipal interests nearly always carried greater weight than national unity, and that very few Italians were excited by the prospect of unification. Great moments heavily laden with symbolism were more myth than history, such as the Battle of Calatafimi in Sicily, a minor military encounter that was nevertheless remembered as a major battle won by Garibaldi's forces. That said, the Risorgimento was crucially important after 1860 as a source for Italian identity and in providing positive lessons in patriotic behaviour. Italy needed an inspirational foundation myth, a larger-than-life epic in which men of faultless reputation were united in common struggle to achieve the noblest of aims. In post-unification Italy, the necessity of retaining an uncritical rendition of the Risorgimento was made all the more important because of the disappointments that followed 1860. Unified Italy never measured up to the expectations of even the political class, who along with other groups in society looked back nostalgically to the Risorgimento as a heroic and romantic age.

The symbolic importance of the Risorgimento myth distracted even the best of historians from its distortions; the great Benedetto Croce famously described Italian unification as a 'masterpiece of liberal nationalism', while another great historian, Luigi Salvatorelli, claimed it was the result of a century of moral and political struggle. After the Second World War, however, a new orthodoxy emerged among historians, one that placed a great deal more emphasis on accident and sheer luck in the making of modern Italy. Indeed, historians both within Italy and beyond have demonstrated that Italian nationalism was not as decisive an influence as once thought, and that, more specifically, the nationalists were too few and marginal to precipitate a major political revolution. More will be said of the growing popularity of the idea of Italian nationhood; suffice it to say here that historians nowadays stress causal factors that were perhaps more decisive. In particular, all Italian states in the post-Napoleonic period continued to struggle to find a viable political order in the face of profound social and economic change, and in an ideological environment that was becoming more polarized. They lived under the constant threat of revolution, either from dissident groups or from the discontented masses below. Most importantly, Italy's ruling regimes found it increasingly difficult to ignore the opinions and aspirations of the middle and upper classes, which collectively made their presence felt through an expanding public sphere. By the 1840s, this emergent 'public' had found ways to express its disenchantment and exert pressure, effectively serving notice that political legitimacy was now dependent on public approval.

State formation and civil society

In March 1814, France was defeated by the Grand Alliance (Austria, Russia, Prussia and Britain), after which Napoleon found himself once again in Italy, though now as a prisoner on the island of Elba. After Napoleon's brief but disastrous attempt to revive his empire in 1815, the victorious powers carried on with the process of dismantling his empire, and, having savoured some of the lessons of two decades of incessant conflict, carefully organized an effective system for maintaining international stability. The Congress of Vienna set in place the so-called 'Balance of Power', a system that worked against any single Great Power claiming a mastery over Europe, and which was generally successful in regulating relations among these powers until July 1914. The Congress also demonstrated the extent to which Italian states were perceived as mere pawns. The Savoy dynasty reigned once again over Piedmont and Sardinia, but now also ruled Liguria. The Kingdom of Italy was broken up, with Habsburg Austria recovering Venice and Lombardy. The Grand Duke Ferdinand III made his way back to Tuscany, which incorporated Elba after its abandonment by Napoleon, and the Duchy of Lucca in 1817. Of the smaller states, only Parma, Modena and the Republic of San Marino survived. The Papal States were restored, while the Bourbons returned from Palermo to Naples, which grated with the Sicilians. The realm was renamed the Kingdom of the Two Sicilies.

Although the political geography of the peninsula did not appear radically different to what it had been in 1796, Italy had nevertheless been reorganized in a fashion that suited the Grand Alliance, Austria in particular. The Habsburgs controlled most of northern Italy directly and effectively dominated the duchies of Modena, Parma and Tuscany. As a buffer zone between France and Austria, Piedmont was able to remain the most independent of the Italian states, but for the rest of the country, Austria more or less acted as a policeman, intervening in domestic affairs whenever the *ancien régime* or any other Habsburg interests were threatened.

The period following the Congress of Vienna, the Restoration, was characterized by the *ancien régime's* attempt to undo the French Revolution and take Europe back to how things were before the Bastille had been stormed. In Piedmont King Vittorio Emanuele I was so keen on restoring the *ancien régime* that he reinstituted customs barriers within his own kingdom, gave back to the nobility their privileges, and abrogated all laws introduced under the French. Much the same was done in Modena, where Francis IV practised absolute rule and administered the duchy through his court. Within the Papal States there was a similar attempt to put back the clock in areas ruled directly from Rome, but in the Legations, the provinces that were administered from the cities of Bologna, Ferrara, Ravenna, Forlì and Pesaro, Napoleonic structures remained largely intact. Indeed, Italian rulers recognized that by maintaining the structures inherited from Napoleon, especially centralized government and administration, they were shoring up the power of the state. In the interests of preserving central state power and administrative efficiency, the impact of reactionary politics was quite limited in Naples and Tuscany, as well as in Habsburg Lombardy and Venice.

Restored rulers nevertheless had taken some steps to appease reactionary opinion and to satisfy their own urges to settle scores with the *epoca francese*. After all, for the *ancien régime* it had been an utterly humiliating experience. For years the Italian aristocracy watched their world being pulled apart by an authoritarian, ideologically zealous, excessively secular, and illegitimate adversary. The *ancien régime* and other sections of the population that wilted under French oppression, such as the peasantry, which suffered punitive taxation and watched the desecration of their religious institutions, had many reasons to be nostalgic for an earlier age. The

Restoration period therefore witnessed attempts by Italian rulers to broker a compromise between reaction and revolution, to revive Church power and influence, and renew values such as privilege and tradition, while at the same time retaining features of the Napoleonic state that strengthened state authority. Thus Ferdinand I of the Kingdom of the Two Sicilies took a conciliatory approach towards officials and military officers who had served under Murat, and he retained the system of government and administrative personnel as he found them. Yet at the same time, he would allow no constitution: Sicily's constitution of 1812 was therefore suspended. In Tuscany the nobility had willingly collaborated with the Napoleonic regime and were generally in favour of the reforms that eliminated privileges and promoted commercial life. The returning archduke was similarly unwilling to make all but the most minor gestures to appease reactionaries. The Austrians chose to rule Lombardy and Venice through their own officials, which meant that locals were excluded from the most important administrative and official postings. Yet here too the Austrians were not particularly keen on wholesale change, so administrative, judicial, police and financial structures were left substantially intact.

This amalgamation of revolution and reaction, however, did not necessarily bring stability. In economic terms the thirty-odd years following the defeat of Napoleon were difficult ones for the Restoration states, in which conscious efforts to modernize did more to exacerbate social turmoil than bring economic growth. In political terms, Italian society was too polarized to respond positively to any amalgam of revolution and reaction. Reactionaries vigilantly opposed the diminution of traditional authority and clamoured for the restoration of their lost privileges. Meanwhile, a whole new generation of nobles, bureaucrats, professionals and officers could not accept the absence of constitutional safeguards and bitterly resented all re-manifestations of the feudal order. Regarded by many as going either too far or not far enough, Italy's ruling regimes functioned throughout the Restoration period without an adequate social support base. In the Papal States, for example, Cardinal Ercole Consalvi and successive ministers sought to modernize this most archaic polity, but opposition was fierce and very difficult to overcome. The Legations were not willing to surrender their autonomy to a centralized state based in Rome. Consalvi could not stop the clergy from taking full control of state administration, and from preventing powerful interests retaining tax exemptions that, in turn, seriously weakened the state's financial position. For progressives who looked back nostalgically to the *epoca francese*, the main goal was to have the Restoration regimes adopt constitutions, but the only prospect of realizing that dream was through revolution. In 1820 in Naples, 1821 in Piedmont, and in 1831 in central Italy, liberals launched revolutions that quickly revealed the weaknesses of these states, but each insurrection was efficiently crushed by Austrian troops.

There were other sources of tension that destabilized the Restoration states in Italy. In Lombardy and Venice, for example, competent administration was nevertheless resented because foreigners dominated it, and because local access to official positions was blocked. The Sicilian nobility resumed their quest for independence when the Neapolitan government formally abolished their feudal privileges. The greatest threat to social stability throughout Italy, however, came from the lower orders. Throughout the Restoration period, peasants would continue to suffer from the sale of common land in places such as Lombardy and the Kingdom of the Two Sicilies. The commercialization of agriculture persisted in swelling the ranks of the destitute, but so too did the dramatic rise in population that out-paced any improvements in food production. Peasants were also affected directly by the price slumps in the latter phases of the *epoca francese* and the early Restoration period. The Italian countryside was therefore characterized by rural indebtedness, begging and banditry, and pauperization, which inevitably made the propertied classes feel more insecure. Their solution to the social problem was to seek greater state protection. The upper and middle classes of Italy acquired an obsessive fear of crime and were terrified at the prospect of social revolution, but Italian rulers were generally too weak to suppress banditry and could do little to alter the impression that crime was out of control. The failure to provide adequate security for the propertied classes did much to diminish the legitimacy of the Restoration states, though Piedmont was the exception to the rule. After the *epoca francese*, the Kingdom of Sardinia continued along its anomalous course as a highly centralized and economically progressive state, and had an exceptional record in suppressing banditry. By the 1840s, Italy's propertied classes were not only looking to Piedmont for inspiration but even for direct intervention.

One of the expectations of centralization was that the state would now shoulder far more responsibility for the welfare of society, and an expanding 'public' was ever more determined to hold the state to its responsibilities. Despite the restoration of monarchies and the absence of constitutions, the first half of the nineteenth century did witness the revival of civil society and public opinion. Put simply, individuals and associations of individuals took an increasingly active interest in the functioning and destiny of the state, and state authorities found their opinions and moods difficult to ignore. Social mobility during the *epoca francese* had expanded the number of professionals, officers and bureaucrats who, along with younger members of the nobility, were becoming more insistent about their right to participate in state decision-making and to influence political processes. In most states, attempts to discuss matters of public interest openly were muffled by official censorship and the police, but there were less open ways in which people could function as a public. Affluent individuals who took a deep interest in politics, the arts or other fields of learning often opened their homes to regular social gatherings at which public issues were discussed. These salons or *case* were particularly important in times of government repression, and even when the subject of conversation was not political, these private residences, which temporarily served as public spaces, had the effect of promoting a public consciousness. Cafés, schools, universities and the opera houses were also public gatherings spaces that allowed for the exchange of views and news. Even in authoritarian states such as Piedmont it was becoming more and more difficult for the state to ignore public opinion, and state decision-making was increasingly conditioned by it.

In response to the growth of the public sphere, state authorities sought to establish formal links with society without diminishing the powers and privileges of the ruling dynasty. Some states sought to attain direct access to public opinion through the creation of sectional consultative bodies, as happened in Habsburg Lombardy and Venice. Interest groups that constituted these bodies could make their feelings known to the state, provided the state chose to consult them. A similar system was introduced in Piedmont and the Kingdom of the Two Sicilies in the 1830s, and the Papal States after 1846. Another indication of this new sense of responsibility for society's welfare was demonstrated in the greater interest shown in public works and poor relief. On his accession to the throne in Naples in 1830, Ferdinand II denied his kingdom a constitution but was nevertheless determined to bring progress by promoting state reform and economic development. The Naples of Ferdinand II was a vibrant city, swarming with students from throughout the realm, full of organized cultural societies, learned societies and *case*, and with a very lively publishing industry. Although the Neapolitan public was prohibited from discussing politics openly in 1830s and 1840s, there was nevertheless much discussion of the kingdom's condition and pressing state matters, which brings us to the chief difficulty facing Italy's rulers. No matter how progressive and enlightened an absolute ruler might try to be, or how great his achievements, civil society was nevertheless insistent upon its right of involvement. The king could not stop polite Neapolitan society from exchanging views on the kingdom's backwardness, its lack of roads and its retarded agricultural sector. Although the Restoration monarchies continued to maintain that their legitimacy was based on divine right, the reality was that they were becoming much more dependent on public approval.

The revival of civil society in Italy presented the most formidable challenge to the Restoration states, for not only did it provide a context in which public opinion and disquiet could be formulated, but it also allowed for the development of alternative political cultures. The ideologies that begin to have a major impact in European history, such as liberalism, socialism and anarchism, found receptive audiences among members of the public who were frustrated with the status quo and who yearned for fundamental societal and political change. Within developing civil societies malcontents could exchange information on such matters as socialism, or could seek out others who shared a similar political outlook. More than ever before, polite society, and the educated public generally, were increasingly receptive to new ideas that offered a critique of society and prescriptions for renewal. One, albeit vague, solution that was becoming popular was national unity. The absolutist monarchies of the Restoration states were deemed incapable of sufficiently modernizing Italy and keeping it free of foreign domination. By the 1840s and the especially the 1850s, the idea that Italy's future prospects were better served by some form of unity had gained considerable currency especially in the north and the centre.

In retrospect, then, the unification of Italy in 1860 was partly attributable to the growth of civil society, which allowed the idea of national unity to spread, but why that particular idea came to achieve such prominence requires more detailed explanation. A logical starting point for any answer would be to consider the growth of nationalism as an ideology.

From national to nationalist movement

To students of Italian history the Restoration is better known as the period in which Italian nationalism made its first appearance. Above all, it is the age of Giuseppe Mazzini, the father of Italian nationalism and creator of the first self-consciously Italian nationalist movement. His chief contribution to the history of nationalism in Europe was not so much as an intellectual but in having created a movement that was specifically dedicated to realizing the national ideal. His movement breathed new life into an Italian dissident scene just when existing approaches to revolution had been exhausted. The period witnessed a profound transition in Italian revolutionary activity, as the secret societies were phased out and replaced by a unified and intellectually coherent movement that made national unification its primary goal.

However reform-minded some Restoration monarchs might have been, they were nevertheless dedicated to preserving fundamental features of a feudal past, especially absolute rule, that grated with many Italians. Moreover, the prominent role that reactionaries played in the Restoration period, the strict regime of censorship and prohibitions on political organization that many states had imposed had convinced those of a more progressive mindset that Italy had gone backwards. Under the restored *ancien régime*, Italy, as far as they were concerned, had once again been submerged in darkness. For Mazzini's generation, the great struggle for national unity was one between tradition and progress, darkness and light. Those who were particularly susceptible to this mood were the victims of reactionary revenge attacks after 1814, or those who lost their offices or administrative posts either because of their political affiliations, or because of government cost-cutting exercises. The Restoration period created a new pool of disgruntled Italians who were willing to join secret societies and would later join Mazzini's movement. In Lombardy and Venice, where Austrian administration was every bit as efficient as its predecessor, the fact that local notables were barred from top postings was motivation enough. In the Papal States, members of the laity were particularly incensed by the fact that all administrative positions were once again reserved for the clergy. Within the army of the Kingdom of the Two Sicilies, there were officers of all ranks that had been loyal to Murat and who remained committed to the ideals of the *epoca francese*.

What most opponents of the Restoration wanted was a constitution. Only a constitution could guarantee individual liberties and a progressive system of government. Liberal-minded Italians looked to progressive and powerful Britain for inspiration, where constitutional government was an essential accompaniment to economic prosperity, technological advancement and individual rights. Under the dead weight of the *ancien régime*, progressive Italians, who had always looked to 'Europe' as a measure of Italian backwardness, were dogged by a sense of frustration and humiliation. The concerns of some northern progressives found expression in the Milanese weekly, *Il Conciliatore*, which initially dealt with non-Italian literature but had become a powerful voice of political dissent before it was closed down by Austrian authorities a little over a year after its first publication (September 1818–October 1819). Among its contributors were some of the leading lights of this 'Age of Risorgimento', including Silvio Pellico and the economist Melchiorre Gioia. Piedmontese, Lombard and Tuscan aristocrats discussed and debated methods and programmes of reform, and considerable prominence was given to educational and economic matters. Another notable feature of *Il Conciliatore* was the renewed interest in the promotion of Italian history, which effectively promoted Italian patriotism. *Il Conciliatore* was not a nationalist publication in the sense that it campaigned explicitly for the creation of an Italian nation-state, but its contributors were considering *Italian* solutions to *Italian* problems. This disposition was becoming more commonplace among middle- and upper-class Italians through the Restoration period, as awareness of a common Italian predicament had the effect of strengthening a sense of common identity.

In the meantime, the political struggle against the Restoration states had been waged largely by the secret societies. They operated in much the same fashion as before, with their unique rituals and symbols, their rigid internal organizations, and their conspiracies. Plotting the overthrow of reactionary regimes and imposing constitutions was their main goal. Given their secrecy, it is difficult to know precisely how they hoped to reshape society once in power, though we do know they did not necessarily have common aims. There were many groups, such as the *Federati* and the *Guelfi*, though the most pervasive was the *Carboneria*, which had cells in most parts of Italy and imitators in many parts of Europe, especially France. Within the *Carboneria* could be found a diversity of views, though there was considerable support for the Spanish Constitution of 1812, a very liberal document that provided for a parliament, and an executive whose membership was chosen by the monarch from a list compiled by the parliament. Feudalism in all its forms was to be abolished. The Spanish liberals who devised the constitution were denied the opportunity to implement it, but for radicals within movements such as the *Carboneria*, the Spanish Constitution not only espoused their political aspirations but was also a powerful symbol in itself.

In reality, the secret societies were quite small and no match for the Restoration regimes or the Austrian garrisons stationed on Italian soil. The societies regarded themselves as part of an international movement against a common enemy, but they were incapable of co-ordinating action across Italian states, let alone across Europe. What these conspiratorial groups did have in their favour was that they were unknown quantities. Their mere existence was unnerving to state authorities, whose responses were punitive. Large numbers of spies were employed to monitor suspected members, mail was intercepted and opened, and long prison sentences were meted out to convicted radicals. The societies as such were too small to constitute a threat to established authorities, but they could prove dangerous if they successfully tapped more powerful forces within society, such as the disgruntled peasantry or sections of the army. Serving and former military officers were heavily represented in the secret societies, especially those that had experienced the *epoca francese* and who were ideologically committed to revolutionary ideals. On these grounds, commissions were terminated and career paths blocked. Moreover, there were thousands of soldiers who had been demobilized and could not find alternative employment. Many of them had joined the legions of bandits in the countryside, while others could conceivably be mobilized in insurrections being plotted by the secret societies.

Local *Carbonari* and officers that had been loyal to Murat planned the revolt that took place in the Kingdom of the Two Sicilies in July 1820. It began in Nola from where its spread to much of the Kingdom, and was joined by one of Murat's former generals, Guglielmo Pepe, who incidentally had just been commissioned to raise 10 000 troops to suppress banditry. The monarchy fell within a matter of days, but so rapid was the collapse that the more radical members of the *Carboneria* managed to outmanoeuvre their moderate counterparts and impose the Spanish Constitution. The insurgents quickly fell into disarray. Murat's former officers sought a return to Napoleonic authoritarianism, while those supporting the Spanish Constitution demanded extensive social and political reform. The revolution in Naples was followed quickly by another in Palermo, which was based on a whole range of grievances but which was overtaken by Sicilian elites seeking Sicilian independence. The most formidable obstacle to change, however, was the Habsburg monarchy, which forbade any Italian state from introducing constitutional government. The revolution collapsed when Austrian troops invaded the Kingdom of the Two Sicilies and defeated Pepe's army at Rieti in March 1821. An Austrian occupation force remained there until 1827.

Revolutionary forces in Piedmont encountered similar difficulties. In this most reactionary of Italian states, liberals thought they might be more successful if they secured the support of sympathetic members of the royal family, including the king and particularly Prince Carlo Alberto, who was widely thought to be a liberal. The revolt broke out in Alessandria in early March 1821 and spread to many cities in the kingdom, but it quickly transpired that the conspirators were not at all a united group. Those who had seized control of Novara and Alessandria were of a much more radical temperament than those in control of Turin, while members of the Genoese movement were driven by the desire for independence from Piedmont. As it happened, neither king nor prince responded positively to the insurrectionaries, who in turn failed to organize a co-ordinated response to an imminent invasion of Austrian and Russian forces determined to restore legitimate rule. The revolution was quashed with little difficulty.

For the genesis of Italian nationalism, the repression that followed these revolutions was probably more important that the revolutions themselves. The Austrians and the more reactionary ruling elites embarked on a wholesale persecution of *Carbonari* and members of other secret societies throughout Italy, and they did not discriminate between moderates and radicals. The reactionary cardinals that ruled the Legations, and groups such as the Sanfedisti of the Papal States and the Calderari in Naples, seized the opportunity to persecute their political opponents. Numerous dissidents were put on trial, many were given death sentences, and others had long prison terms imposed upon them. The repression lived long in the memories of Italian progressives, as did Austrian participation. For the fact that Austria was primarily responsible for suppressing the revolutions merely confirmed to Italians that they were not free, and that freedom from foreign domination was a necessary precondition for instituting liberal reforms. It was in this period when the incarcerated Silvio Pellico wrote his famous *Le mie prigioni* (My prisons), which was interpreted later as an evocation of Italy's predicament as a captive nation. Austria also confirmed its use as a focus of Italian antipathy. Moreover, the court trials that followed launched a new set of national heroes, such as the Lombard Federico Confalonieri, whose death sentence was commuted to life, and who wrote of his ordeal in *Memorie politiche*. He would also inspire later generations of dissidents to act selflessly for liberty and progress.

The 1820s were dark years for the secret societies, but by the end of the decade they had re-grouped, had spread to new places such as Rome, and were ready for their next assault. In 1830, revolution in Paris once again reverberated through much of Europe, and this time found a response in central-northern Italy. In February 1831 revolutions broke out in the duchies of Modena and Parma, and among some of the Papal Legations. These uprisings were orchestrated by the Modenese liberal, Ciro Menotti, who had organized committees in Bologna, Parma and Mantua, as well as a handful of other cities. Significantly, Menotti and some of the conspirators had hopes of liberating the whole of Italy and creating an Italian state. As it happened, the *ancien régime* quickly collapsed in the face of revolution, and the conspirators involved in each of the fallen cities were expected to appoint representatives to the so-called 'government of the united Italian provinces'. But it quickly transpired that these localities were far more interested in attending to local issues and meeting local aspirations. And as with the previous revolution, there were serious differences between moderates and radicals within each of the cities.

Needless to say, the Austrians had no trouble in crushing this central Italian revolution as well, yet it served as a real turning-point in the history of Italian dissent. As ever, particularism was shown to have much greater purchase on the Italian mind than Italian unity, but 1831 convinced many among the secret societies that the Italians would never be free unless they could achieve unity. The solution lay in the creation of a centralized nation-state on the French and British model, or perhaps a federal system that reflected Italy's political and cultural heterogeneity. Suffice it to say that progressives throughout the peninsula were weary of failure and began to see national unity as their salvation. Giuseppe Mazzini was just one among many activists who were disillusioned by the futility of old methods and who were now prepared to take a wholly new direction. The quest for Italian unity, or the Risorgimento, really started when the earlier unstructured approaches to Italian emancipation were finally recognized as unworkable.

Mazzini and the Italian nationalists

The emergence of a new generation helped to effect the transformation of Italian political dissent in the 1830s. Among the new crop of energetic youth was Mazzini himself. Born in 1805 in Genoa, the son of physician and professor of pathology, Mazzini read law at university and showed some talent as a literary critic. As a young Genoese, he resented the fact that his homeland had been ceded, by the Congress of Vienna, to authoritarian Piedmont. In 1829 joined the local *Carboneria*. The following year he was caught and imprisoned for three months, after which he began a life of exile and hardship, thus following in the footsteps of the great poet whom he greatly admired, Ugo Foscolo. He chose to live in Marseilles, where he made contact with many more exiled *Carbonari*, and it was during this period that they conceived of a new progressive movement. In July 1831, they formed an association called 'Young Italy', which in many ways resembled the secret societies in terms of its membership, which was also drawn wholly from the middle and privileged classes. The major difference, however, was that this was a truly national movement. Whereas the *Carboneria* was essentially a loose alliance of regional cells that often had different aspirations, Young Italy was a single, national movement dedicated to the unity of Italy. Whereas the secret societies had vague and contradictory programmes, Young Italy had well defined objectives. As far as Mazzini and his group was concerned, Italy could only move forward as a community of free people, and the liberties of all Italians could only be guaranteed against external and internal antagonists if they had a republican form of government. Some form of constitutional monarchy might be acceptable as a provisional solution, but for Mazzini freedom and republicanism went hand in hand.

This new movement struck a chord among dissidents throughout Europe. Soon after the creation of Young Italy, Young Poland and Young Germany and other such named movements also appeared. The new emphasis on nationalism did not signify a change away from the internationalist perspective characteristic of early nineteenth-century political ideologies – 'Young Europe' was also formed in Switzerland in 1834. Mazzini abhorred chauvinism that resulted from extremist patriotism, a malady that he incidentally identified as 'nationalism'. Rather, he shared the view held by other thinkers, such as Herder, that the nation offered the best prospects for the betterment of humankind. Mazzini advocated a continent containing a family of nations, and in 1857 he specified that Europe could contain twelve viable nation-states, including one that contained Serbs and Croats.

In some ways Young Italy resembled a modern political party. It had a formal recruitment programme that covered every province, and which was designed to recruit people who could demonstrate their commitment to the cause. Young Italy had great success in recruiting members in the vicinity of Mazzini's birthplace, in Piedmont, Liguria and Lombardy, but less so in central and southern Italy. Each new member took an oath and an alias. Initially, they had to be less than forty years of age so the movement could truly be a fellowship of young people, who, frankly, would be more willing to struggle and suffer deprivations than older brethren. The movement also had a journal, in which Mazzini and leading figures of Young Italy elaborated their views, and which supporters managed to circulate throughout Italy.

Given the unity and persuasiveness of Young Italy, state authorities had reason to believe it was a more dangerous movement than the secret sects. The movement seemed to be constantly looking for that revolutionary moment, and authorities managed to uncover a number of plots. Mazzini himself was the victim of an international manhunt that forced him to spend much of his time either indoors in lonely isolation, or as a fugitive moving from place to place. He was to spend most of his life in the relative safety of England.

Yet prior to 1848 the men of Young Italy had very little to show for their sacrifices. Plots were uncovered before they could be launched, or crushed before they had achieved any momentum. The first was particularly disastrous. Young Italy planned its first revolution in 1833 in Piedmont, where it found recruits within the military. The plot was betrayed to authorities, and as a result the Piedmontese branch of Young Italy was almost destroyed, with its leaders arrested and 12 men executed. Neapolitan, Lombard and Tuscan branches of Young Italy were also suppressed in the aftermath. In 1834 another rising planned in Genoa, which promised to be Garibaldi's initiation in the nationalist cause, was also uncovered before it was launched. In Venice in 1840, Attilio and Emilio Bandiera founded the Mazzinian movement *Esperia*, and in 1844, with the support of nineteen followers, tried to launch an uprising in Calabria. They were betrayed and apprehended, and the Bandiera brothers and Domenico Moro, another leader of *Esperia*, were executed. The main reason why revolutionary activity in this period has such a pathetic record is that it failed to establish any popular support. As with the *Carboneria* before them, the nationalists were not prepared to exploit the massive potential of Italy's discontented masses because they believed (perhaps rightly) that these masses could not be trusted to follow their lead.

At the same time, they naively hoped that members of their own class would rally to their cause once a plot had been initiated, an expectation not warranted by past experience. Among Italy's upper and middle classes, Mazzini's calls for active support for national unification, republicanism and, more particularly, revolution, had limited appeal. There was, however, a great deal of sympathy for aspects of the nationalist programme. The Piedmontese aristocrat, Massimo d'Azeglio, was an important sympathizer. He spent some time among struggling artists in Rome and, unlike other members of the Piedmontese upper class, had seen enough of Italy to become emotionally attached to it and appreciate some of its more pressing problems. He spent many years in the Papal States, where he made contact with Mazzinian groups and wrote about a failed revolt in Rimini in 1845. The book, *Degli ultimi casi di Romagna*, was published the following year. In it he made it clear that fundamental change through revolution would never succeed, and that public opinion needed to be convinced of the need for reform. That thousands of copies of his book were sold after its publication indicated that there was strong public interest among political moderates who had no truck with Mazzinian calls for revolution and republicanism.

D'Azeglio was representative of a strand of national opinion that developed in parallel to Mazzini's democratic nationalism and was hopeful of

replacing the moribund *ancien régime* with a liberal political order dedicated to serving the interests of the propertied classes. Moderate opinion
sought constitutional government and parliamentary institutions, but was
resolved to keeping the masses under a tight rein. Thus the 'moderates' were
politically liberal yet socially conservative advocates of national unity,
though they did not constitute a movement in the formal sense. Rather, the
moderates, whose views increasingly reflected a growing proportion of
educated Italians, in d'Azeglio's words constituted 'a conspiracy of public
opinion in broad daylight'. This emergent public opinion was not of a single
mind and many prescriptions for Italy's problems were canvassed, although
it can be said that very few if any moderates were attracted to the idea of
an integrated Italian nation-state. A fair indication of moderate opinion
might be sampled by considering three of the best known proponents of
national unity: Balbo, Cattaneo and Gioberti.

Count Cesare Balbo (1789–1853) was a politician and historian who
had served in the Napoleon's armies and was later to become Piedmont's
first prime minister. For Balbo and other moderates like him, the essential
goal of national unity was to rid Italy of foreigners. He yearned for an Italy
that resembled Britain, a land free of foreign domination, which enjoyed
constitutional monarchy and the guaranteed protection of civil liberties. In
common with many moderates, he regarded Mazzini's ideas as fanciful.
Such views were expressed in his famous 1844 publication, *Delle Speranze
d'Italia*, in which national unification was denounced as childish, but in
which he advocated the virtues of federation. Balbo's Italy would have no
single centre of power but a series of centres, namely Turin, Milan,
Florence, Naples, Rome, Parma and Modena. While confederation reflected
Italy's cultural diversity, it did not necessarily weaken Italy, as the Lombard
League had demonstrated many centuries before in its encounters with the
Holy Roman Empire and the Papacy. Balbo's solutions to Italian problems
were largely found by looking into Italian history.

A better known exponent of federalism and one of the more subtle minds
of the Age of Risorgimento was the Milanese Carlo Cattaneo (1801–69).
Cattaneo shared Balbo's desire that Italy should once again become a
respected part of Europe, but he looked for solutions in science and
economics rather than Italian history. Unlike those moderates who sought
to rally the support of Italy's ruling elites, Cattaneo and other more radical
liberals advocated a new political order that was dominated by the productive classes, or more specifically, the entrepreneurial middle classes. He had
little time for revolution and the romantic nationalism of the Mazzinians,
but he did believe that the solution to Italy's problems lay in the implementation of wide-ranging practical reforms, especially rapid economic
modernization. Through economic change, which could only be secured
through the auspices of states dominated by the concerns of entrepreneurs,
Italy could then deal with its other problems. Cattaneo did not believe a

single Italian state was desirable, but he did see the practical economic and political benefits of a federation of states. He believed that the commune was the cornerstone of liberty, and in 1864, Cattaneo would oppose the Italian state's policy of merging smaller communes with larger ones.

Tellingly, the man whose ideas had the greatest impact on the Italian public was also the least radical. Vincenzo Gioberti (1801–25) was a priest who at one time had served as professor of theology in Turin, the city of his birth, and who had also been implicated in revolutionary activity in the early 1830s. He was best known, however, for his *Del primato morale e civile degli italiani*, published in 1843, which sought to convince Italian elites of the wisdom of instituting some form of Italian unity. Much like Balbo and Cattaneo, he advocated a confederation of Italian states, but believed this arrangement had to be led by the pope and protected by the Piedmontese military. The *Primato* showed no interest in constitutions, nor did Gioberti share Cattaneo's belief in reason and science as a cure to Italian backwardness. He argued that any Italian project which ignored the Church was tantamount to forging a state system without reference to Italian culture. Needless to say Gioberti did not convince the papacy of the wisdom of national unity, but his book was very widely read. His chief service to the cause was to make national unity palatable among Italian elites that previously associated unity with revolution.

Italian civil society's receptivity to the ideas of Balbo, Cattaneo, Gioberti and other moderates signified the extent to which opposition to the settlement of Vienna extended far beyond radical circles. It also demonstrated that the belief that Italian unity as a means of solving problems was gaining ground. One popular solution to Italian backwardness was to imitate the Germans, who were also distributed in small states, but who in 1834 had formed an economic union (the Zollverein) that was mutually beneficial to each of its members. An Italian economic union was expected to bring with it a standardized set of weights and measures and a common currency, as well as the removal of internal trade barriers, such as tariffs and customs duties. Liberals were particularly attracted to the vision of economic unification, as they tended to imagine Italian regeneration in terms of an economic revival. The main inhibiting factor was the Austrians, who controlled the most economically advanced part of Italy (Lombardy), and the *ancien régime*, whose political and economic prerogatives often violated the workings of free market capitalism.

The growing popularity of national solutions to Italian problems was reflected somewhat indirectly by the development of specifically 'Italian' educational and scientific societies. The best known venture was the Congresses of Italian Scientists, which met regularly from 1839. The Congresses were not meetings of nationalists but of dedicated scholars from a range of scientific fields, but the mere fact that these were 'Italian' gatherings was of some concern to Austria's chief minister, Clemens von

Metternich. Indeed social science subjects and statistical studies were deemed too politically sensitive to be noted in congress agendas, and delegates were quite aware that the very act of information exchange could be construed as a form of political dissent. One of the great achievements and patriotic duties carried out by these Congresses was to collect and consolidate information, such as inventories of natural resources, that contributed to a scientific portrait of Italy. Thus scientists were now adding to the corpus of raw materials hitherto found in historical, philological and artistic work that enabled descriptions of Italy. In other words, Italy was being consolidated as a subject that could be readily imagined.

Public discussion on railway construction also reflected the view that progress was achievable if there was Italian unity. Italian commercial interests had been hoping to capitalize on growing commercial traffic coming through the Suez Canal, and they were equally keen to connect with Europe's expanding network of railways. What could be more essential for the establishment of an Italian economic union on the German model, and what could be more effective in breaking down Italian parochialism than a uniform railway network traversing the entire peninsula? Supporters of unity, such as Cattaneo and the Piedmontese nobleman and future Italian Prime Minister, Camillo di Cavour, had foreshadowed the crucial role that railways could play in effecting an Italian confederation. Railway construction was a key subject at the Congress of Italian Scientists in Genoa in 1846, where delegates discussed whether Italy should have one north–south rail line or two running along the Adriatic and Tyrrhenian coasts respectively. The railway question did, however, confirm the extent to which national unity was regarded more as a means to other ends, as most schemes did not include economically under-developed central or southern Italy. The most famous publication on the topic, Ilarione Pettiti di Roreto's *Delle strade ferrate italiane e del migliore ordinamento di esse* (The Italian railways and an improved plan for them) (1845), did as much. Although people were beginning to think in terms of 'Italia', such imaginings were quite contingent on more pressing matters.

The road to 1848

Perhaps the clearest indication of the significance of the new 'national opinion' was the importance ascribed to it by the king of Piedmont, Carlo Alberto. By 1845, particularly after having read Balbo's *Delle Speranze d'Italia*, the Savoyard monarch was keen to assume leadership of the movement for Italian unity. He probably had not acquired a passion for Italy or *italianità*, but he was certainly driven by the need to save the country from the growing influence of liberalism, and to ensure that no other Italian dynast took the leadership initiative. In fact by June 1846 he was goaded into action by the sudden emergence of a rather reluctant rival: Pius IX. 'Pio Nono' appeared to be of liberal and reformist disposition, and by most accounts an affable character, all of which made him very much unlike his stern and reactionary predecessors. Judging from his friendly demeanour and some of his early acts as pope, such as the emancipation of the local Jewry, many assumed that Pius was the man that Gioberti had anticipated, the pope to lead the charge for Italian unity. It transpired later that Pius differed very little from his predecessors on most issues, including the question of national unity, and any critical assessment of Pius's earlier record would have shown that he had little sympathy with progressive issues. Rather he was a confused man, overwhelmed by the adulation showered upon him. Quite simply, he was not the man he was meant to be, and he actually threatened to abdicate. 'I do not want to do what Mazzini wishes, I cannot do what Gioberti wants,' he said.[1]

That so much was expected of Pio Nono was indicative of the restive mood that characterized Italy in the mid-1840s. All social classes could sense that a crisis was looming. For liberals, the urgency to secure economic and political reforms was based on their own fears of the rural and urban masses, and their belief that the continuing intransigence of the *ancien régime* guaranteed revolution. And as will be discussed in the next chapter, revolution did come soon enough.

---

[1] Quoted from Frank J. Coppa, *The Modern Papacy since 1789* (London, Longman, 1998), p. 88.

|4|

The unification of Italy,
1848–1860

The revolution of 1848, much like the relatively minor outbreaks of 1820, 1821 and 1831, ended in failure, yet each revolution in its turn demonstrated the fragility of the Restoration states. On each occasion, the ruling regime collapsed suddenly in the face of insurrection and had to be rescued by the Habsburgs. What made the Restoration states so brittle, apart from their profound economic difficulties, was that they had failed to cultivate a support base within civil society. In their determination to remain faithful to the settlement of 1814, to preserve absolute rule and prohibit wider participation in matters of state, the Restoration monarchies cut themselves adrift from an emergent civil society, which in turn was becoming ever more sophisticated and demanding of its political authorities.

In the meantime, Italian society was becoming increasingly polarized and difficult to manage from above. The *epoca francese* unleashed a series of conflicts between advocates of reaction, conservatism, liberalism, nationalism and socialism; and even the traditional rivalries between municipalities, between municipal factions and between the generations appeared to have become more competitive and bitter. Militating against open social and political conflict throughout Italy was the ever watchful eye of Metternich's Austria, and it is significant that the massive scale of revolutionary activity that erupted and persisted through 1848 had much to do with the fact that the Habsburg monarchy was at that time preoccupied with suppressing revolutions closer to home. The Habsburgs managed belatedly to restore their authority over the peninsula by early 1849, but not before the whole panoply of political and social tensions were played out in open conflict. More importantly for our purposes, the revolution of 1848 did provide a conclusive outcome in the struggle between the *ancien régime* on the one hand, and proponents of national unity on the other. Moderates and democrats alike regarded 1848 as a temporary setback. The *ancien régime* was deemed a spent force, but the question of Italy's future remained unclear and it took more than a decade before a firm answer was found.

To this point we have sought to understand the history of Italian nation formation through long-term structural processes, especially state formation, economic modernization, social change and the ideological impact of the Enlightenment. The *epoca francese* was dealt with in some detail if only because it intensified the above processes, and because in so many ways it fixed the terms for Italy's political and cultural development. Long-term factors were important in setting the stage for the events leading to 1860, but they can never sufficiently account for the events themselves. It must be remembered that those who shared Mazzini's desire for an Italian nation-state prior to 1860 were but a tiny minority, that neither Piedmontese leaders, moderates nor many democrats, anticipated or desired an Italian nation-state. Unification was less a product of design and more of the accidents and twists of fortune. Hence the events leading up to that moment, specifically 1848 to 1860, merit close attention.

Italian unity and 1848

By the mid-1840s, Italy and indeed the entire continent had unmistakably entered a period of crisis. Europe was not only wallowing in an economic recession but was also beset by a series of poor harvests that produced social upheavals on a scale not seen since the *epoca francese*. Food shortages were so desperate that municipal authorities in the affected parts of Europe organized relief work to avert a complete catastrophe. The sense that the continent was on the cusp of another major revolution was widespread.

The inevitable social and economic crisis had political ramifications. Indeed liberals and radicals were determined that it would. Liberals feared that without reform the chances of averting revolution would be lost, an argument they exploited with great force when goading the absolute monarchies to effect change without violence. Piedmont's Carlo Alberto, who in his younger days was thought to have been a liberal, had taken an oath on accession to never allow a constitution, and had ever since shown that he was rigidly devoted to the principles of absolutism. He had the support of a like-minded minister in Solaro della Margarita, and from sections of the nobility, bureaucracy, clergy and army, but there were also members of these same institutions, as well as of the professions and commercial classes, who believed the time for liberal reforms had come. Count Cesare Balbo was among the chorus of influential liberal subjects who sought to influence the king to relinquish much of his power, but it was outside events that would impel the obstinately absolutist Carlo Alberto to do so, particularly developments in Rome. The election of Pope Pius IX on

16 June 1846 was a turning point in Italian history, and it was certainly interpreted as such at the time. Decades of pent-up frustration among liberals and radicals in the Papal States were suddenly given expression with the advent of a pope who was keen to introduce measures that might relax social and political tensions in his realm. In doing so, Pius unwittingly unleashed forces that he found almost impossible to harness and which would envelop the whole of Italy. Revolution was in the air. Between June 1846 and the collapse of the Venetian Republic in August 1849, Italian politics was to be in a state of flux. Age-old structures and conventions were challenged and overhauled, and a whole array of social and ideological tensions exploded.

Pius's early days as pope appeared to confirm the aspirations of liberal and radicals. He immediately issued an amnesty to political prisoners, and followed with a spate of progressive measures. Thus positions within the Papal government that had previously been reserved for clergymen were opened to the laity, and a 'consulta di stato' (council of state), containing representatives from the localities, was created to serve as an advisory body. Jews were allowed to move out of the ghetto, and Pius also talked of the need for railways and an Italian customs union. Yet the new pope was no liberal, and his reforms were not really the product of a progressive vision. In most cases he was bending to public pressure for change, but each concession merely whetted the appetite for further reform. Pius's calls for a customs union between Italian states appeared to suggest that he was interested in the question of Italian unity, but it later transpired he had no such interest. He simply was not the man the adoring crowds had imagined him to be, and he found the momentum he had naively unleashed deeply troubling.

Pius's reforms precipitated developments elsewhere. In Vienna, his concessions had become a major source of consternation. The Austrians sent signals of their willingness to use force and restore order, given that they believed Pius was the captive of radicals in Rome. The seasoned Austrian general, Joseph Radetzky, without Pius's approval, decided to occupy Ferrara in July 1847, but the move appeared to everyone else as a declaration of war on the Papacy, and Pius had no choice but to retaliate. He moved forward with the idea of an Italian customs union that included Tuscany and Piedmont, and a treaty was signed in November. In excluding the Austrians, the treaty symbolically asserted Italy's desire for independence, and Metternich, having offended Catholics all over Europe with the occupation of Ferrara, was not in as good position to enforce order as he had been in 1821 and 1831.

Italian society continued to live under the cloud of imminent war, especially as the Austrians were faced with resistance from other quarters as well. Carlo Alberto of Piedmont in particular was eager not to allow Pius's running as leader of Italy to go unchallenged. He appeared to relish the opportunity of taking up the cause of Italian independence, partly to deflect domestic attention from the issue of liberal reform, and largely because he hoped to dominate Italy in the event of an Austrian defeat. For the Piedmontese monarch, dynastic ambition was the prime motivation, but to secure public support he would be forced to implement reforms. And for moderate opinion throughout Italy, independence and reform went hand in hand. Before joining the customs union with Pius and Leopold II of Tuscany, Carlo Alberto had already conceded to a few modest reforms, including a relaxation of censorship and changes to local government. Then another stunning development in southern Italy gave further impetus to the cause of political reform. A revolution in Sicily in January 1848 prompted Ferdinand II to grant a constitution, compelling Leopold in Tuscany and Carlo Alberto in Piedmont to follow suit in February and March respectively.

Within two years of Pius's accession, a great deal had changed in Italy. Many states now had a constitution, an Italian 'Zollverein' was in the making, and all the while Austria had been kept at bay. Yet like Pius, Ferdinand, Leopold and Carlo Alberto were unsympathetic to liberal reform. The dynasts ensured that each constitution was as conservative as possible, and as for the customs union, Pius showed a marked reluctance to push things along. These rulers were captives of events and of a broadening public desire for reform and independence, yet for the most part they had temporarily succeeded in appeasing the desire for change. In the spring of 1848, however, events shifted into a higher gear, making the developments of the previous two years appear comparatively benign. One particularly frightening feature for Italy's propertied classes, let alone the reigning monarchs, was the prominent role played by democrats and the lower classes in the ensuing struggles.

On 25 February 1848 yet another revolution had broken out in Paris. Once again this precipitated revolutions elsewhere in Europe, including in the capital of the Habsburg monarchy itself on 13 March. Other centres of the empire followed suit: revolution broke out in Venice on 17 March, and the following day in Milan, where its residents fought a desperate struggle against Radetzky's troops and drove them out of the city. Throughout Italy, the force of popular revolution swept the Austrians away. In Lombardy and the Veneto, it was the artisans and workers who made the revolution, with the support of Italian troops who had deserted from the Austrian garrisons. As elsewhere in Europe, the outbreak of revolution and the stunning victories against the established authorities produced a carnival atmosphere, or what is commonly remembered as the 'springtime of peoples'. Insurgents throughout the cities and towns of Italy celebrated in unison, even if the only things they had in common were their opposition to the Austrians and their desire for independence. Italy's rulers were once again faced by powerful movements from within society that were hard to resist. And Carlo

Alberto was the one dynast with enough guile to harness this force in order to realize his personal ambition to dominate Italy.

In Lombardy and the Veneto, provisional regimes were set up in the wake of the departing Austrians. Inevitably, the most pressing issue for the insurgents was the preservation of their newly won independence, but how this was to be secured precipitated confrontations between democrats and moderates. The initiative was with the democrats, particularly Mazzinians, for many of them had taken a leading part in the insurgency and won public acclaim. Yet as it also became clear that the insurgents would need the support of Piedmont, given that the Austrians were bound to retaliate at some point. So important was Savoyard support that leadership in the liberated northern cities soon reverted to the moderates and the traditional urban elites. Even Mazzini acknowledged, to the frustration of many of his followers and allies, that Italy's best hopes for independence lay in conceding leadership to the Savoyard monarchy.

Although horrified by the upheavals, not least because the revolutionaries in Lombardy might seek the assistance of the French, Carlo Alberto decided he would champion their cause and that of Italian patriotism generally. The Italian tricolour was raised, but with the Savoyard crest fixed on it. Indeed from the very beginning, Carlo Alberto's actions made it clear that he was essentially pursuing his own interests. He took full advantage of Lombard and Venetian vulnerability to insist that the price of his support was Savoyard rule. The issue was hotly debated among the political factions in the region, with some like Cattaneo arguing that the price was not worth paying, while Mazzini was in accord with moderates in thinking that it was, at least for the time being. The Lombards and the Venetians, except Venice itself, voted overwhelmingly for unification with Piedmont, but Carlo Alberto's image as a shameless opportunist remained fixed in Lombard and Venetian minds.

On 23 March Piedmont declared war on Austria, and what had begun as a popular revolution reverted to a dynastic war between the Savoyards and the Habsburgs. From March to July Italy was preoccupied by the military campaign to drive the Austrians out of Italy. Tuscany and the Kingdom of the Two Sicilies, under pressure from patriotic sentiment, followed Piedmont's lead, though Carlo Alberto, who had no desire to share the spoils of victory with other Italian princes, made little effort to utilize their support, or that of volunteer groups. His slogan, that 'Italy shall do it alone' (*Italia farà da sé*), supposedly evoked commitment to the patriotic cause but it was more a case of the Savoyards doing it alone. It proved a foolish strategy, as did everything else Carlo Alberto did once he had declared war on the Austrians. His incompetence in the field was impossible to hide. For the Habsburg monarchy the revolutions of March 1848 had been so disastrous that it actually decided to come to terms with Piedmont, but Radetzky, noting Carlo Alberto's failure to take advantage of initial Austrian disarray and convinced that the Italian campaign could be destroyed in one decisive battle, persuaded his superiors to fight on. The octogenarian general had long experience of defeating Italian armies, and his instincts were once again proven right. Much like a feudal monarch, Carlo Alberto had taken command of the military campaign personally instead of allowing more experienced and competent officers to take the helm. He led his poorly armed and supplied force of 60 000 into contested terrain without maps, and made no attempt to prevent Austrian forces from regrouping and from being re-supplied. After a series of minor battles between Austrian and Piedmontese forces, there was a major encounter on 24 July at Custoza, where Radetzky won a decisive victory.

The utter failure of the Piedmontese campaign was attributed by Cavour and Balbo, both senior ministers in his government, to the fact that Carlo Alberto waged the Italian campaign as if it were his personal, dynastic war. The king's actions following Custoza confirmed the extent to which he was out of step with public opinion. Thus he preferred to sign an armistice with Radetzky than accept the assistance of the French, who were prepared to send 60 000 men to continue the campaign for Italian independence. His strategy, which was meant to buy time in which to organize another Savoyard-dominated campaign, was widely criticized for allowing the Austrians to resume their control of Lombardy and the Veneto. His own parliament refused to ratify his armistice. In the meantime, another major setback in the midst of the military campaign was the decision of Pius IX to declare his opposition to the war against Catholic Austria. He finally showed his true colours when he denounced the Piedmontese invasion of Lombardy, being Austrian territory, and on 29 April he denounced the war and the independence movement. Having been for so long the focus of patriotic hopes, Pius was now a villain.

With Carlo Alberto's dynastic war adjourned and his reputation in tatters, and with Pius having betrayed the patriotic cause, it was now the turn of radical elements to carry on the struggle. Mazzini proclaimed it was now time for the Italian people to take charge. Even before the royal debacle at Custoza, democrats and others were already actively pursuing a separate agenda. Through much of Italy, patriots had formed groups or 'circles', and after Custoza they exerted pressure on their governments, dominated by moderates, to maintain the struggle for independence. These circles were quite successful in Tuscany. In late August 1848, popular discord rocked the cities of Livorno, Arezzo, Pistoia and Lucca, and by 12 October the government of moderate Gino Capponi had been overthrown. His replacement was Giuseppe Montanelli, who was well known as an advocate of Italian independence, and whose social and political ideas put him firmly in the democrat camp. Tuscany travelled so far down the radical path that on 23 February 1849 Leopold II took fright and fled to the Kingdom of the Two Sicilies. The democrats were also in the ascendancy in Piedmont. In the eyes of local democrats, Custoza and Carlo Alberto's ignominious armistice had discredited the patriotic credentials of the moderates as much as the *ancien régime*. Among those championing the resumption of war against Austria was Gioberti, who was eager to focus the energies of the democrats away from issues of political and social reform, and have them concentrate on the struggle for independence instead. By December 1848, Gioberti had formed a government with democrat support.

In Rome, Pius's allocution of 29 April suddenly made his life very difficult. The Civic Guard which had been formed during the exuberant early days when Pius seemed a progressive, and which he had blessed with great reluctance, defiantly ensconced themselves in the Castel Sant'Angelo. Sensing his grip on power had been weakened, Pius appointed Count Terenzio Mamiani as minister of the Interior on 4 May. Mamiani was a man whose integrity was recognized by most Romans, and he managed to keep some sense of stability in Rome through to July. But Pius then sought to act as mediator between what he termed the 'German' and 'Italian' nation in the wake of Custoza, which again incensed the patriotic sensibilities of the Romans. Through late summer and autumn, relations between the pope and the Romans worsened, especially when those who had volunteered to serve in Carlo Alberto's military campaign returned to the city. Pius had appointed as chief minister Count Pellegrino Rossi, who hated Mazzini and was determined to impose order on the unruly Romans, but on 15 November Rossi's throat was slit by an assassin. This incident sparked the next revolution. The following day the Civic Guard bombarded the Quirinale, one of the Papal residences. On 24 November, Pius fled south to Gaeta, which was in Neapolitan territory. Rome was ruled by a provisional revolutionary government until 5 February 1849, when power was handed to a popularly elected constituent assembly (the *Costituente*), which formally ended Papal rule and proclaimed a republic. Mazzini was able to put his democratic stamp on the Roman Republic when he arrived in March, in company with many others who were involved in the struggle for Italian independence.

The other major popular revolution took place in Venice. In March 1848 Daniele Manin led a popular insurrection that forced the Austrians to flee. Most other cities in the Veneto region, except Verona, managed to do the same, but as with the cities of Lombardy, they put their faith in the Savoyards to secure their independence. Venice alone refused to do so, and after Custoza, when the Austrians managed to recapture most of the Veneto, the city's effectively organized military defences and spirited population, led by Manin, kept the Austrians at bay until the summer of 1849.

The democrats were in the ascendancy through much of Italy after Custoza, but they were no more successful than the Piedmontese monarchy in uniting Italians against Austrian might. In October 1848, Montanelli in Tuscany led calls for the formation of an Italian constituent assembly, whose initial purpose was to orchestrate a united Italian military offensive against the Habsburg empire. By January 1849, with Rome itself a republic, calls for an Italian constituent assembly had gained momentum. Through January and February there was much discussion between the Italian states, especially Piedmont, Venice, the Roman Republic and Tuscany, on the level of representation which each state should have in an assembly that, in the aftermath of war, might decide the future of Italy. The Venetians resisted calls by the larger states for proportional representation and insisted that each state, including small states like their own, should have equal representation.

The mere fact that discussion on the question of Italian unity went this far is significant. While few shared the Mazzinian dream of an Italian nation-state, the circumstances of 1848 more than ever impressed on the insurgents the need for unity if they were to defend their newly acquired liberty. Patriots sought unity of purpose to protect their new Italian world, but they were equally determined not to sacrifice local liberties and rights to a centralized nation. The limits of Italian patriotism were made obvious in the ensuing political bargaining. The Piedmontese insisted that their delegates would represent a kingdom of upper Italy, which included all territories that had voted to join Piedmont before Custoza. Venice entered negotiations half-heartedly, fearing that any association with radical Tuscany and the Roman Republic might compromise its image in France and Britain, whose help Manin depended on to secure a favourable settlement with the Austrians. Overall, Manin sought to distance his revolution from that of Mazzini and the democrats. Though a republican himself, he used his moral authority over the Venetian population to keep social order, and would not countenance disruptive democratic ideas lest social order be compromised. Manin was not a supporter of Mazzini, and Garibaldi was not warmly received when he visited Venice in November 1848. Tuscany came close to forging a union with Rome in February, but social disorder in the Tuscan countryside, caused by peasants loyal to Leopold, had a chastening effect on the less radical among the democrats, who aligned with moderates to reject the union in March. Worse still, Gioberti revealed a capacity for treachery. Though the head of a democrat-supported government in Piedmont, he was no democrat, and before his dismissal from office on 21 February 1849, he had been plotting to restore Pius in Rome and Leopold in Tuscany. The trade-off would have been their support for a new Piedmontese-led war against Austria.

With the democrats having failed to form an effective union, Italians once again looked to Carlo Alberto, who, by March 1849, was ready to resume his dynastic war against the Habsburgs. Public opinion in Piedmont had been demanding the resumption of war, and the king needed to atone for the humiliations of the previous year and salvage the reputation of his dynasty. The renewed offensive against Austria caused considerable excitement throughout Italy, but only for a mere two weeks. Radetzky proved again his reputation as Italy's nemesis and routed the Piedmontese at Novara on 23 March. Once again, the campaign was poorly prepared and conducted. Carlo Alberto had no choice but abdicate and be replaced by his son, Vittorio Emanuele II. Italy's first war for independence was all but over.

Austria soon re-established its authority over central Italy, as did Ferdinand II over Sicily. The Venetians and Romans, however, fought on indomitably in the face of overwhelming odds until August. In Rome, the Republic's resolve to continue the fight had a great deal to do with Mazzini's good governance. The French Republic, now under Louis Napoleon, sent an expeditionary force to capture Rome and restore Pius. A citizen's militia of some 10 000 men, expertly led by Garibaldi, valiantly defended the city and inflicted heavy casualties. The desperate defence of Rome lasted two months, after which Garibaldi escaped with his men to fight for a cause not yet lost in Venice, which was being besieged by the Austrians. Manin hoped, in vain, that Britain and France would intervene on his city's behalf, but on 24 August, having suffered considerable hardships, including acute food shortages and an outbreak of cholera, the Venetians also capitulated.

Hopeless as the last months of Roman and Venetian resistance might have seemed, the gallantry displayed by the citizenry and the democrat leadership left a substantial symbolic legacy for Italian patriotism. Mazzini and other leaders of the Roman Republic were consciously setting an example for Italian patriots with their inspirational, albeit foolhardy, struggle and the valiant stands taken in Rome and Venice meant that the democrats emerged from 1848 with their prestige greatly enhanced. Garibaldi and Mazzini were fixed firmly in the popular mind as leading figures of Italian patriotism. For the moderates, on the hand, 1848 was a significant setback. What they hoped for during the revolution's dying stages was the defeat of their democrat counterparts. From their vantage point in Piedmont, Balbo, Cavour and d'Azeglio were kept abreast of developments in Rome and were to welcome the French victory in August.

Triumph of the moderates, 1849–59

Despite defeat, Mazzini and his followers emerged from the Revolution of 1848 with a fair degree of optimism. Italy had surely come alive during those heady days. Mass participation accounted for the success of the republican states, and it was the republics that demonstrated the greater will to fight. Although the *ancien régime* was again restored it was difficult to imagine how it could survive in a patriotically 'awakened' Italy. Although daunted by an anticipated wave of political repression, the democrats also sensed that 1848 had all but destroyed the *ancien régime's* legitimacy. And as both the dynastic and moderate campaigns had been found wanting, the democrats, with their credibility intact, could look forward to leading the next attempt to create an Italian nation and a republic.

Yet the symbolic victory claimed by the democrats was not a real victory, and it did not appear to advance their prospects through the following decade. The movement survived and remained a dangerous political force, but hopes for a democrat-led revival of the Italian independence struggle receded as the hardships of prison, exile or police persecution gradually took their toll. Moreover, the symbolic victory of 1848 was in some ways deceptive. Mazzini took heart from his experiences as leader of the Roman Republic and saw no need to change course. He viewed the defeats of the summer of 1849 as temporary, and imagined that another revolution in France, which he anticipated in 1852, would spark another more successful one in Italy.

However, to many leading democrats, such as Carlo Cattaneo and his fellow Milanese federalist, Giuseppe Ferrari, the lesson of 1848 was that Italian independence was an insufficient motive for popular participation. Skilled workers had been captivated by the revolutionary atmosphere and had emerged as a politicized group, but the great mass of the population, who found that the revolution had nothing to offer, remained either noncommital or hostile to the national cause. A wholly different approach was required, one that combined patriotic aims with social and political reform. While Cattaneo stressed the attractions of liberty and federalism to most Italians, Ferrari was convinced that popular support could only be gained through promises of social reform. The revolutionary potential of the great mass of the population remained untapped because neither moderates nor democrats had been interested in dealing with poverty and land reform. Ferrari advocated a people's revolution that not only entailed implementing democracy but socialism as well. Thus Cattaneo, Ferrari and other democrat leaders aimed to appeal to issues that cut deeper with the Italian masses than Italian unity, but Mazzini would not countenance any change to his uncomplicated approach of first securing Italian independence and unity. In his opinion, matters of reform could be dealt with later. Intolerant of opposing opinions and of calls for a change in direction, Mazzini alienated other democrat leaders, who had no choice but to create splinter groups.

The restored regimes also did their best to prevent the democratic movement from capitalizing on the kudos they had won in 1848–49. Pius IX and Ferdinand II revoked reforms they had been compelled to introduce under public pressure, including the constitutions, and waged a campaign of persecution which filled their gaols with political prisoners. The luckier democrats managed to flee into exile, most of them to Piedmont, the only

state that did not experience political reaction. Others clustered in such
places as Marseilles, Paris, Brussels, London and Zurich. State persecution
thus effectively fragmented the democratic movement, but could not
prevent the plotting of insurrections, the first of which went disastrously
wrong. Mazzini decided to support a revolution that was planned to take
place in Milan on 6 February 1853, organized by a variety of dissident
elements. Two weeks before the chosen date the leaders of these groups met
in Locarno, where it transpired that many of their aims were incompatible.
Whereas some pushed for a social as well as a political revolution, moderates at the meeting made it clear that they favoured minimal change. The
meeting fell into disarray, and some of the moderates proceeded to sabotage
the planned uprising. On the day of reckoning, the Austrians were lying in
wait, only a small number of expected insurgents turned up, and sixteen of
them were killed.

   This rather pathetic showing in Milan in 1853 was not only a devas-
tating setback for the democrats, but it finally discredited revolution *per
se* as a means of effecting change in Italian political life. Revolutions
created heroes and myths, but in practical terms they proved to be futile.
Another vain attempt at revolution in 1857 merely confirmed that revolutionary movements were not capable of securing Italian independence.
Mazzini remained devoted to his political course, but his authority among
the democrats waned. He remained the figurehead of democratic nationalism, but he was no longer in a position to lead or influence any comprehensive political strategy for Italian independence. Many of his most
influential allies now rejected revolution and were forced to concede that
only the Kingdom of Piedmont–Sardinia could lead Italy to independence.
Manin, the republican hero of Venice, and Garibaldi himself had come to
share this view. They harboured deep suspicions of the Piedmontese and
of the Savoy monarchy, but so poor were Italy's prospects that, as patriots, they felt they had no choice. Despite Carlo Alberto's disastrous military campaigns in 1848 and 1849, Piedmont remained an independent
state and continued to pursue an independent foreign policy. As such it
was unique among its Italian counterparts. As democrat fortunes sank
through the 1850s, Piedmont began to earn the support of disaffected
democrats whilst also winning back the moderates.

   One reason why Piedmont inspired renewed confidence was its quick
recovery as a middle-ranking power. Ironically, the dynasty's humiliating
showing in 1848–9 was one of the key reasons for the recovery, for it
removed the possibility of a political reaction. The kingdom emerged from
the war with its constitution and parliamentary system intact, and with
governments that consciously and effectively pursued political and
economic reform. Under the leadership of Count Camillo Benso di Cavour,
who had a series of key ministerial positions between 1850 and 1853, and
who was Piedmont's prime minister for most of the period 1853–60, the

kingdom benefited from a state-directed economic development agenda. His government's commitment to economic modernization was most apparent in heavy public spending on infrastructure and in the subsidization of very expensive, yet economically crucial, transportation services like railways and shipping. The costs would leave a heavy burden of debt on the future Italian state, but for the moment it appeared to most Italians that Piedmont was the harbinger of progress. Cavour spent much of his energy forging formal trading links with other European states and promoting the export of Piedmontese goods. His reduction of tariffs had the effect of stimulating a threefold increase in the export of key commodities. The kingdom's enhanced trading links with the wider world not only improved state revenue (though not nearly enough to meet state expenditure), but meant Piedmont could appear to other Italians as a 'serious' state. Its success was made to look all the more striking because the other Italian states were struggling with economic difficulties.

Another dilemma facing these states in the 1850s, and which had to be remedied if the restored regimes were to survive, was the continuing crisis in law and order. In the Papal States, particularly in the Legations, crime was thought to be out of control. Papal authority in the Legations was backed by Austrian troops, who were quick to establish order in the cities and towns, but the countryside was another matter. Bandit groups appeared to have free rein, robbing travellers and attacking the homes of the wealthy at will. Whether there really was an increase in crime is hard to assess, but what can be said with certainty is that people believed that crime was out of control. The propertied classes looked in vain for protection to the *ancien régime*. In the Papal States troops were regarded as too corrupt and incompetent to restore order. A more efficient police corps was eventually formed, but the brutal and arbitrary methods it employed when hunting for bandits had the effect of alienating the urban and rural poor, without an appreciable improvement in crime reduction. The failure of Papal authority in the Legations was one major reason why propertied Italians were not merely content to look to Piedmont for inspiration, but were beginning to countenance political unification.

Furthermore, many Italian elites could not fail to notice that much of the country was experiencing economic difficulties at a time when the rest of Europe appeared to be enjoying a boom. The Revolution of 1848 was followed by an age of prolonged and unprecedented economic expansion, but among Italian states only Piedmont, Lombardy, Tuscany, Parma and Modena seemed to reap any benefit. Worldwide developments gave added force to the commonplace lament that Italy languished as Europe forged ahead. Debt was a major problem. The suppression of secessionism in Sicily and massive spending on the armed forces imposed crushing financial burdens on the Kingdom of the Two Sicilies. Here too, in the south, crime and banditry appeared to be out of control.

In those parts of Italy ruled directly by Vienna, discontent amongst the social elites had a different source. Here the Austrians, in accordance with their reputation for administrative efficiency, were more thorough in countering banditry. They were also determined to punish the Lombards and Venetians for their disloyalty during the Revolution of 1848. There was a wholesale purge of the legal system and the bureaucracy, while Lombards who fled after the 1853 rising in Milan had their properties sequestered. The punitive measures taken against dissidents reflected Radetzky's belief that the Italians had to be ruled with a firm hand. The Habsburgs signalled a more relaxed style of governance in 1857 with the recall of Radetzky and the issue of amnesties to political prisoners (25 January), but by then anti-Austrian feeling was firmly embedded. The propertied classes were particularly incensed by the imposition of a whole range of tax rises and the introduction of new taxes designed to bankroll the debt-ridden Habsburgs. There were increases in land, income and indirect taxes, and there was a one-off 'loan' procured from Lombard and Venetian communes to help pay for the Emperor Francis Joseph's wedding to Elizabeth of Bavaria in 1854. In all, the Italian provinces contributed an extra 58 million lire to the empire's coffers after the revolution of 1848, and it was obvious to local elites that Lombardy and the Veneto were being milked with impunity. There were other economic factors which, in addition to Austrian fiscal exactions, made life more burdensome under the second restoration. Silk was an important export of northern Italy, but production was severely affected by plague in 1853, from which the industry took over a decade to recover. In these oppressive and economically regressive times, the Lombards and Venetians would once again look to Piedmont for leadership.

In general, support for the *ancien régime* in Italy during the 1850s was wafer thin. Even in Tuscany, where the economic outlook was not so bleak (despite having to shoulder the costs of an Austrian occupation force for the first half of the 1850s), the mood for political change remained strong. Memories of how Grand Duke Leopold II had betrayed the revolution and had been restored by the Austrians could not be easily erased. Moreover, the dissolution of parliament and the abolition of the freedom of the press, were among a series of violations that many Tuscan elites would not tolerate forever.

Piedmontese foreign policy and the national society

Of the Italian states, only Piedmont did not suffer a crisis of political legitimacy. Here the state managed to expand its social support base by retaining the liberal reforms enacted under Carlo Alberto, by demonstrating a capacity to promote the local economy through a series of active measures, and in being the only state that retained a strong interest in Italian independence.

Of course, Piedmont's interest in the matter was self-serving. The Savoy dynasty continued to covet Lombardy and the Veneto, and its main ambition was to force the Austrians to relinquish these territories, probably with French support. Piedmont had hopes of dominating the rest of Italy without having to acquire it, particularly as any venture into Papal or Neapolitan territory would antagonize the French. Yet at the same time, it was difficult to ignore the calls from moderates and democrats all over the country for another Piedmontese-led push for Italian unity. With Cavour as prime minister through the 1850s, Piedmont was to find a way of accommodating aspirations for Italian unity and independence on the one hand, with Piedmontese foreign policy ambitions on the other. As for Italian national unification, that was an outcome few contemplated or desired.

One of the hard lessons of 1848, and one which was well understood by Cavour, was that Italy, let alone Piedmont, could not 'do it alone' (*farà da sè*). The active support of a major European power was crucial. So, too, was another international crisis which would enable Italy to declare war against Austria without incurring censure from the other Great Powers. Cavour's greatest contribution to national unification would be his acute sense of how Europe's Balance of Power worked, knowing how and when to exploit the opportunities presented by that system, and, better still, how to actively destabilize it. His first major intervention in European diplomatic affairs came in 1855 with the Crimean War, when Piedmont decided to support Britain and France against Russian encroachments into the Ottoman Empire. The king was keen to wage war on Russia, and Cavour was supportive because he initially hoped Austria would side with Russia, but when Austria did the opposite, Cavour maintained that intervention would nevertheless raise Piedmont's profile and standing among the European powers. A small Piedmontese force of 10 000 made a modest contribution to the defeat of Russia in 1855, and Cavour led a delegation to Paris where the victorious powers settled the peace in early 1856. There he managed to publicize Italy's problems, particularly the ways in which Austrian-backed reactionary regimes had left much of the country in a parlous economic condition. Cavour appeared to tap an anti-Austrian mood among the British and French leaders, who began to seriously question Austria's domination of Italy, and who began to exert pressure on the two most archaic Italian polities, the Papal States and the Kingdom of the Two Sicilies, to introduce liberal reforms.

More importantly, Cavour made an impression on Napoleon III, an ambitious and aggressive imperialist who could claim strong links with Italy, not only through his great uncle but through his own experiences as a young and active *carbonaro* in Rome. It was something quite bizarre and completely unforeseen, however, that precipitated a Franco-Piedmontese alliance against Austria. A foolhardy attempt on Napoleon III's life on 14 January 1858, by an Italian patriot named Felice Orsini, had the unlikely effect of enhancing the emperor's sympathy for Italy's struggle against Austria. The failed assassin was guillotined, but Napoleon was keen to publicize the fact that his would-be assassin was a martyr of a national cause. He published Orsini's last letter, which contained an emotive appeal to the emperor to support Italy's quest for freedom. He even insisted the letter be printed in Piedmont. Patently moved by Orisini's dedication to this principle of nationality, he also sensed an opportunity to expand French territory and displace Austria as the dominant power in Italy. Cavour and Napoleon III plotted a strategy against their common enemy at a famous meeting at Plombières on 20 July, where the emperor clarified that the price of French support was Nice and Savoy.

Piedmont's other great contribution to the Risorgimento was as a safe haven for Italian patriots: only the more radical democrats such as Mazzini were not welcome. With its constitution, free press and comparatively lively political scene, Piedmont became a beacon for political exiles from all over Italy. Here they could mingle openly, debate issues freely and plan the next struggle for independence. From within Piedmont emerged a new Italian independence movement in the mid-1850s that did much to rally 'respectable' opinion behind the cause of Italian unity. Although its membership was small, this movement became influential because it explicitly rejected the Mazzinian approach in favour of a Piedmontese-led liberation movement. What by July 1857 became known as the Italian National Society (*Società nazionale italiana*) also attracted support because of its practical plan for national unity. Its leadership profile reflected a truly Italian organization, for among its ranks could be found the Venetian Daniele Manin, the Lombard Giorgio Pallavicino, the Sicilian Giuseppe La Farina, and, in 1856, it secured the allegiance of Giuseppe Garibaldi of Nice.

Initially the National Society set itself the task of mobilizing public opinion. Its main challenge was to advocate an agenda that could attract support across the middle and upper classes, which it did by pursuing a simple strategy of achieving Italian unity and independence first, and leaving other substantive issues, such as how an independent Italy would be organized, to be debated later. Although the Society never managed to attracted a large membership, which was at its height was little more than 4000, its influence permeated the Italian peninsula and did more than any other movement to shape patriotic opinion in the late 1850s. The great achievement of the National Society was not just in rallying Italians behind a Piedmontese-led bid for independence, but in attaining the support of Cavour. Hitherto Cavour had shown disdain for the idea of Italian unification; this future icon of the Risorgimento was similar to many members of the Piedmontese nobility in that he could barely speak Italian, and knew very little about Italy south of the Po. Influential members of the National Society were instrumental in swaying Cavour behind the cause of Italian unity, or rather, each recognized the similarity of their respective aims, and the mutually beneficial role they could play in each other's designs. The Society saw in Cavour a statesman who was serious about driving the Austrians out of Italy, and who appeared more capable than anyone in securing that aim. In turn, Cavour recognized that the society was actively encouraging Italians everywhere to follow Piedmont's lead.

War of unification, 1859–60

When thinking of the events that precipitated the unification of Italy between the summer of 1859 and October of the following year, one can pose any number of counterfactual propositions that would have produced very different outcomes. In other words, fortune played a crucial role. The most optimistic outcome that the Italian National Society could have hoped for in April 1859 was that some form of unity might have been worked out between the Kingdom of Piedmont on the one hand, and Lombardy, Tuscany, Modena, Parma and the Legations on the other. Cavour was not at all comfortable with anything bigger. Throughout the 1840s and until the very end of the 1850s, national opinion did not aspire to an Italian nation-state, a prospect that would have horrified all but Mazzini and his diminishing cohort of supporters. The call for unity, which had often been heard in Italian history, normally implored Italians to work in unison to guarantee Italian liberty, not to bring the Italies under the direct control of a central authority. Yet through the course of 1859 and early 1860, the idea of an Italian nation quite suddenly became agreeable and even palatable to the Italian public. More importantly, events appeared to run ahead of both Cavour and his king, after which Italian unification was presented to them as a *fait accompli*. As will be detailed below, Plombières gave Cavour much more than he could ever have bargained for.

After the meeting at Plombières, Piedmont launched into its secret (in fact fairly obvious) preparations for war with Austria. There was much excitement among patriotic circles throughout Italy. The National Society collected money to transport thousands of volunteers from all over Italy to Turin, while Cavour and the Society began organizing supporters in the Legations, Parma, Modena and Tuscany. In the event of war breaking out, these supporters were expected to seize control of their localities and declare their allegiance to the Savoyard monarchy. In the meantime, Cavour allowed relations with Austria to deteriorate. To help things along, the Austrians were subjected to a series of provocations: thus the Piedmontese were accused of supplying armaments to Hungarian nationalists. Yet just when Vienna was ready to retaliate, the Great Powers threatened to solve the issue and destroy the scheme that was hatched at Plombières. The Russians decided to defuse tension between these two European powers by calling an international congress. To make matters worse, Napoleon III was reconsidering his position. To Cavour all now seemed lost. On 19 April, while he was supposedly contemplating suicide, Austria came to his rescue by issuing an ultimatum. The Austrian foreign minister, Karl Ferdinand von Buol-Schauenstein, feared the international congress would side with Piedmont and that Austria might lose its grip on the Italian provinces. In the event of war, he also counted on Prussian support if the French chose to intervene on Piedmont's behalf. As it happened, the Habsburg ultimatum alienated international opinion, and while Napoleon III, as predicted, came to Piedmont's aid, Prussian support for Austria was not forthcoming. On 26 April, Piedmont rejected the ultimatum and the Italian Question had to be settled by war.

The second war for Italian unification began in earnest in May 1859, when the Austrians crossed the Ticino River. About 200 000 French troops, led by Napoleon III in person, were rapidly transported by rail to Piedmont. They were supported by 60 000 Piedmontese troops who were duly led by their monarch, and a further 20 000 volunteers. After a series of minor clashes in which Garibaldi played a distinguished role, this war was decided in two major battles between French and Austrian forces. The Austrians were defeated at the Battle of Magenta on 4 June, and again at the Battle of Solferino on 24 June.

In the meantime, according to Cavour's script, Parma, Modena, Tuscany and most of the Papal States were meant to overthrow their ruling regimes and declare themselves for Piedmont. In Tuscany the old regime collapsed as soon as the war started. Leopold II fled Florence on the second day, and leaders of the National Society played a leading role in forming a provisional government. The Duchess of Parma and the Duke of Modena absconded almost as quickly as Leopold, and only in Parma did an army loyal to the Duchess obstruct the National Society in setting up a pro-Piedmont regime. That task was achieved by other nationalists. In contrast to 1848, there was little popular participation in these bloodless revolutions. The duchies collapsed because of the withdrawal of the Austrian forces from central-northern Italy, and in most cases the National Society had the relatively easy task of filling the vacuum. In the Papal States, however, Austrian troops remained at their posts until early June, and the National Society had no choice but to wait until they were recalled by Vienna. In the Romagna region the National Society was largely successful in seizing control of cities once Austrian troops had gone, but in the Marches and Umbria the story was quite different. Here support for Piedmont and the National Society was weak, thus in Perugia a pro-Piedmontese coup was brutally suppressed by Papal troops. Further south, the National Society was so weak that it did not even try to challenge the Papal government.

That said, by late June things were going as well as could be expected for Cavour. The duchies and Romagna was already secured, Lombardy was

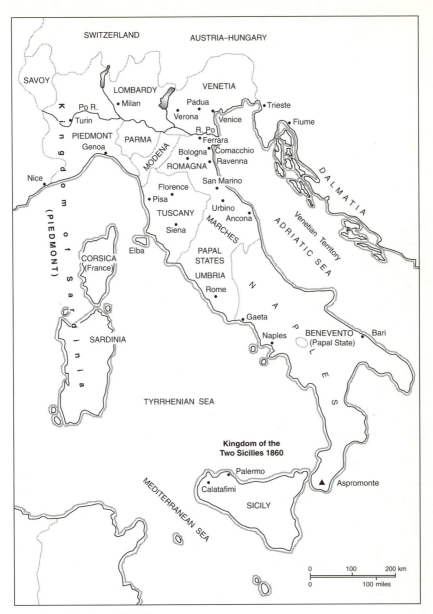

3 Italy at the time of Unification
After J.M. Scott, *Italy* (Ernest Benn, 1967)

effectively reconquered for Piedmont by the French, and all looked set for the Society to do its work in the Veneto. But Napoleon brought the war to a sudden halt. The Austrians were confined to the fortifications known collectively as the Quadrilateral, but on 8 July an armistice was announced and on 11 July a peace was signed at Villafranca. Napoleon III had been troubled by a series of problems, including the serious possibility of Prussian intervention and waning public opinion back home, but he was particularly concerned about developments in central Italy. Piedmont had gone way beyond what had been agreed at Plombières, and its successes in Papal territories were always going to cause problems for Napoleon with his Catholic constituency.

It appeared that Italy's second war for independence was over. The parties met at Villafranca, where it was decided Piedmont would take most of Lombardy except those parts still under Austrian control, while Tuscany and Modena were to be returned to their former rulers. Napoleon III and Emperor Francis Joseph agreed that Italy should form a confederation under the leadership of the pope, and that Austria, which retained control of the Veneto, should be a member. Cavour resigned after his king counter-signed the agreement. But neither France nor Austria was in a position to enforce their plans for central Italy, let alone oversee the formation of a confederation. Nor were the British happy to see the old regime restored in the duchies, or the Legations handed back to the Papacy. In Tuscany the moderates had consolidated their power. Baron Bettino Ricasoli, the prime exponent of unity with Piedmont, formed a government that resolved to stop Leopold from returning. At much the same time, Luigi Carlo Farini, who represented the Piedmontese government in the Legations, was installed as governor there in November, after already having established pro-Piedmontese governments in Parma and Modena. In each of these provisional states public opinion had been mobilized to push for unification with Piedmont, and in September and November they sent formal requests to Turin which stated their desire for unification. Under French pressure, Vittorio Emanuele reluctantly declined, so by the end of the year, Parma, Modena and Romagna were formally united under the name 'Emilia'.

In January 1860 Cavour had been reinstalled as prime minister, by which time Napoleon III had withdrawn his objection to a Piedmontese annexa-tion of Tuscany and Emilia. The proviso was that popular plebiscites had to be conducted in these territories, as well as in Nice and Savoy, where the anticipated results would see them annexed by France. The National Society did everything possible to ensure a high voter turnout in the hope that it would produce a resounding vote for Piedmontese annexation. In early March (11–12), all Tuscan and Emilian males above the age of twenty-one voted overwhelmingly in favour of unification, though induce-ments and intimidation were employed to secure the desired result. Corruption was also suspected in the plebiscite in Nice, which voted for unification with France even though outside observers sensed the city was distinctly pro-Italian. In any event, on 18 and 22 March, Vittorio Emanuele formalized the annexations of Tuscany and Emilia by decree.

Less than a year after war was first declared against Austria, the territory ruled by the House of Savoy had more or less doubled in size, but success had the effect of stimulating greater public enthusiasm for *Italia*. At the same time, Cavour was well aware that however stunning the results of his foreign policy might have been thus far, he could only work within the parameters allowed by much greater powers. Further annexations along the peninsula, especially Rome, would probably prompt the intervention of France and undo whatever had been achieved thus far. The Italian public, however, remained hungry for more success as long as much of Italy remained unredeemed. Venice remained the captive of Austria, and Cavour incurred howls of protest for having conceded Nice and Savoy. The idea of unifying the whole of Italy had suddenly become popular among the middle and upper classes, now that it seemed within the realms of possibility. The incorporation of central Italy and Rome itself seemed the next obvious step. Indicative of the new mood was the popularity of Garibaldi, who had been able to build upon his already legendary military stature during the war against Austria. Garibaldi was more outraged than most about the secession of Nice, his home town, and in April 1860 he made public his ambition to liberate Sicily. Cavour thought this a dangerous move, given his fears of Great Power intervention, but there was little that he could do to prevent it. Garibaldi had popular support and enjoyed the king's favour, hence Cavour could only foil his expedition through surreptitious means.

Public opinion was way ahead of Cavour, and it was to be carried further ahead as Garibaldi's venture succeeded beyond everyone's wildest expectations. The expedition came in response to calls from Sicilian democrats, including the future prime minister, Francesco Crispi, to take advantage of a major revolt that followed a failed plot against the Bourbons on 4 April. The Bourbons soon lost control of western Sicily, and the rest of the island appeared ripe for revolution. On 6 May 1860, Garibaldi set sail for Sicily with a pitifully small, yet highly committed, force of volunteers – his so-called 'Thousand', which was technically 1087. He arrived on 11 May at Marsala, on the far western tip of Sicily, and began his amazing conquest of the island in the name of King Vittorio Emanuele II and Italy. The mere presence of the hero was enough to regenerate a rebellion that appeared to have run its course, and he boosted his chances of success by appealing to the discontented lower classes with promises of wide-ranging social reform. By 26 May he had captured Palermo, and by 20 July, Bourbon troops had been driven out of Sicily. Success brought its own momentum. The bankruptcy of the Bourbon monarchy was completely exposed by the relative ease with which Garibaldi carried on with the conquest of Naples, where the opposition also appeared to dissolve before him. His expeditionary force did have some difficulty in evading the Neapolitan navy, reaching the Calabrian coast on 19 August, but by 7 September he had already occupied Naples. At he beginning of October he defeated a major Bourbon army at the Battle of Volturno. Cavour did his best to thwart Garibaldi's progress at every turn, having even sponsored a plot against the Bourbons before Garibaldi could reach Naples, but almost nothing could really stop the momentum created by this living legend.

Garibaldi then set his sights on Rome, but here the Piedmontese government decided to actively intervene. The Great Powers were not particularly concerned with the collapse of the Bourbon monarchy in Naples, but the Papacy was a different matter altogether. An attack on Rome would not only bring direct Great Power intervention but a direct confrontation between Garibaldi and French forces stationed in Rome. A drastic solution was necessary. On 11 September, and with Napoleon III's assent, Cavour sent Piedmontese troops to invade and occupy what remained of the Papal States, except the Lazio region, in order to intercept Garibaldi before he moved on Rome. The Marches and Umbria were now part of Italy, though an attempt earlier (3 September) by Cavour and the National Society to orchestrate another series of pro-Piedmontese revolutions in these regions had fallen completely flat.

September 1860 therefore witnessed Garibaldi's conquest of the south and the Piedmontese acquisition of most of the centre. Vittorio Emanuele II led his army during the latter stages of the campaign and met Garibaldi on 25 October at Teano, where the latter signified unequivocally his loyalty to the crown. To legitimize Piedmont's substantial territorial acquisitions, prospective subjects of the Savoy monarchy were made to vote in plebiscites. As happened earlier in Emilia and Tuscany, vote rigging helped to secure the desired result. On 21 October, 1 312 666 voted for annexation in the south, with a mere ten thousand against, while in Sicily, it was 432 720 in favour, 667 against.[1] Similar results were to be had in The Marches and Umbria the following month. Italy was finally born.

Conclusion

Thus in 1860, most of what we now recognize as Italy had been brought together in rapid fashion. Earlier pages detailed the long-term factors that set the stage for unification, such as the declining legitimacy of the *ancien régime* and the emergence of an Italian public sphere. At the same time,

---

[1] R.P. Coppini, 'Il Piemonte sabaudo e l'unificazione (1849–61)', in G. Sabbatucci and V. Vidotto (eds), *Storia Italia*, 1. *Le premesse dell'unità dalla fine del settecento al 1861* (Rome-Bari, 1994), p. 426.

Italy was also made possible by a series of accidents and unexpected outcomes, most notably Garibaldi's military successes in the south.

Yet when all is said and done, it is hard to deny that Italy was largely the creation of Piedmontese foreign policy. Cavour and Vittorio Emanuele II sought to expand the borders of the Kingdom of Sardinia and transform it into a Great Power. The support of a major power was crucial, but there were other factors that enabled Cavour to radically exceed Piedmont's foreign policy ambitions. The social elites of Emilia and Tuscany were more or less prepared to accept Piedmontese hegemony because the *ancien régime*, particularly after 1848, had failed to establish a viable political and social order. In 1859, public opinion in Florence and Bologna declared their acceptance of the Savoyard constitutional monarchy, not for any love of the Savoyards, but in expectation of progressive government and effective law and order. The elites of minor cities had an additional motive in that they hoped to escape the domination of their regional capitals once they were incorporated into a much larger state.

Piedmont and the House of Savoy were therefore set to play a determining role in the construction of an Italian nation-state. What form that nation-state was to take is the subject of the next chapter.

|5|

Inventing the Italian nation: from the Risorgimento to the Great War

It was the early twentieth-century Polish leader, Josef Pilsudski, who asserted that it is states that create nations, not the other way around. The claim may not apply across the board, but it does in our case study. Public enthusiasm for national unity through 1859–60 had the effect of goading the Piedmontese government into a more adventurous foreign policy, and it inhibited Cavour from foiling Garibaldi's conquest of the south. Moderates and democrats had also played their role in promoting the idea of national unity. Yet what had essentially taken place in 1860 was the fulfilment of Piedmontese foreign policy aims, and hence the Risorgimento really amounted to the Piedmontese conquest of Italy. Dubious plebiscites conducted subsequently in the centre and south could not screen the fact that to the great bulk of Italians Italy was an imposition that was neither called for nor desired. Piedmont's viceroy in Naples, Carlo Farini, reported that he could not even find a hundred locals in favour of unification.

When discussing 'national opinion', 'civil society' or 'the public' in the mid-nineteenth century Italy, it is worth keeping in mind that each term referred to a small fraction of the population. The peoples of the peninsula and the islands did not speak the same language: most scholars accept that in the year of unification, no more than 2.5 per cent of the population were Italian speakers.[1] The slenderness of the new state's support base is hard to exaggerate. Among the middle and upper classes that constituted the Italian public, a fair proportion were devout Catholics who shared the pope's hostility towards liberalism and Cavour's government, or who remained committed to the deposed old regimes.

The survival of the new nation-state therefore depended on expanding its social support. Above all it needed more Italians. Massimo d'Azeglio spoke

---

[1] Tullio de Mauro, *Storia linguistica dell'Italia unita* (Laterza, Bari, 1963), p. 41.

for the new ruling order when he reputedly asserted, 'Now we have made Italy, we must make Italians.' The challenge was to take *italianità* from something that, for the vast majority, meant nothing, and transform it into an intrinsic feature of personal and social identification. 'Making Italians' was therefore a monumental task for the new political order.

D'Azeglio's famous words usefully encapsulate a standard assumption held by most scholars of nationalism nowadays: that nations are historically contingent, and that they have to be invented and re-invented. Yet for an invented nation to be seen as legitimate, the very fact that it *was* constructed had to be concealed. As Benedict Anderson has often noted, the nation had to appear to be innate and a matter of fate. Somehow, Italy and Italian-ness was to be legitimized by making each seem natural and self-evident. Thus the absence of *italianità* in the lives of the great bulk of Italians was not merely a matter that had to be addressed, but an absence that had to be forgotten. A great deal needed to be erased from collective memory, such as the fact that Cavour, the great architect of 1859, until near the end of his life thought national unification a repugnant idea. Along with other founding fathers of the Italian nation, he had to be recast as an Italian patriot.

The reconstruction of Cavour was part of a broader myth-making exercise. The Risorgimento myth would tell of the inevitable triumph of the national movement and the selfless struggles of nationalist, but re-writing history was only one of a series of projects that contributed to the invention of the nation. The purpose of this chapter is to consider some of the active steps taken by state and non-state agencies in developing a national culture and a national identity at a time when the meaning of *italianità* was not at all obvious. The exceptional strength of municipal identities and the fact that the Italian masses had never shared a supra-local form of identification, other than the fact that nearly all of them considered themselves *cristiani*, were serious obstacles to political and cultural integration. Yet Italy's heterogeneity was not an insurmountable barrier at this critical stage in the nation's formation. As a matter of course, nation building always involved various degrees of 'ethnocide': the destruction or diminution of ethnic difference within the nation's territorial boundaries. Whether through attrition or acculturation, the nation had to domesticate particularism in order to secure its own cultural and political dominion.

Piedmontization

The immediate problem faced by Cavour's government was the political consolidation and administrative integration of vast new territories, and how 'regional' political elites were to be accommodated to the new national political order. The leaders of Lombardy, Emilia and the duchies anticipated that constitutional arrangements would be negotiated and that the new state would respect most existing local institutions. Federalism remained by far the most popular choice, and there were signs that Cavour's government was prepared to countenance that option despite Piedmont's position of strength. Lombard leaders were made to think initially that they could retain many of their institutions and traditions, particularly after a commission of Lombard notables had been appointed to advise the Piedmontese government on the matter. And in 1861, one of Cavour's ministers, Marco Minghetti, introduced a bill for regional devolution into the parliament. Yet Piedmontese parliamentarians generally were hostile to talk of compromise, nor did Cavour entertain the requests of regional elites with much conviction. The Lombards were not appeased, nor was Minghetti's half-baked bill passed. The dominant opinion in Turin was that Piedmont had nothing much to learn from the rest of Italy, and that Italy should be incorporated into Piedmont. Southern Italy, or the Mezzogiorno, was treated as if it was occupied territory: Piedmont's legal code and institutions were imposed nationally without much consultation.

As far as nation formation was concerned, these were not auspicious beginnings. There were signs that the Savoy monarchy had exploited public enthusiasm throughout Italy simply in order to realize selfish dynastic aspirations. An explicit signal that the king had annexed Italy for dynastic purposes was his insistence on remaining 'Vittorio Emanuele II' rather than 'I', a matter that offended regional leaders. The king claimed sovereignty over Italy by right of annexation, and the kingdom's first parliament was formally described as the eighth, which was in line with the Piedmontese succession.

Admittedly, Tuscan, Emilian, Modenese and Parmese social elites voted in favour of unification in order to share the progress and security offered by the Piedmontese state. To put it simply, but not too inaccurately, they welcomed the extension of Piedmontese administration to the rest of the Italy, but they were taken aback by the extent to which regional interests were ignored by early Piedmontese-dominated governments. The first capital of the new nation-state was Turin, and Piedmont's constitution, or the Statuto Albertino that had been in force since 1848, was now the constitution of Italy. Piedmont's parliamentary system, legal code and administrative structures were extended to cover the new territories. Educational institutions, which included some of the world's oldest universities, were brought under the control of the Ministry of Education. Schools and universities were all subject to uniform curricula. The 'Piedmontization' of Italy meant that traditional institutions had no place in the new order. Nor was the government in Turin prepared to make allowances. Count Giuseppe Pasolini of Ravenna, future Italian foreign minister and close friend of Minghetti, complained in a letter to his friend that he would never forgive him for assisting the Piedmont government to 'destroy everything old'.[2] Only Bettino Ricasoli's Tuscany had enough standing to retain many of its institutions and its own penal code, but Tuscany was an anomaly, and even Ricasoli had to tolerate the less appealing features of the Piedmontese state, such as its extremely powerful monarch. The *statuto* gave the king full control over the armed forces and foreign affairs, the right to formulate policy without reference to his ministers, and his person remained as 'sacred and inviolable' as those of his predecessors. Piedmont's two parliamentary chambers, which included a senate whose members were appointed by the king, and the chamber of deputies whose members were elected by very limited suffrage, were automatically adopted for Italy. Vittorio Emanuele retained the right to dismiss elected governments and appoint new ones. He also continued his ambiguous relationship with the legislature, for the king retained a right of veto and the right to issue decrees.

The fact that Piedmontese nobles were over-represented in positions of authority in the new state was interpreted as a sign of 'Piedmontization'. The division of the country into provinces did, more or less, accord with historic boundaries, but the subdivision of regions into administrative departments, in accordance with the French model, was arranged to undermine parochial loyalties. There was recognition, however, even among some regional elites that devolution would be likely to threaten the achievements of 1859–60. Some parts of Italy might even revert to the *ancien régime*, or rally behind the immensely popular Garibaldi: the incapacity of Italian states to co-operate effectively in times of crisis, as happened in 1848, was one of the most poignant lessons of recent history. Much of the Mezzogiorno was in open rebellion through the 1860s, while Austria always loomed as a threat: the Habsburgs initially refused to recognize Italy. Centralization was therefore defended by Ricasoli and his Piedmontese counterparts on the pragmatic grounds that the consolidation of the newborn nation needed the protection of a strong state, at least temporarily.

The first decade of Italian independence witnessed the continuation of 'Piedmontization'. The Italian army was essentially built on the foundations of the Piedmontese army, which had been significantly reformed by General Alfonso La Marmora in the 1850s. Piedmont had five divisions, but after the overthrow of Grand Duke Leopold II, the Tuscan army was simply added to that of Piedmont. It became the ninth division, while the Lombards added divisions six to eight. The army that Garibaldi had amassed in the south, which included 50 000 men and 7300 officers, was deemed too dangerous to retain. Cavour and General Manfredo Fanti, the architect of the integration of the northern forces, were stoutly opposed to simply adding these men to the king's army. 30 000 men from this so-called

---

[2] Quoted in Adrian Lyttelton, 'Nation, Region, City', in Carl Levy (ed.), *Italian Regionalism: History, Identity and Politics* (Oxford, Berg, 1996), p. 41.

southern army were disbanded with six month's pay, while the rest were integrated into the Piedmontese army. Garibaldi's officers, who led the most successful Italian military force in the wars for unification, were basically fobbed off.

There were limits to Piedmontization, however. The political system was accessible to Italy's regional elites, who in the years that followed unification had been progressively making their mark in parliamentary life and in government. Cavour headed the first government of Italy, and Piedmontese nobles dominated the ministries and the commissions that were meant to organize the administrative and legal structures of the nation-state. But there were clear signs that Piedmontese domination was abating when Ricasoli replaced Cavour in June 1861. The Modenese Farini held the post from December 1862 to March 1863, followed by the Bolognese Minghetti, (March 1863–September 1864). Two of the more prominent late nineteenth-century prime ministers, Agostino Depretis and Francesco Crispi, were from Pavia and Sicily respectively. In transferring the capital from Turin to Florence in 1865 Piedmont made its the most decisive gesture of commitment to Italy, though it was mainly meant to reassure the French that Italy did not have designs on Rome. Many Piedmontese nobles were so enraged, however, that they called for secession from Italy, and quite serious popular disturbances rocked Turin. Vittorio Emanuele himself was reluctant to move from his beloved Turin. (He made little effort to improve his Italian accent, and he was only really interested in touring the country so long as he could also pursue his passion for hunting).

Piedmontese political domination was much resented by other Italian elites. The new state was seen as too rigid, impersonal and authoritarian, but it would not take long before Italy's regional elites found ways to manipulate the state in ways that served their private interests. The imposition of Piedmontese government structures was relatively easy, but ensuring the system operated as it did in Piedmont was a much more difficult proposition. At the regional level the state relied heavily on the co-operation of local elites, who manipulated the system in order to shore up their own power and that of their localities. The organization of Italy into provinces and municipalities provided a poignant example of the disparities between form and reality in Italian political life after 1860. The country was divided into sixty-nine provinces and contained well over 8000 municipalities or *comuni*. While the key regional offices were appointed by the state, namely the prefects of each department and the mayors, all other local and regional positions were elected locally. Yet men of influence quickly asserted their control of provincial and municipal elected bodies and offices, which in turn gave them control over the distribution of state resources. Not only did local government become an important source of illicit income for influential locals, who distributed jobs and resources to their clients, but it also gave local government considerable leverage in dealing with the central state. Politicians relied on power brokers in their constituencies to secure votes, and deputies and centrally appointed prefects were expected to press local issues in parliament and secure government funding for local needs.

Neither central nor local governments were supposed to operate in that fashion, but the weakness of the state and the realities of social power made for the development of at least two Italies after 1860: one 'legal' and one 'real'. Of *Italia legale* and *reale*, more will be said later. Suffice it to say here that it was a dichotomy that worked at many levels, and its ramifications for nation building were important. As we shall see in the next chapter, the mutation of the state system into something that served private interests at the public's expense ensured that the state never managed to secure its legitimacy in Italian society. And without legitimacy, the state was never really in a position to nationalize the population.

Territorial integrity

Concerns about Piedmontization were not enough to distract public opinion from its obsession with Venice, Rome and the incompleteness of the Risorgimento. Spectacular though the achievements of 1859–60 might have been, the public consensus was that the new nation was not quite Italy, and that further territorial conquests were necessary. Implicit in this yearning was a spatial understanding of Italy – of Italy being a geographical entity as much as a political and cultural unit. Size was very important. Until the fall of Mussolini, making Italy bigger was the state's fundamental role. Whether through redeeming lands believed to be culturally Italian, such as the border regions with Slovenia and Croatia, or building a Mediterranean empire, Italy's integrity as a nation was judged according to its size on the map. From the very beginning, territorial expansion took precedence over all other matters of state.

In spatial terms, Italy was relatively easy to imagine. Its heartland was the peninsula and the Po river basin. When Metternich contemptuously dismissed Italy as a mere 'geographical expression', he had a reasonably clear geographical space in mind. Few could argue that it was not an historic entity. Since antiquity, rulers, scholars and travellers had recognized the territory south of the Alps through to Apulia and Calabria as Italy, and most agreed that it certainly formed a cultural unit. Hence for the new nation, geography provided a ready source of substance; the map gave the Italian public an important means of imagining who they were, and for demarcating their relationship with the wider world. As the reading public became familiar with the political map of their new state, they came to a much firmer sense of 'us' and 'them', of Italians as 'we' and of non-Italians as 'other'.

While Italy's basic geographical location was a given, the positioning of its boundaries was not at all clear. The *italianità* of the borderlands and the islands had always been nebulous, but the inclination of Italian nationalists was to be as inclusive as possible, if only to claim more territories for the nation. Thus 'national opinion' maintained with great conviction that the Alto Adige was Italian; that the peoples of this region might have identified more with German than Italian culture was irrelevant. Corsica, the Trentino, Trieste and the Dalmatian coast were also widely believed to be part of Italy's patrimony, and Garibaldi remained adamant that his home-town Nice was Italian. To be sure, Italy could persist with some semblance of integrity without these territories, but Venice and Rome were of a different order. Their acquisition was necessary for the nation to feel whole.

Irredentism, the 'redemption' of territories believed to belong to the nation on ethnic and historical grounds, was a public obsession as well as a useful political distraction. As Cavour's successors struggled with pressing domestic issues, such as popular rebellion in the south and other forms of reaction against the imposition of nationhood, public opinion was focussed on how to seize Rome. The problem for the Italian state, however, was that in order to meet public expectations on this matter it had to take very dangerous risks. That Venice and Rome should belong to Italy was not in doubt: the real question was how quickly they should be acquired. The king and his governments agreed that irredentism was a national priority, but the reality was that Italy could not really afford a confrontation with any Great Power. The Risorgimento left the new nation-state in a parlous financial condition, and the existing massive military budget could certainly not be maintained. That Italy should risk war against the Habsburg monarchy over Venice and the Second French Empire over Rome, was foolhardy in the extreme. Once again, Italy's only possible solution was to secure the support of a greater power, and this time it was Prussia.

Serious tensions between Prussia and Austria in 1866 afforded the kind of opportunity that gave Italy's aggressive foreign policy its only chance of success. In April, La Marmora, who was now prime minister, and the Prussian chancellor, Otto von Bismarck, concluded an alliance against Austria. Fearing a war on two fronts, the Habsburgs actually offered Venice to La Marmora, but he declined because there was not much prestige in receiving Venice as a gift. Italy's military record thus far had been so unin-spiring that the new nation and the House of Savoy were desperate for glorious conquest. The state also sought a great victory without Garibaldi. Thus when hostilities broke out, Italy's greatest military leader was given a small and under-armed retinue, and was kept away from where the main fighting would take place. On 16 June 1866 Prussia declared war and the Italians did the same a week later. An Italian army double the size of its counterpart made its way to the north-east frontier, but it was badly led, poorly organized and under-equipped. The Italians not only repeated most of the mistakes of recent years but also lost yet another battle at Custoza. It was not a decisive battle, in fact the Austrians suffered heavier casualties, but so unco-ordinated were the Italians that they were forced to retreat. Worse still was the disastrous defeat of a large Italian naval force against a much smaller Austrian fleet off Lissa. Adding insult to injury, Garibaldi acutely embarrassed the government by making significant territorial gains against the Austrians in the Trentino. It was Prussia's victory against the Austrians at Sadowa on 3 July that saved the day for the Italians. Austria was forced to relinquish the Veneto, although it had to pass through the hands of France first, given that the Habsburgs did not officially recognize Italy.

The annexation of Rome was an equally inglorious affair. In 1862 Garibaldi had led a force from Sicily that was intercepted *en route* by Italian troops at Aspromonte in Calabria. The government feared provoking France, but public outcry after the assault on Italy's greatest hero prompted the dismissal of the then prime minister, Urbano Rattazzi. Garibaldi and his followers made a second attempt at Mentana, near Rome, in 1867, but this time they were well beaten by French and Papal forces. There were serious doubts that Italy would ever acquire Rome, but hopes were soon to be renewed with the escalation of tensions between France and Prussia in 1870. The outbreak of war between the two powers in July caused much deliberation over which side to support, but the matter was settled with the Prussian victory in September and the demise of Napoleon III. Prussia's decisive victory at Sedan and the absence of French troops made it reasonably safe to absorb Rome into the Kingdom of Italy on 20 September.

The Risorgimento was thus brought to a close by an anticlimax, for there was nothing inspiring about the seizure of Rome. The Papacy's forces defended pitifully, while the people of the city were not particularly interested in being liberated. There had been some anticipation of a popular insurrection in favour of annexation before the arrival of Italian troops, but nothing of the kind took place. Local indifference was a sobering reminder that ordinary Romans, along with the great bulk of Italians, did not share the aspirations of 'national opinion'. Indeed, Vittorio Emanuele was so uncertain of the kind of reception he might be given in Rome that no triumphal entry was organized. He waited until late December to visit, and only when locals were preoccupied by floodwaters from the Tiber. Since the war of unification first began in 1859, glory had eluded the House of Savoy and the Italian nation at every turn. Without the exploits of Garibaldi and his 'garibaldini', it would have been extremely difficult to create a national foundation myth. That said, the formation of such a large territorial state within a short space of time was a significant achievement, and as will be discussed later, the truth was no impediment to the creation of a glorious and yet believable foundation myth.

Maps and inventories

Many 'Italians' continued to exist outside the national borders, and until the Second World War, territorial expansion, whether to redeem supposedly 'Italian' lands or to build an empire as the Romans of antiquity did, remained a noble objective for patriotic Italians. Yet with Rome and Venice in hand, irredentism was not such a pressing issue. According to the new map, Italy now *looked* like Italy. Cartography provided the crucial means for visualizing the nation. Pre-unification states such as Piedmont and Naples did have sections within government departments that mapped their territories, but it was not until after 1860 that a state agency could produce a scientifically constructed map of *Italia*. The *Istituto geografico militare italiano* was given the task of constructing a fully detailed official map, an undertaking that was so massive that it was not completed until 1907. In the meantime this institute and many others like it produced less detailed maps for public consumption, especially for schools where students could have constant access to images of Italy.

Indeed, the sciences were to play an important role in making Italy more familiar. Hitherto, nearly all references to what constituted Italy and *italianità* could only be drawn from history. Thus Rome was automatically assumed to be the capital, and without Rome the nation was thought to be somehow disembodied. (The only serious objections to Rome being the capital came from the Florentines, who in 1870 were left in considerable debt after trying to make their city a suitable national capital.) But history was not really an adequate source for imagining the *new* Italy. After all, this new Italy sought to break away from the past; it constituted a rejection of a long history of political fragmentation, and *ancien régime* and Catholic Church domination.

Maps and collated scientific data offered alternative means for making Italy imaginable. Part of any nation-building exercise is the urgent requirement to measure, quantify and describe. Thus in 1885 the *Istituto geografico militare* measured Italy to be 286 588 square kilometres. The state familiarized itself with the nation by overseeing a massive inventory of its properties and peoples, as well as collecting ethnographic statistics and written descriptions of the nation's human geography. A precedent had already been set by the Congresses of Italian Scientists before unification. A scientifically constructed portrait was meant to counteract foreign characterizations of Italy as a land of backwardness and crime, and offer an alternative picture based on systematically gathered and processed information. The key political motive was to show that Italy was worthy of independence.

An additional motive for collecting information after 1860 was to secure the economic and political consolidation of the nation. Simply put, for the

French-speaking Piedmontese nobility, Italy was a foreign country, and what they needed urgently was credible knowledge of national human and natural resources for the practical purposes of government. By European standards, Italy was quite a large country. In October 1861 the 'Division of General Statistics' was created within the Ministry of Agriculture, Industry and Commerce to compile the necessary information. Under its first director, Pietro Maestri, the division produced about sixty volumes of statistics, including eleven on population, eight on industry, twelve on commerce, nine on schools, and three on meteorology. Maestri's outfit was equally committed to educating the Italian public about their country, publishing a thousand free copies of each volume.[3] Maestri and his collaborators also expected that their work would be exploited by the relevant state agencies when deciding the manner in which the nation was to be subdivided into administrative units. Here the challenge was to combat regional and local identification by apportioning the country into units based on scientific rather than cultural criteria. Maestri's colleagues paid special attention to the rational division of the entire country into comparably sized and populated communes, and into larger *compartimenti* or regions. His division of the country into regions (Piedmont, Liguria, Lombardy, Emilia, Umbria, The Marches, Tuscany, Abruzzo and Molise, Campania, Appulia, Basilicata, Calabria and Sicily) worked reasonably well because they corresponded with some of the pre-1860 states. These *compartimenti* became the principal means of understanding Italy through its constituent parts. Students of Italy, whether they were state administrators, scientists, statisticians, school children or foreign travellers, would begin to make sense of this complex country by studying its components. In other words, the regions served to make Italy more digestible and therefore knowable.

The rational division of the country into parts as a means of understanding the whole could not, however, detract from the real difficulties posed by the country's profound cultural complexity. The imperative to 'make Italians' meant that Italy was supposed to become a cultural unit as much as it was now a political one. Ethnographic studies were employed during the early stages of nation building to identify those features of traditional cultures – e.g. vocabulary, dress, songs, folktales and family rituals – that could be identified as cultural variations of a national norm. In other words, the state sought to overcome the complications posed by the country's heterogeneity by ascribing to local cultures a domestic status; thus distinct, yet related, languages were redesignated as 'dialects'.

Taming cultural disparities was an important means of establishing a composite 'Italian' culture, but Sicily, Sardinia and the southern half of the mainland were considered too alien by many northern commentators.

---

[3] Silvana Patriarca, *Numbers and Nationhood: Writing Statistics in Nineteenth-Century Italy* (Cambridge, Cambridge University Press, 1996), pp. 181–2, 184.

Indeed, many such critics believed that 'the south' threatened the integrity of *italianità*. As one Piedmontese envoy reported in 1860: 'What barbarism! Some Italy! This is Africa: the bedouin are the flower of civilized virtues compared to these peasants.'[4] The brutal war that flared in southern Italy between 1861 and 1867, which took a greater toll on lives than the wars of the Risorgimento, played an important role in the formation of enduring typecasts of southern society. 'Il Brigantaggio' was officially likened to a war on criminal elements and against unruly, primitive peoples who were languishing in ignorance and superstition. Thus the suppression of a popular insurgency against an oppressive regime was represented by the state as a civilizing mission. The Mezzogiorno was therefore ascribed many of the characteristics that the state and 'national opinion' believed were inimical to *italianità*. Thus the Mezzogiorno was typecast as a useful opposite or 'other' against which the Italian 'self' could be fashioned.

Attempts to explain the Mezzogiorno continued well after the suppression of the insurgency, and particularly from the mid-1870s, when it became an established subject of scientific study. Although the Mezzogiorno had been quelled, locals continued to harbour a deep-seated hostility towards state authority, and the persistence of high crime and poverty were read as manifestations of a biological problem, i.e. cultural backwardness in the Mezzogiorno came to be attributed to race. In likening southerners to Africans and other categories who were perceived as being racially inferior, scientists such as the famous criminologist Cesare Lombroso found their explanation for southern hostility to national integration. This so-called 'Southern Question' (*questione meridionale*) was investigated with great rigour by statisticians, scientists and bureaucrats. To the Tuscan senator Leopoldo Franchetti, a leading commentator on the *questione meridionale*, the Mezzogiorno was so exotic that it was not European and hence not Italian, while others such the Sicilian Alfredo Niceforo, who wrote perhaps the most influential tract on the Southern Question, *L'Italia barbara contemporanea* (1898), southerners were racially distinct but were still Italians. Overall, the *questione meridionale* offered a way of determining what Italians were not or what they should not be. If southerners could be pronounced inferior on racial grounds, then *Italianità* too was a racial condition: by implication, Italians were, in biological terms, European. Either way, Italian identity was being defined through the development of stereotypes of the Mezzogiorno.

---

[4]   Quoted in John Dickie, 'Stereotypes of the Italian South', in R. Lumley and J. Morris (eds), *The New History of the Italian South: The Mezzogiorno Revisited* (Exeter, University of Exeter Press, 1997), p. 122.

The new Italy: progress and symbolic forms

Science afforded a useful means for making the nation known as well as underscoring its relationship with progress and modernity, but science could not 'make' Italians. The legitimation of the Italian nation could only be secured through the formation of a common identity that bound Italian society to the nation-state and the new political order. If science and statistical information provided a rational basis for explicating the nation, other means were necessary if an enduring emotional bond between society and nation was to formed. In particular, Italy would need to appeal to the senses.

Since time immemorial, all sovereign powers have recognized the importance of symbolic representations of authority, especially as a means of reifying the legitimacy of that authority and establishing a connection between rulers and the ruled. Since the idea of the nation in the nineteenth century was so novel and abstract, political symbolism was particularly germane. Symbols had a way of tricking the mind into thinking of the abstract as concrete, and hence making the nation both imaginable and affecting. The Italian tricolour that first appeared during the *epoca francese* was a natural choice for the national flag and as an emblem of nationhood. Less explicit references to both the nation and the political order were to be found in items such as coins, postal stamps and statues, or in public buildings, streetscapes, public festivals and commemorations. Italy was supposed to be commonplace and awe-inspiring at the same time. By altering the material environment and offering publicly visible references to nationhood, it was hoped that Italians would be constantly reminded of their individual nationality and the greatness of their nation. Railway construction and monumental buildings were supposed to draw a symbolic link between *italianità* on the one hand, and greatness and progress on the other. Throughout the late nineteenth century, the Italian state and patriotically minded associations did make some headway in fashioning a national culture that reflected the ideals of the political order. These nationalists at the end of the century had much in common with the martial spirit of the House of Savoy and little in common with the cosmopolitan and socially progressive Mazzinians.

Symbolic representations of nationhood were concentrated in urban environments, where audiences were naturally larger and where the 'public' resided. The focus on cities in the Italian case was especially necessary, given that the new nation would need to compete with deeply entrenched municipal loyalties. In the decades following unification, many of Italy's major cities were substantially renovated in much the same way as George-Eugène Haussmann reorganized the Paris of Napoleon III. Old neighbourhoods, such as the Jewish ghetto in Florence, were cleared to make way for major rectilinear thoroughfares that linked the key points of the city. Piazzas were created or expanded to provide ample space for public commemorations and informal gatherings. Many residents were displaced by massive construction projects that were designed to enhance the property values of the owners of real estate, and yet which modernized the cities in ways that made the movement of traffic and policing much easier. No city experienced more reconstruction than the nation's capital: Rome. In 1870 Rome was comparatively small by Italian standards, roughly a quarter the size of Naples and half that of Milan, but in the years following its seizure much effort went into transforming it into a suitable European capital as well as a focus of national identity. Some of the major thoroughfares of the city, such as the Via Cavour, the Corso Vittorio Emanuele and the Via del Tritone, were created after old neighbourhoods had been torn down, yet each served to enhance the city's many-layered historical heritage. The reconfiguration of Rome was intended to break-up an urban plan that symbolized the domination of the Church, that had the main arteries linking the city's major basilicas. In 1882, the state launched a major competition for the design of a monumental structure dedicated to the deceased King Vittorio Emanuele II, which was to be constructed between the Piazza Venezia, the Roman Forum and the Capitol. When the monument was finally opened in 1911, it sought to evoke the same martial spirit and the grandeur that was conveyed so evocatively by the Roman ruins nearby. The close proximity of classical ruins and the Victor Emmanuel monument in this part of the city was supposed to be read as a symbolic alliance between ancient Rome and the new Italy. This part of Rome was also expected to displace the Vatican as the new city centre. With the new thoroughfares that cut across the old city, and linked the king's monument with the Piazza del Popolo and the Stazione Termini, the urban plan that reflected the Church's dominion was now broken.

Urban transformation signified the new national order, though it was equally important to stress the ascendancy of the nation over the city, and after 1860 nothing symbolized the diminution of the Italian city more than the destruction of its walls. Milan, Bologna, Modena, Bari, Palermo, Florence, and many other cities witnessed the systematic removal of walls that hindered urban modernization and which signalled their absorption into a nation-state. Certain wall sections made way for large avenues that connected the city centre to newer developments and the new ring roads that often ran in parallel with the walls. It was especially important to construct a major link between the city centre and the main train station, which was normally situated outside the old walls.

As with any other new nation, Italy had many of its significant streets and town squares re-named after patriotic heroes, battles and dates: 'Via Garibaldi', Via Settembre XX and so on. While town planning reflected the new national order, monuments did the same more explicitly. Urban centres were endowed with all types of monuments that celebrated battles and individuals that made the Italian nation. Representations of the Risorgimento were inevitably to face strong competition from Italy's exceptionally rich heritage of monuments, but changes to urban environments made it possible to place the nation's grand statues, columns, obelisks, mock altars and mock temples in prominent locations. Municipalities sought to demonstrate their patriotic worth by finding a conspicuous place for their own national monuments in piazzas and parks. Columns with statues fixed on top were usually erected to commemorate locals that perished in the struggle for the 'patria' (fatherland).

Statues relating to the Risorgimento were often male or female allegories of 'victory', 'liberty' or martial values, while others depicted specific heroes. The most commonly depicted figure was Vittorio Emmanuele II. This rather reluctant Italian was over-represented in national iconography because the state initially sought to create a national culture that focussed on the Savoy dynasty, which was in line with the king's belief that Italy was his patrimony. The greatest monument of the post-Risorgimento or Liberal period was Rome's Victor Emmanuel monument, the 'Vittoriano', which was widely likened to a massive marble typewriter in the Piazza Venezia in Rome. The Vittoriano was unequivocally a celebration of martial values and the anticipated glorious imperial destiny of the Italian nation, each of which were reflected in the person of the warrior king himself. The decision to erect a major monument to the nation's first king was confirmed in the parliament very soon after he died in 1878, and was presented to deputies by Giuseppe Zanardelli as reflecting the unanimous will of the nation. Making the king the focus for symbolic depiction of national culture was the least divisive choice. Ideological divisions between democrats and moderates continued through the early years of the Italian nation; the legacies of Garibaldi, Cavour and especially Mazzini were much disputed. Mazzini was far too radical a figure to be celebrated publicly, and the only major city to defiantly erect a monument in his honour in the nineteenth century was his birthplace, Genoa. There were not many monuments dedicated to Cavour either, mainly because it was difficult to glorify a statesman who died in his bed. Vittorio Emmanuele II did not personally engage in battle, but he did take part in military campaigns and hence was commonly depicted in military garb and on horseback. And given the extent of his constitutional powers, neither side of politics was willing to dispute his newfound status as national military hero. The king's rival, and the only real hero to enjoy public acclaim, was of course Garibaldi. His enormous national and international profile also made him a problematic choice for depiction, as he could not be allowed to overshadow the king.

The House of Savoy dominated representations of nationhood in museums as well. From 1885 a number of Risorgimento museums appeared through much of Italy, each of which were dedicated to providing an historical portrait of the nation. The state had already promoted an extensive inventory of Italian artefacts from the many different stages in Italian history, but it was the Risorgimento that was in vital need of historical reconstruction. On 26 April 1884, an exposition was opened in the Parco del Valentino in Turin, which sought to celebrate the New or 'Third' Italy's achievements, such as in science and technology, but the exposition put an emphasis on 'reflection'. It made a special effort to celebrate the heroes and struggles of the Risorgimento, and as the location was Turin, Cavour as well as the Savoy monarchy featured prominently. After the exposition, a series of museums were created as permanent shrines to the history of the nation's foundation: by 1906 there were twenty-nine Museums of the Risorgimento, of which six were in central Italy and twenty-two in the north.[5]

Creating national memories and loyalties

The Vittoriana, the museums and the flag could influence the formation of Italian identities, but Italians were not passive recipients of symbolic projections of nationhood, and the socializing role of forms depended heavily on how they were received and consumed. Nation-building projects therefore depended more heavily on formal education as a more direct means of effecting a new cultural outlook. Nothing could make peasants into self-aware nationals as could the schoolteacher and the curriculum, and the most essential starting point for 'nationalising' the masses in nineteenth-century Europe was the primary school. It was here that the state could begin to spread the national language, where children would be forced to acquire a facility with Italian and hopefully make it their everyday medium of communication. It was also at this level where minds were at their most impressionable, where young people could be moulded into law-abiding subjects, and where love of king, flag and fatherland could be instilled on a daily basis. One of the most urgent initial steps taken by state authorities in France, Germany and Italy was to break the hold of the Catholic Church on education, a weighty undertaking that was perceived as a struggle for hearts and minds. The Catholic Church regarded education as the major battleline between the forces of God and secularism, while its opponents sensed that the survival of the nation was at stake. These 'culture struggles' were ideologically charged and highly acrimonious, and the struggle played out in Italy was particularly acute. Rome, after all, was the centre of both Catholicism and the Italian nation-state, where the Papacy refused recognition of the Italian nation, and from where Catholics had been directed not to participate in its political life.

---

[5] Massimo Baioni, *La "Religione della Patria": Musei e istituti del culto risorgimentale (1884–1918),* (Quinto di Treviso, Pagus, 1994), p. 39.

Prior to unification, Piedmont had launched the most concerted effort to remove clerical influence from education. In 1859, the parliament in Turin passed the so-called Casati Law, the express purpose of which was the establishment of a secular education system whose graduates would owe their primary loyalty to the Savoy dynasty. To achieve these aims the state established its authority over most aspects of the education system, such as its structure, curriculum, education certificates, and teacher training. In true Napoleonic and Piedmontese fashion, the system was supervised by a branch of the state bureaucracy and monitored by teams of inspectors. The Piedmontization of Italy included the extension of the Casati Law across the board, an undertaking made all the more feasible because of a lack of any alternative modernized educational system in the other states.

Italy's cultural heterogeneity and the obvious fact that very few people considered themselves 'Italian' meant that a heavily co-ordinated, nation-wide socialization programme was essential. Of immediate concern was the fact that the great bulk of the population could not understand the national language, and that only 25 per cent of Italians were believed to be literate. The literacy problem was most severe in Basilicata, Sardinia and Calabria, where in 1861 rates of illiteracy were about 90 per cent, and lowest in Piedmont and Lombardy (52 and 54 per cent respectively).[6] The state hoped to provide primary education for all Italian children, regardless of social background. There were two levels of secondary school, the *ginnasio* and *liceo*, which were meant for the children of middle- and upper-class families, who then could proceed to university. The majority of students entering secondary education were normally the children of the middling or petit bourgeois families and went either to institutions that provided vocational training (*scuola tecnica*, followed by the *istituto tecnico*), or to institutions that trained teachers.

Formally, the system provided the structure and bureaucratic support base that was necessary for nationalizing the population, and official rhetoric was clear about education's role in creating a dutiful, loyal and orderly population. The chief difficulty was securing the resources necessary to make such a massive education system function as it was intended.

Funding was a constant dilemma, and much of what could be spared for the education budget was channelled to secondary schools. Teachers were supposed to receive a salary worthy of their status, but salaries were never sufficient to support individual teachers. The *comuni* were expected to bear the costs of the primary school system, but more than often they were totally unable or quite unwilling to do so. Where primary schools were actually established, one found that most Italian families, particularly in

---

6 Giovanni Vigo, 'Gli italiani alla conquista dell'alfabeto', in Simonetta Soldani and Gabriele Turi (eds), *Fare gli italiani: Scuola e cultura nell'Italia contemporanea*, Vol. 1. *La nascita dello stato nazionale* (Bologna, Mulino, 1993), p. 50.

rural regions, could not afford to do without the free labour that their children provided. Nor were they easily convinced that education was worthwhile. Laws making two years of schooling compulsory were meant to overcome expected obstruction from the illiterate classes, but the Italian state was quite adept at issuing rules that it could not enforce. In France the primary school was considered the most important vehicle for spreading French civilization to its citizenry, but the French state had the means to make schooling free and widely accessible, and it succeeded in impressing upon parents the advantages of schooling, and particularly literacy. Because of Italy's radically inferior financial position, and the reluctance of the political order to spend money on 'the masses', the primary school system made very few Italians, and it was not much better in improving literacy levels. In the period 1871 to 1911, as the supply of teachers and the costs of primary school education became more manageable, the rate of national illiteracy dropped from 68.8 to 37.9 per cent, though in Calabria and Basilicata the rates were still rather high: 69.6 and 65.3 per cent respectively. The growing prestige attached to proficiency in the national language, and the increasing recognition of the importance accorded to acquiring literacy encouraged more and more people over time to regard education as a necessity of life. Yet such self-conscious Italians were being made at much slower rates than were, say, Britons, French and Germans. Nationalism was still not a popular phenomenon in Italy at the end of the century, and the outbreak of war in 1914 was not greeted with the kind of patriotic response that could be found among the other participating nations.

Schools were deliberately meant to produce patriots, hence students were expected to write essays on subjects such as 'Why do you love Italy?', or on the heroic feats of Vittorio Emanuele II. As in most nation-states, schools were decorated with large wall maps of Italy, which usually identified the unredeemed Italian territories, such as the Trentino, and with portraits of national heroes and the national flag. Yet as impressionable as young minds might have been, they were usually not retained at school long enough for the nation to make an enduring impression. The great majority of children that did attend school did so for no more than two years. Primary schools could impart basic literacy and numeracy skills within such a short space of time, but making 'Italians' was a far more laborious undertaking, and was only possible when retention rates were noticeably improved under Fascism.

Those who were more likely to emerge from school 'feeling Italian' were secondary school graduates. The *ginnasi* and *licei* were very much like elite schools in northern Europe in that they were preliminary training grounds for the nation's ruling class and its state functionaries. The number of students that passed through these institutions clearly indicated their social exclusivity, as the *licei* collectively had a mere 4672 students in 1862–3, and only 15 713 by 1891–2. In 1862–3, 65 per cent of *ginnasi* students and 76 per cent of *licei* students were the children of major landholders, and most of the rest were the progeny of merchants.[7] Students were mainly trained in the classics, and it was at this level that they could be fully immersed in Italian literature and history. In effect, thorough tutoring and reading could make students fully appreciative of Italy's mission. Thus schooling could have the desired effect of making Italy's foreign policy, for example, a matter of personal and emotional involvement. In knowing their Italian history, students at this level could be expected to know what being Italian supposedly meant, and could think of themselves as national beings and living in national history.

Indeed after unification the Italian public took a great interest in history, which also happened to be the primary focus of the arts. Painters, sculptors, musicians, novelists, poets and journalists dealing with Italian historical themes were legion: Garibaldi attracted the most painters and writers, including one of the leading poets of the late nineteenth century, Giosue Carducci. Carducci, who saw himself as the *vate d'Italia* (bard of Italy) also produced an epic poem called 'Risorgimento'. The Tuscan school of painters known as the Macchiaioli dedicated much energy to depicting scenes from the Risorgimento, particularly the great battles, which they helped to mythicize on canvas, with striking colours and in intricate detail. But what history were artists and writers of the post-Risorgimento period referring to? What counted as the nation's history? What kind of history was being celebrated by those museums that were dedicated to the Risorgimento? More to the point: how could the recent history of Italy be made a source of national values and pride? There were so many lost battles, so few heroes, and so few patriots. How could the House of Savoy, which produced such poor military leaders and such fickle proponents of Italian unity, be then made the focus of Italian national culture?

The actual past has never provided a serious obstacle to new nations seeking glorious histories, and Italy was no exception. As the French scholar Ernest Renan argued at the time when national histories were being invented throughout late nineteenth-century Europe, 'getting history wrong' was part of the course. The real 'Age of Risorgimento' was too unheroic and embarrassing to be reconstructed faithfully by historians, but concerted efforts were made by the state to dominate the nation's memory and determine the construction of a more useable, self-serving history. Thus the state took great interest in the manner in which history was taught and ensured that it became a central feature of schooling at primary, secondary and tertiary levels. From September 1862 it required that Italy's ancient and modern history be taught in universities where philological subjects had been long established, and subsequent years witnessed a spate of new

---

[7] Marzio Barbagli, *Education for Unemployment: Politics, Labor Markets and the School System – Italy, 1859–1973* (New York, Columbia University Press, 1982), pp. 67, 69.

professorial chairs and courses dedicated to the teaching of history. The Ministry of Public Education took a keen interest in appointments to teaching posts in history, ensuring that only 'reliable' people were allocated places. One of the important contributions of such historians was to the training of school teachers, who were expected to impart patriotically charged history lessons to generations of students, thus expanding social awareness of Italy's great past and its destiny.

Italy invented its 'Age of Risorgimento', which in due course inscribed itself in public memory. Its construction was the work of professional and amateur historians, who saw no problem in producing a narrative that served the national interest. Indeed, historians generally regarded history writing as a patriotic exercise, and it is no coincidence that the rise and expansion of history as an academic discipline and as a field of public interest coincided with the ascendancy of nationalism. According to Pasquale Villari, one of the major historians of late nineteenth-century Italy, a narrative demonstrating the continuities of Italian history was 'not merely a scientific need, but a patriotic duty'. There were, of course, major obstacles. Firstly, if the nation's history before 1860 had been characterized by political fragmentation, how could one produce a single, digestible narrative? Moreover, if the new Italy was a secular state that had been recently denounced by the Papacy, was it also possible to produce a history of Italy that diminished the role of the Church? Yet as Villari told a national Italian history conference in Florence in 1889, Italy's long continuous history was not in doubt. Rather, the purpose of the critical historians was to 'uncover' it. Historians charged with patriotic conviction could always find ways to refashion the past or explain away inconvenient facts in their quest to uncover a national narrative. For example, conflicts between Italian states could be recast as 'fratricidal' struggles, and Cavour's aversion to Italian unification and his many attempts to thwart Garibaldi's conquest of the south could be simply overlooked. Given the undeniable political fragmentation of Italy before 1860, scholars often found the most plausible narrative lines were those that referred to cultural continuity, which plotted the production of Italian literary, scientific and philosophical classics along a single timeline. Among the most important and most influential histories produced in the late nineteenth century was Francesco De Sanctis' *Storia della letteratura italiana (1870–71)*, which sought to demonstrate the growth of Italian national consciousness through writers stretching as far back as Dante.

The re-invention of the period leading to unification as the Age of Risorgimento, in which like-minded patriots waged a deliberate struggle for independence, and with the intention of creating the Italian nation-state, proved to be a remarkably successful achievement. The period 1814 to 1860 was now re-remembered as a heroic age. Vittorio Emanuele II was 'Re galantuomo', an epoch-making monarch who exuded the martial and valorous spirit of those times. So successful was the Risorgimento myth that later generations found it an onerous heritage to maintain. As the Italian public grew increasingly disenchanted with the nation's unadventurous foreign policy, its economic backwardness and the manifest level of political corruption and ineptitude, nostalgia for the mythical Risorgimento grew stronger. Contemporary political leaders could never measure up to, and indeed they came to be seen as the antithesis to, Garibalidi, Foscolo, Mazzini, Pellico and Vittorio Emanuele II.

Another relatively efficient 'nationalizing' agency was the Italian military. The state required males to serve in the army once they reached the age of twenty-one, though a large percentage of them were exempted on the basis of poor health. Initially the term of service was eight years, but in 1871 it was reduced to four, then three in 1875, and finally two in 1910. Regardless of how long these men were held, they were subjected to rigid process of nationalization, for conscription was widely recognized as an important means of securing commitment to the political order. One of the expectations of the demobilized soldiers was that they would carry their newfound identity and enthusiasm for *italianità* into their communities. Military service also involved travel, which expanded a young man's horizons. Conscripts were normally posted away from their locality and were blended with men from other parts of Italy, meaning that they initially began in groups without a mutually intelligible language. Regiments were deliberately composed of recruits from many districts, and even if this mixing of different cultures was a cause of hostility among conscripts, mixing groups could also promote friendship and cross-cultural camaraderie. Until the early 1880s, military service required conscripts to achieve an acceptable level of literacy before being discharged, which meant that young males were returning to their localities with some facility in Italian. And even when the regiments had their literacy programme abolished in 1892, the level of illiteracy among discharged soldiers was about 25 per cent, much lower than the national average. The soldier's education also included doses of nationalist culture, through lectures, newspapers such as *La caserma* (The Barracks), and books that recounted heroic episodes of history, including myths from the Risorgimento.

The limits of nationalization

Military service was supposed to develop a religious reverence for national symbols such as the House of Savoy, and hence a passion for Italy. Such outcomes were never guaranteed, however. The hardships and abuses suffered by all conscripts could just as well foster antipathy towards the nation. Moreover, while some regions seemed to offer conscripts that were amenable to socialization, those from Genoa and much of the South were notoriously difficult to shake from their anti-state and anti-patriotic dispositions. Schools and conscription could make Italians in theory, but there was always a marked discrepancy between theory and practice in Italy, as there was between national ideals and national realities. Only in 1911 did the state channel sufficient funding to primary schools, and only then did it make it compulsory for all municipalities to build schools of an acceptable standard.

That it took so long to enact serious education reforms reflected not only financial handicaps but also the state's disingenuousness when it came to making Italians. Education policy was poorly funded and not carried through with much conviction. In reality, the 'masses' were not the target of nationalization: peasants and the urban poor were too dangerous to the social order and best kept under tight rein. Education was a two-edged sword, which could politicize the masses instead of making them them loyal subjects, a prospect that the political order feared above all else. Rather, all efforts to create a national culture were aimed at influencing the middle and upper classes. It was the expanding ranks of the bourgeoisie in particular who had access to secondary school education and who could read books on the heroes of the Risorgimento, or the newspapers and periodicals, such as the *Illustrazione italiana*, that covered items of national interest. Yet in concentrating its efforts on the middle and upper end of the social scale, the state was exacerbating class tensions and effectively dividing the nation. The following chapter details the ramifications of the incompetence of the Liberal regime, among which was the failure to spread Italian national consciousness beyond the middle and upper classes, and in allowing the mutation of nationalism into an anti-state ideology.

|6|

Stillborn nation: Liberal Italy and its malcontents

One early afternoon on 11 April 1864, Giuseppe Garibaldi emerged from Nine Elms Station near Waterloo in London, where he was confronted by vast crowds of adoring admirers. So dense were these crowds, so eager were Londoners to catch of glimpse of the great man, that it took him several hours to work his way through to his destination, which was a mere three miles away.[1] People of all classes had lined the streets to see him, for Garibaldi was nothing less than a legend in his own lifetime. So redolent was his name that it was employed to advertise clothes and biscuits, and his famous red shirt became fashionable attire. Mazzini could also count on legions of admirers across the length and breadth of Europe, for both men symbolized political values that had great purchase among progressives, while their heroic deeds and self-sacrifice also appealed to the romantic imagination. It was not just Mazzini and Garibaldi, but the Risorgimento itself that captivated the world during those middle years of the nineteenth century. For a short while at least, Italy, normally associated with opera singers and the high arts generally, enjoyed the limelight as a land evoking more outwardly masculine values.

It did not take long, however, before this focus of inspiration became the butt of jokes in some quarters. Dismissive remarks were common among foreign statesmen and diplomats who were irritated by Italy's unfounded pretensions to world power status, by the impertinence of its territorial claims, and the sly methods its diplomats employed to attain their unrealistically ambitious goals. When Lord Salisbury famously quipped that the Italians were a nation of 'sturdy beggars', he added his voice to a chorus of

---

[1] Derek Beales, 'Garibaldi in England: The Politics of Italian Enthusiasm', in John A. Davis and Paul Ginsborg (eds), *Society and Politics in the Age of the Risorgimento* (Cambridge, 1991), p. 189.

condescending asides and racial slurs that inferred that Italy, try as it might, could not be 'great'. In fact Italian diplomats were all too aware that their country did not have the wherewithal to behave as a genuine Great Power: their insidious approach to foreign relations was conditioned by the nation's weaknesses. Towards the end of the century, patriotic Italians were becoming increasingly frustrated that their country had not lived up to the glories of the Risorgimento. In their eyes Italy was shame-fully mediocre.

Fin-de-siècle Italians, at least that minority who had any ardour for 'Italia', were also melancholic about it. An unadventurous foreign policy and a few military debacles had highlighted the nation's mediocrity, as had certain, more disturbing, domestic deficiencies. Despite massive public works programmes, the extension of railway networks, the renovation of urban landscapes and other symbolic manifestations of progress, Italy was still a predominantly backward nation. Poverty and crime had, if anything, worsened since the Risorgimento. Millions of Italians were abandoning their nation for northern Europe and the Americas. During the first half-century of Italy's existence, 16.6 million departures were recorded, with approximately 10 million Italians applying to migrate between 1896 and 1915.[2] The Risorgimento was supposed to have united Italians as one community, but class divisions appeared to be deeper than ever, so much so that through the 1890s class friction threatened to undo the Risorgimento. The rise of radical movements such as the anarchists and the socialists, and the insoluble 'Social Question', were convincing proof to the middle and upper classes that Italy was going backwards rather than forward.

As usual, these classes targeted their frustration at the poor, the victims of economic modernisation, but much of their angst was also directed at the Liberal political order in whose incompetent hands the promise of united Italy remained unfulfilled. Indeed, the interests of state and society had become inimical. Government at each level afforded opportunities to politi-cians to pursue their private interests and for local power magnates to exert influence in order to secure their portion of the nation's wealth. With signs of stagnation and even degeneration everywhere, the state was accused of negligence and culpability, yet all the while Italians were being educated to think of their nation's intrinsic greatness and its glorious destiny. Inevitably the gap between public expectations and the realities of Liberal Italy produced a culture of disillusionment. By the end of the nineteenth century, what counted for Italian public opinion had developed an utter contempt for the present and an unwarranted nostalgia for the heroic days of the Risorgimento. As the philosopher and future politician Giovanni Amendola, lamented, 'The Italy of today does not please us.'

---

[2] Donna R. Gabaccia, *Italy's Many Diasporas* (London, UCL Press, 2000), p. 58.

Ironically, an increasing number of those Italians that had been 'made' were also the leading exponents of political revolution. They advocated the complete overhaul of the political system in favour of a more authoritarian regime, specifically one committed to the glorification of the nation through imperialism. Italy was certainly not alone among European powers in equating greatness with territorial expansion, but by 1922 it was the first power to have a radical nationalist regime. This chapter examines the reasons why national opinion in the lead-up to the Great War became increasingly receptive to the rhetoric of the radical right. It also traces the development of reactionary politics before the Great War, which saw the mutation of Italian nationalism into an elitist, chauvinistic and imperialist ideology. The political establishment's claim to the mantle of patriotism was vigorously contested by extra-parliamentary groups, which did not as yet have the means to seize power, but which acted as pressure groups that harassed the state at every turn. Through the expanding medium of print, particularly newspapers and periodicals, the new Right not only exacerbated public disillusionment by its attacks on the political order, but it set the stage for the rise of the world's first fascist government. Certainly these pre-war nationalists provided the principal ideological inspiration of Mussolini's regime. When the nation's disastrous showing during the Great War dealt a mortal blow to the Liberal order, the only political alternative that was acceptable to the nation's elites was a movement whose extremist ideas and aims were already familiar.

Catholicism, the political order and Italietta

The political leaders who were left with the task of consolidating Italy from the latter months of 1860 had few illusions about the difficulties that lay ahead. Their role was to establish the state's authority over a very large and often unfamiliar territory, but a much more difficult undertaking was making the new nation knowable, attractive and affecting to its inhabitants. Creating a common culture was fundamental to any nation-building project, part of which involved the 'nationalization' of traditions and identities with which common people were already familiar. The invention of nations has usually included an extensive ethnographic exercise in which disparate folk traditions, religious cultures and popular myths have been collated and sometimes modestly re-interpreted in order to fit them into an overarching national culture. In recasting distinctive cultures as 'regional variations' and by placing local histories and traditions into a national historical framework, it became possible for ordinary folk to identify with something as utterly abstract as a national community.

Given Italy's cultural heterogeneity, the creation of a national culture seemed a particularly difficult undertaking. Hence Cavour, d'Azeglio,

Ricasoli and others were deeply conscious that the state would need to play an intensive role in its creation, yet they were determined to disregard the one factor that nearly all Italians had in common: Roman Catholicism. The great bulk of Italians readily identified themselves as *cristiani*, yet the new political order envisaged a nation that was secular and free of Papal political influence. Until Mussolini finally managed to secure Papal recognition for the Italian nation-state in 1929, relations between the Italian state and the Vatican ranged between estrangement and hostility. Thus Italy was denied something that made nationalism such a popular phenomenon in Poland, Croatia and Spain, where nationality and Catholicism had been conflated. Religion had been the most powerful marker of ethnic identity in pre-modern societies, and while the nation is often regarded by social scientists and historians as a major symbol *and* vehicle of modernity, the success of the nation depended on its ability to feed off existing cultural capital, *especially* religion. In the eighteenth century, Protestantism was to be the vital underpinning of British identity, much as Catholicism is to modern Irish national self-identification. If the affecting power of religion is transferred to national culture, nationalism becomes a form of religion, in which the nation becomes God's chosen people, national heroes are venerated like saints, and national enemies likened to the devil. There were modest signs of this in Italy in connection with Garibaldi, adoration of whom could resemble the devout homage normally paid to saints.

The Catholic Church in Italy was the one institution that enjoyed real moral authority throughout the country and which was capable of rallying the great mass of the population to the new order. Its refusal to play that role, however, owing to its general intransigence towards secularism and modern ideologies, its recalcitrance towards an irredentist nation-state that usurped its temporal possessions, and the anticlericalism of the Italian political class, meant the construction of the Italian nation began with a very serious handicap. It is difficult to exaggerate the hostility of the Papacy. After having dominated life in the city of Rome since late antiquity, the clergy suddenly found themselves dispossessed of their properties and their place in public life. Soon after Rome's walls had been breached in September 1870, all religious houses were dissolved and monasteries were metamorphosed into public buildings, such as state ministries and prisons. One-fifth of Rome's residential property had been in the hands of the Church, but was now at the disposal of the state. A brooding Pius IX could do little but withdraw behind the walls of the Vatican and hope that God or some Catholic power might come to his rescue. The claim that he was now 'a prisoner of Vatican' was not purely rhetorical. The pope himself was often the target of insults from people in the streets. In 1871 a mob was reported as having smashed madonnas outside his walls, and in 1874 another mob of 300 chanted death threats at the Pope. The anticlericalism of Italian patriots and the political class generally had become as much cultural as it was political. Insults and jibes against the Church were commonplace among politicians and the press, and devout Catholics were often harassed by authorities when religious ceremonies were conducted in public. On 11 May 1874, a religious procession in Milan was officially banned when an alternative Liberal procession in honour of Garibaldi specifically set out to spoil the occasion.[3] When the Law of Guarantees was issued in March 1871, which included Italian recognition of the pope's standing as a sovereign authority, opposition within the parliament was fierce.

The estrangement between Church and State was not absolute, however. The Law of Guarantees did something to reassure the wider Catholic world that the papacy was not a captive of a secularist Italian state. Throughout Italy, parish life continued to function as it had done before, the bishops and priests continued to play their vocational roles. And even most of the political class, including some anticlericals, were privately Catholic. In other words, the Church was not persecuted to the extent that it had been in Jacobin France, and there was scope for future Church–State rapprochement and accommodation, though not during the lifetime of Pius IX. No matter how conciliatory the Savoy monarchy and its governments tried to be, Pius was implacably hostile to Italy and denounced it repeatedly. And his recalcitrance had major implications for Italian nation formation. In directing his flock not to take part in the political life of the new state and to refuse to vote in national elections, as per the so-called *non expedit*, Pius effectively had a majority of eligible voters pitted against the Italian state. Such implacable Papal opposition was a major reason why the social support base of the Liberal Italian state remained so thin. At the broader level, the clergy enjoyed much greater access than did state agencies to Italians of all social classes, and did their best to kindle antipathy towards a political order that denied the people the Church's charitable functions, and whose excessively materialist outlook and liberal economic policies had worsened the plight of the poor.

Thus whereas Catholicism became a pillar of national identities elsewhere, it was undeniably subversive in Italy. The formation of lay Catholic organizations throughout Italy from the mid 1870s, known as the *Opera dei congressi*, constituted an attempt to organize Catholic opinion against the political order. The Papacy approved of the *Opera dei congressi*, which supported Pius's stance on all matters, including his intransigence towards the Italian nation. In due course the Papacy took control of these organizations. In the 1890s, Pope Leo XIII had found effective ways of gaining the allegiance of the Italian faithful by taking an active interest in the plight of the lower classes. Social and welfare services were offered as a means of

---

[3] Owen Chadwick, *A History of the Popes, 1830–1914* (Oxford, Oxford University Press, 1999), pp. 238–9.

alleviating the suffering caused by liberal economic policies, although the new Church initiative was also motivated by competition with the newly emerging socialist movements for the hearts and minds of the lower orders. Indeed, it was the threat of socialism, a much more militantly anticlerical force than liberalism, that did more than anything to force Catholics into direct involvement in Italian political life. The threat to completely remove the Church from education in 1908, and the massive extension of the franchise in 1913, which opened the real prospect of an unconscionably large socialist presence in the parliament, convinced the Papacy that strict application of the *non expedit* was political folly. Although the *non expedit* still formally applied until 1919, the Church allowed for 'expedient' participation where Church interests were deemed to be directly at risk. Through the so-called Gentiloni Pact, Catholic deputies formed an alliance with Liberal deputies in 1913 that kept the socialists from power, but the experience confirmed that a more active and permanent presence in the political system would safeguard the interests of Italian Catholics. The 1913 elections demonstrated the massive electoral potential of a Catholic party, and hence in 1919 the *Partito popolare italiano*, with Vatican approval, contested its first election and gained 1 176 473 out of 5 682 000 of votes cast. The only other single party to gain more votes was the Italian Socialist Party.

Thus Catholics had finally been integrated into Italian political life, but almost fifty years had elapsed since the seizure of Rome, during which time the Italian faithful had been encouraged by their spiritual leaders to reject the Italian nation as something akin to evil. Meanwhile, competing for the hearts and minds of the Italian population was a rather sterile secular nationalism that was focussed on the myth of the Risorgimento and on the House of Savoy. Rather than facilitating nation building, Catholicism was its major obstruction, hence it is not hard to see why the Italian masses were not 'nationalized' during the Liberal period.

To be sure, the French Third Republic managed, quite successfully, to establish a secular national culture, largely because ordinary folk eventually (and after much hardship) came to see the benefits of being 'French'. Although France had a long history as a state, the country itself was culturally diverse, and before 1870, 'France' had no emotional appeal for most of its subjects. As in Italy, the French had to be 'made', but here the state had far greater success. Most ordinary folk would succumb to the nation's 'civilizing mission' by the outbreak of the Great War, in large part because 'France' was capable of imposing itself on so many aspects of their daily lives, and because citizens could see some benefit flowing back from taxation, conscription and other sacrifices demanded of them. The nation was at once burdensome and beguiling. Schools, roads, railways, postal services and other manifestations of the nationhood succeeded in making the nation relevant to ordinary folk, and the connection with progress made the nation something with which the French people wished to identify. In contrast, most Italians found nationhood onerous and oppressive, and were not convinced of its legitimacy. They were incensed by its excessive demands and its miserly benefits. Material prosperity might have proved an alternative, yet equally persuasive, emissary of the national mission to Catholicism, but Italy's economic performance was altogether quite poor until the very end of the century. By northern and central European standards, its agricultural and industrial sectors were backward and uncompetitive. Unlike Germany in 1870, Italy did not begin with a national economic infrastructure, and it was encumbered from the very beginning by debts accrued by Cavour's modernization of Piedmont in the 1850s and the wars of 1859–60. Economic modernization and growth was an imperative for the new nation, not least to service debts, but domestic demand was weak and domestic capital reserves and foreign investment limited. The agricultural sector, which conventionally provided the capital surplus necessary for industrialization, actually sank into a prolonged recession which worsened rural poverty and exacerbated social conflict. An unimpressive economic record also meant that the nation was unable to meet many of the expectations it raised, such as making Italy a great imperial power, which in turn only managed to diminish its standing vis-à-vis Italian society. Liberal Italy was therefore caught in a conundrum that eventually brought about its demise.

As national opinion became increasingly disillusioned by Italy's feeble progress, attention turned to the degenerate nature of its political system. Liberal opinion throughout the world lent its moral support to the Risorgimento because it appeared to champion the values of Enlightenment over the *ancien régime*. Post-Risorgimento Italy pretended to emulate liberal Britain, but appearances belied an authoritarian political order that was determined to exclude the great bulk of the population from public life. The system conceded too much power to a dynasty that insisted on maintaining its legitimist aspirations and which interfered constantly in the affairs of state. Moreover, national government gradually assumed a wholly negative reputation. According to the nation's first king, Italians could only be ruled by 'bayonets and bribery', which nicely encapsulates the way the Liberal regime exercised authority over society. While the southern revolt was crushed in ruthless fashion, regional elites, whose support the central government desperately needed, were effectively bought off. The Chamber of Deputies became a forum in which deputies surreptitiously pushed the interests of local elites, on whose support they were dependent. Deputies traded their votes in return for policies and political favours (usually government contracts or civil service posts) that satisfied their backers. This stranglehold exercised by regional power brokers over the centre was made possible by a slender electoral base, for initially a mere 2 per cent of the population was entitled to vote, and of those who were eligible, a large percentage were loyal Catholics who dutifully abstained.

Politics initially appeared respectable when governments were formed by men associated with the so-called 'Historic Right', the *Destra storica*. This grouping carried the mantle of Cavour and the Risorgimento moderates, and they were usually propertied northerners who believed in free trade, minimal government spending and the restriction of the franchise. In 1876 they were dislodged by the so-called 'Left', the *Destra storica*'s ostensible opposition, and supposed descendants of the Risorgimento's democrats. They were normally middle class professionals, often from the Mezzogiorno, who advocated more public spending and the extension of the franchise, if only to expand their own electoral base. They were much beholden to power magnates in their constituencies, and were primarily responsible for *trasformismo*, that fluid system of alliances forged by the trade in favours, and which in turn produced a rapid succession of governments. From 1882, when 'Left' leader Agostino Depretis made an alliance with more conservative elements to form a government, party politics was replaced by a new system in which governments were formed by those that could accommodate enough deputies and maintain a coalition. Depretis demonstrated how effective the system could be, though the most remarkable exponent of *trasformismo* was Giovanni Giolitti, who at the end of the century managed to bring even socialist deputies into coalition. Creating and maintaining ruling coalitions required incredible political skill, but governments came and went in rapid succession regardless. Worse still, they could not be expected to maintain a policy platform lest they alienate supporters and collapse. It was a political order ruled by expediency. In 1919, the educationalist Giuseppe Lombardo-Radice wrote that:

> The ruling class lacked historical awareness, indeed it was totally devoid of it, and consequently its political horizons were narrow. It was easier to find a mentality restricted to the constituency than one that encompassed the nation.[4]

Thus in comparison to Britain, France and Germany, Italian politics seemed to be particularly corrupt. Government was much more about wheeling and dealing than it was about policy formulation and implementation, and corruption was a disease that seemed impossible to expunge. During his two terms as prime minister (1887–91, 1893–96), the former Mazzinian Francesco Crispi sought to capitalize on middle-class disenchantment by bringing the parliament to heel. Crispi appeared to be engineering a drift towards dictatorship, as he greatly strengthened the power of the executive and twice had parliament suspended. For much of 1895 he governed without reference to parliament. He also tried to promote national pride and

---

[4]   Quoted in Alberto Banti, 'Italian Professionals: Markets, Incomes, Estates and Identities', in Maria Malatesta, (ed.), *Society and the Professions in Italy, 1860–1914* (Cambridge, Cambridge University Press, 1995), p. 253.

distract public opinion with an aggressive foreign policy, but the destruction of an Italian expeditionary force by an Ethiopian army at Adowa in March 1896, ended his foreign policy and his career.

Thus a seemingly lively but essentially torpid Liberal regime proved to be no less inert than the pre-Risorgimento rulers. To all and sundry it was clear that the state was almost incapable of serving the nation and its interests. To be sure, in the late nineteenth century and through to the period approaching the Great War, some political reform was inevitable if the state was to maintain any hope of meeting the new challenges posed by profound socio-economic change. Economic modernization and modest spurts of growth helped expand the ranks of the middle and working classes. Extending the franchise was one way to bridge the gap between the state and a fast-modernizing society. In 1882, the percentage of eligible voters rose from something above 2 per cent to just under 7per cent, which placed Italy almost on par with Britain but behind Germany and well behind France. Only literate males over 21 who could pay 19 lire in direct tax could vote, which meant many more northerners were enfranchised than southerners, but electoral boundaries ensured that on average, southern deputies were distributed among smaller constituencies and needed less voters than their northern counterparts. However progressive the extension of the franchise might have appeared, it was introduced by Agostino Depretis, during his third and longest term as prime minister (1881–7), in order to shore up his support in parliament. His opponents, meanwhile, hoped to extend the franchise further in order to undermine him.

A polarized society

Far from improving the relationship between state and society, incremental extensions of the franchise merely exposed the former to the deepening resentments of the latter. Indeed social discontent had been threatening to derail the nation-building project ever since the Risorgimento. The most spectacular affirmation of resistance to the state had been the civil war in the south during the 1860s, while the next major uprising took place in the 1893–4 in Sicily, when widespread peasant dissent prompted the prime minister, Francesco Crispi, to impose martial law. In the early months of 1898, the whole country seemed out of control. In May a hike in wheat prices precipitated riots in Milan, where, at a conservative estimate, 80 protesters were killed and 450 wounded. The fact was that national unity had not solved the peninsula's pauperization problem, the so-called 'Social Question'. The virulent nature of popular protest reflected desperate social conditions. So too did criminal activity. According to the socialist Filippo Turati, only in crime did Italy have primacy in Europe. More shameful was the Liberal state's typically unimaginative answer to the 'Social Question', which was to bludgeon dissenters into submission. Although Crispi gave modest thought to social policy, he and another authoritarian leader of the *fin-de-siècle* period, Antonio di Rudinì, believed that only seditious enemies, such as the French or the Church, could have fomented such turmoil, and hastily resorted to guns and bayonets. When it came to the 'Social Question', successive Liberal governments were firmly resolved in believing that stronger government and the expeditious show of force were the solutions.

The countryside remained as overcrowded, under-productive, ecologically degraded and as socially divided as ever it had been. Landlessness, indebtedness, malnourishment and disease continued to be an all too common affliction of the peasantry. Poverty was exacerbated by state policies that subscribed blindly to free-market ideas, which included the complete abolition of common land and ecclesiastical property, and by the imposition of taxes that targeted the common people. The immensely unpopular *macinato*, or grist tax, paid on the milling of grain, had been abolished in 1860 to celebrate the new nation. Its reintroduction on 1 January 1869 provoked mass rioting all over Italy. In the meantime, conditions among the urban poor were not much better. It was not illegal to employ children under 9 years of age until 1886. Unions and strikes were dealt with brutally. Without the support of any welfare provisions from the state, workers resorted to forming mutual aid societies that provided some relief for the unemployed and the sick. Because of the steady expansion of industry, but also because of the oppressive conditions experienced by the Italian working classes, these aid societies grew rapidly after unification, and served as the basis for the formation of trade and industrial unions.

Poverty and instability in the post-Risorgimento period were partly attributable to sluggish industrial growth and a wilting agricultural sector, but the boom years that followed 1896, and carried through almost uninterrupted to the Great War, only made a marginal difference to poverty levels and fostered more potent forms of social dissent. The boom was characterized by highly impressive growth rates (5 per cent per annum on average), by the expansion of heavy industry, engineering, the rise of major firms such as Fiat, Pirelli and Olivetti, and by more stable financial institutions. Inevitably, the period also witnessed the emergence of an Italian working class, and a transition in urban protest from traditional plebeian rioting to disciplined strike action. Mutual aid societies began to take on the appearance of unions, and the strikes recorded in Italy increased from 45 in 1881 to 410 in 1900. The number of estimated participants in 1881 were 8000, but by 1900 there were 93 000. In 1901 and 1902 there were 1671 and 1032 strikes respectively, between 1906 and 1912, the figure never dropped below 1000, and in 1907 there were 2258 strikes that involved well over half a million workers. During the first decade of the new century, a series of labour confederations had formed, each of which had up to 200 000 members. The state and the middle and upper classes were therefore confronted by a new, increasingly organized and self-conscious working class which was not afraid, despite punitive reprisals, to press their claims for better pay and conditions.

Perhaps more frightening, though, was the politicization of workers and the seditious ideologies to which they were drawn. Initially the most serious ideological force was anarchism. Introduced to Italy in the mid-1860s by the Russian Mikhail Bakunin, anarchism gained a foothold among peasant and urban strata in various regions and was particularly strong in Emilia Romagna, Tuscany and Sicily. However, anarchism failed to provide a sufficiently potent rallying cry for the downtrodden. The movement lost its momentum after 1877, and thereafter Italian anarchists were best known as assassins: Vittorio Emanuele II's successor, Umberto I, who was assassinated in 1900, was among their most celebrated victims. As far as imported political ideologies went, however, socialism proved to be far more formidable and successful. A variety of socialist parties existed in northern Italy's industrial heartland, but in 1892, a national political party dedicated to promoting the interests of Italian workers generally was created in Genoa. In 1895 it adopted the name *Partito socialista italiano* (Italian Socialist Party – PSI), and unlike the parties within Italy's parliament, it managed to gain a mass following among urban and many rural workers. Despite the limited franchise, the number of socialist deputies elected to the national parliament between 1892 and 1900 increased from 6 to 32. By 1913, the PSI had 74 deputies elected and was the largest opposition party in the parliament. Overall, these deputies, along with the PSI and organized labour, were never capable of operating in unison, but their mere existence was a frightening reality for liberals, conservatives and Catholics. The undeniable ascendancy of socialism and organized labour posed serious dilemmas for the political order. For one thing, the socialists were assiduously 'internationalist' and outwardly rejected the imperialist and 'Savoy-centric' nationalist culture propagated by the state. The political order and this new 'Left' were each aware that they held contradictory political visions. Where the king, his executive and many within the parliament believed the nation's *raison d'être* was to be a Great Power, the Left preached social revolution. Thus when it came to the Great War, the Italian socialists were among the small minority of Europe's socialist movements that did not rally behind the nation. Hence, in the latter years of the Liberal period, an increasing proportion of the Italian population was more receptive to notions of class solidarity and revolution than to statues of Vittorio Emanuele, nationalist rhetoric and the flag. Socialism and social change were therefore undermining the state's admittedly feckless attempts to make Italians.

During the Giolittian period the state tried to absorb the Left, partly because Giolitti was an unusually gifted statesman who recognized that the

Liberal order could survive by becoming socially inclusive. After all, Italy was fast becoming a mass society, which not only denoted demographic concentration and cultural homogenization, but also implied a more inter-active relationship between state and society. Interest groups (trade unions, political parties, extra parliamentary pressure groups) were better orga-nized and increasingly determined to influence state affairs. Even within highly authoritarian states, such as Russia, with rising literacy rates and greater availability of affordable newspapers, the public sphere was expanding and becoming more self-conscious.. The question facing Italy as much as Russia was whether to preserve the existing power structure through repression, as Crispi had sought to do, or open up the state to broader social participation. Whereas Czarist Russia chose the former course and was eventually destroyed by revolution in 1917, Giolittian Italy opted for the latter. Thus through much of the period approaching the Great War, *Italia legale* was forced to confront *Italia reale*. Much as the Liberal state had absorbed regional elites some forty years earlier, so now, in Giolitti's view, it could assimilate workers and socialists. He attempted to appease the former with welfare measures and by legalizing strikes, and by bringing PSI parliamentarians into his government coalitions.

In the short term, Giolitti's arrangements gave him government majori-ties, but in accommodating the Left he alienated middle- and upper-class Italians, who denied socialism and labour organizations should have any place in the political order. Employers now sensed that they were being deserted by the state, with new legislation on industrial relations likely to open the floodgates to more industrial unrest. At the same time, many on the Left viewed any accommodation with the Liberal state as a betrayal of working-class interests and therefore continued to preach revolution. Giolitti in any case lost much of his socialist support in 1911 when he ordered the invasion of Libya. That same year, Giolitti flagged the most radical measure ever seen in the life of the Liberal state: the extension of the vote to all literate males over 30, but only those who had completed their military service. The intention was to defuse the growth of radicalism by handing the vote to peasants, who were expected to vote for Catholic candi-dates whom Giolitti hoped to absorb into his government. It proved to be all too clever a strategy. In 1913, after winning a massive number of seats, the Catholics began making the kinds of demands on education policy and social policy (e.g. with regard to divorce) that grated with secular liberals and anticlericals. Worse still, encouraged by their early success and frus-trated by subsequent difficulties with their Liberal allies, the Catholics began to create their own mass political movement.

In a sense the Liberal regime's attempt to come to terms with mass soci-ety by accommodating broader sections of the population came too late. Social classes were becoming more aware of themselves as distinct interest groups and were already too polarized to allow Giolitti's sophisticated political arrangements to function successfully. By the outbreak of the Great War, Italian society was dangerously divided. And as will be shown later, the war experience convinced the middle and upper classes that what Italy needed was new authoritarian state that advocated their interests *as opposed to* those of the lower classes.

At this point it would be useful to consider the role played in the nation-building process during the Liberal period by the middle classes. In many ways the bourgeoisie was the torch-bearer of modernity in Italy, and, as elsewhere in Europe, it was the class that was most receptive to nationalism. Yet it was also comparatively slow in embracing the new culture, and when it belatedly began to do so in the decade or so preceding the Great War, the form of nationalism it embraced was authoritarian and imperialist. Indeed, the reason why fascism succeeded in Italy after the Great War had much to do with the weaknesses and historical peculiarities of the modern Italian bourgeoisie.

'Weakness' may seem an unfair appellation in this context, especially as non-aristocrats dominated the government and bureaucracy of the Italian nation almost from the beginning. After the extension of the franchise in 1882, political life was dominated by professionals, especially lawyers, making the bourgeois ascendancy in politics complete. Its domination even extended to the officer corps, which was conventionally the last bastion of the old regime. Yet while one can speak of 'bourgeois Italy' with justification, the bourgeoisie was also an atomized formation. Its members were reluctant to function as self-aware social grouping. More to the point, until the last few years before the Great War, the average middle-class Italian remained resiliently parochial, as opposed to national, in orientation. There was also the way power and wealth were distributed in Italy. In comparison to its late nineteenth-century British, French and German counterparts late, the Italian bourgeoisie was small and relatively poor: in 1881, it accounted for 6.7 per cent of the population – less than half the French percentage. Moreover, a much larger proportion of the Italian bourgeoisie relied on state employment, and salaries on average were far lower than their French counterparts. The country's universities were over-producing lawyers, doctors, engineers and other professionals, many of whom were forced to emigrate: between 1881 and 1920 35 per cent of graduate sought a future outside of Italy. This portion of the Italian bourgeoisie, therefore, was a particularly vulnerable group, and given their heavy dependency on the state, professionals were caught in the web of patron–client relations that blighted the nation's political life. Clientelism worked against the development of class-consciousness.

The atomizing effect of clientelism, which clearly inhibited the Italian middle classes from thinking and acting as a corporate body, in turn affected the broader evolution of a national public. In France and Germany it was the middle classes which responded most enthusiastically to the promotion of nationhood, and which actively contributed to the nation-building efforts of the state. Thus the latter decades of the nineteenth century witnessed the proliferation of voluntary associations that served such important patriotic functions as establishing and maintaining museums, monuments, public festivals and commemorative practices. They also often served as pressure groups that sought to influence the state in such areas of national interest as colonial policy and military spending. Some of the groups were disruptive, for example the Action française, a political movement formed at the end of the nineteeth century with the express purpose of bringing down the Third Republic in favour of a regime that was more capable of pursuing nationalist aspirations. But movements preaching political revolution in France were out of step with broader bourgeois opinion, which was more supportive of the state. Official efforts to create a national culture through education campaigns or other policies, depended for their success equally on the eager responses and contributions of the middle classes, whose patriotism distinguished them socially from the lower orders.

In Italy, however, the feeble efforts of the state to construct a national culture were complemented by those of a relatively weak bourgeoisie. Certainly, the Scientific Congresses of the pre-Risorgimento period were early examples of associational activities that did much to foster national consciousness, and after 1860 there was a proliferation of institutions such as the *Società Dante Alighieri*, which was dedicated to the propagation of Italian culture and language. Another national association that fostered awareness of the nation was the *Touring Club Italiano*, which did much more than promote cycling. Most bourgeois households had at least one card-carrying member, which meant that middle-class families had access to the Touring Club's accurate maps and informative touring guides, which in turn were intended to tutor readers in the wonders of Italy. In making Italy familiar to its members, the Touring Club was intentionally seeking to make Italians. However, in Liberal Italy such associations were small in number. And of the above-mentioned associations, only the Touring Club had a mass following, mainly because middle-class Italians were generally reluctant to join free associations. For example, only 20 per cent of professionals in Milan had joined locally-formed clubs by 1891, and only 15 per cent of engineers in the Veneto belonged to the relevant professional associations in 1915. Even by the outbreak of the Great War, it was not clear that horizontal loyalties were as yet posing a serious challenge to vertical ones, or that national identity was replacing particularism.

Thus while the middle classes had been thoroughly nationalized and were playing key roles in the development of the national cultures of *fin-de-siècle* Britain, Germany and France, matters in Italy were at a somewhat incipient stage. In due course, in the 1910s and the years approaching the Great War, nationalism did come to influence an increasing number of bourgeois Italians, though it is unclear what proportion of that class was affected. Owing to the nation's poor showing as a Great Power before and after 1915, however, critics of the government were increasingly prone to use the language of nationalism to express their frustrations. Indeed nationalism became an ideology of opposition, deployed against a political order that was seen to have diminished the nation, and whose removal was justified as a matter of national interest. Among the country's social elites, its more conservative parliamentarians, the army, and especially among journalists and writers, antipathy towards the Liberal regime was often expressed in the language of patriotism. The lead in the formation of this oppositional nationalism was taken by journalists whose outlook reflected a recent continental ideological current, in which nationalism was associated with authoritarianism, militarism and imperialism. Although it was not to produce a mass movement before the war, its advocates were an extremely vocal and pervasive presence in public life, and their new brand of radical nationalism was to exert an enormous influence on the course of Italian nation formation.

Patriotic opposition, 1896–1908

Once unequivocally identified with the political legacies of the Enlightenment, of constitutional government and parliamentary rule, nationalism in *fin-de-siècle* Europe had transmutated into a new form of reactionary politics. The nationalism of the *new* Right was an ideology of ethnic chauvinism, war and dictatorship, and one which Mazzini would hardly have recognized. These new nationalists, who founded such major movements as the Pan-German League and the Action française, were characteristically xenophobic, hostile towards immigrants, established minorities – especially Jews – and most foreign nations. They were convinced of the innate superiority of their own national community, which they often perceived as a distinctive 'race', and had a paranoid conviction that enemies were lurking both within and beyond the nation. For these radical nationalists, the 'Fatherland' was in constant mortal danger. The new nationalists preached not only against hostile nations and seditious minorities, but against the degenerative societal consequences of liberalism and the comforts of bourgeois mores. As to working-class and feminist activism, they regarded such developments as an affront to the civilized world. Nostalgic for a highly mythicized heroic past, when ancestral warriors built empires and gave expression to primordial impulses and passions, nationalists viewed many of the contrasting features of modern life with a mixture of loathing and anxiety. Railing against the doom-laden course charted by liberal government leaders, nationalists believed salvation could be found in war and conquest, arguing histrionically that only through the hard lessons of battle and the retrieval of masculine values could society survive the sapping effects of modernity.

The new nationalists identified themselves as bearers of national opinion, and in Germany some of their associations (eg. the German Navy League) were relatively well-organized mass movements. By the turn of the century, nationalist parties in Paris had found ample support in local and national elections from artisans and shopkeepers, who in earlier times had been the natural constituency of republicanism. Elsewhere, however, Europe's (including Italy's) radical nationalists mainly consisted of fringe right-wing movements, usually containing disaffected middle-class intellectuals and professionals. Italian radical nationalists, or *nazionalisti*, were in fact an inchoate grouping of mainly journalists who did not manage to launch a formal political party until as late as 1914, and who gave little thought to mass organization. They nevertheless deserve detailed treatment in any study of Italian nation building, for as a disparate collection of like-minded intellectuals they served as forerunners of Italian Fascism, having formulated many of the ideas and aims. In many ways the *nazionalisti*, much as radical right-wing movements throughout Europe, were symptomatic of a broader cultural condition associated with the revolt against positivism and the crisis of liberalism.

For the *fin-de-siècle* bourgeois world, the pace of change produced as much anxiety as it did exhilaration. Unprecedented technological progress, rapid industrialization, urbanization, mass immigration, mass culture, and other developments that commonly come under the rubric of 'modernization', had produced extraordinary cultural side-effects. Modernity made many nervous. The appearance of motor cars, aeroplanes and moving pictures might confirm that civilization was moving forward, but falling birth-rates and a decline in church attendance and other traditional practices were seen by many as signs that it was heading towards a precipice. Reaction took many forms and occurred at different levels. In the realm of high culture the revolt against positivism involved a turn to the irrational and, as exemplified by the philosopher Friedrich Nietzsche, artist Pablo Picasso, psychoanalyst Sigmund Freud and physicist Albert Einstein, the results were creative and path-breaking. In political terms, reaction to modernity could also be creative but its implications on the whole were decidedly negative. The advent of mass society, and specifically mass politics, fostered a new form of reactionary ideology dedicated to bringing society back under tighter control through the return to authoritarian rule. Much support for the new reactionary politics could be found among social groups that were particularly vulnerable to the vicissitudes of the late nineteenth-century world economy, experienced particularly in the boom and bust years from the early 1870s through to 1896. Small entrepreneurs, particularly shopkeepers and artisans, were often attracted by the new Right. We have already noted that the upper and middle classes viewed the rise of socialism and labour protest with acute apprehension, as they did the extension of the franchise and the social distribution of power generally.

The state's inability to allay these anxieties on the one hand, and adequately respond to the needs of mass society on the other, goes far in explaining why there was a general crisis of liberalism in pre-war Europe. In the meantime, Europeans were mindful of the intensification of inter-state rivalries, of an accelerating arms race and the scramble for colonial empires. Far from forming the brotherhood that Mazzini had envisaged, European nations approached inter-state relations as a contest in which only the fittest would survive and the weak would be vanquished. The new nationalism spoke to those who believed that the essential purpose of the state was to respond to the challenge of this Darwinian struggle between nations, protect the fatherland from hostile enemies, and to seize 'historic' opportunities to attain glory through imperialism. Whether the nation was fit enough to meet the challenges of war and conquest, whether current political leaders were capable of leading the nation to its historic destiny, and whether society had the mettle to wage desperate war, were questions of obsessive concern to the new nationalists. Theirs was a worldview dominated by fantasies of national regeneration through imperial triumph, in which the interests of society were subordinated to the rigours of that eagerly anticipated struggle.

The ideas associated with the *nazionalisti* can be traced back to the fall-out from Italy's earlier foreign adventures, and especially the defeat at Adowa in 1896. One of the earliest nationalist writers, Alfredo Oriani, proclaimed that the Risorgimento was unfinished because Italy had yet to construct its empire. Only with the hard experience of empire building could Italians claim to be a 'great' people. Through the first decade of the twentieth century, the association between empire-building and national renewal found its fullest expression through the press. The first journal to offer consolidated ideas along these lines was the Florentine publication *Il Regno*, which first appeared in late 1903. It focussed on such issues as race, especially the prospects for survival in a world dominated by the Germanic peoples, and on the socially divisive and weakening effects of democracy. *Il Regno*'s chief topic of interest was international relations. One of the founding fathers of Italian nationalism, and who helped launch *Il Regno*, Enrico Corradini, argued that Italy's *raison d'être* was to have an aggressive foreign policy and command a large empire. While he was at the helm of *Il Regno* (November 1903 to March 1905), Corradini was able to develop and elaborate ideas which became the basis of a new right-wing ideology, hostile towards socialism and liberalism but distinguishable from traditional forms of conservatism. While Corradini agreed with many conservative politicians that Italy would be best served by an authoritarian state, he also entertained visions of society in which the interests of the poor were not ignored. He detested social hierarchy as much as did the socialists, but he feared that the socialists were seeking to make the proletariat the new dominant class. Italians of all classes, in his view, could only move forward and fulfil their historic destiny if they functioned as an organic whole, as one people. If Italian society could be converted to believe in the absolute primacy of the nation, he claimed, then Italy would become more socially cohesive.

In these years Corradini pronounced the tenets of Italy's radical right that were to hold until the destruction of the Fascism in 1945: liberalism and Marxism were anathema; Italian society had to close ranks and function as a unit; the national purpose was to build a great empire and restore Italy to its historic ascendancy among nations. For the *nazionalisti*, glory was what the Risorgimento was supposed to have achieved. Instead, as one of celebrities of the age, the flamboyant poet Gabriele D'Annunzio, disparagingly claimed, Italy had become an art museum and a boarding house for European tourists. That Italy was only good for its antiquities, museums, scenery and prostitutes was confirmation that it was not a serious nation. The *nazionalisti*, and later the Fascists, yearned for the day when Italy met with different reactions from outsiders: respect, reverence, fear. Ideally, Italy would achieve the standing of imperial Rome. The solution was to radically recast Italian society.

The most extreme alternative vision of society was advocated by an avant-garde artistic movement known as Futurism. For the best known Futurist, Filippo Marinetti, Italy was encumbered by its history. He notoriously argued that all traces of history should be effaced, and that Italy must be remade along modern, industrial and revolutionary lines. Few were really attracted to Marinetti's outlandish and destructive vision, but his radicalism and virulent tone were shared by the radical Right. A more influential *avant-garde* intellectual movement, advocating the invigoration of Italian society with new generational values, was a loose collection of writers based in Florence. Like Marinetti, they sought to erase the malignant influences of the decadent and effeminate Liberal state by preaching a new culture of activism, vitality and martial values. Through publications such as *La Voce* and *Leonardo*, the Florentine *avant-garde* promoted the virtues of war as an agent that might allow Italians to express a new creative spirit. In accordance with other radical nationalists, they believed the current political order was inherently incapable of fulfilling the promise of the Risorgimento, but they did not regard the nation as an end in itself. They were nationalists in so far as they sought a different nation through which Italian cultural and emotional exuberance could be freely expressed.

The typical nationalist of the pre-war years, however, followed Corradini in emphasizing the absolute primacy of the nation over all other interests. The *nazionalisti* expressed societal disillusionment with the Liberal state in its most acute form, but they did not offer a coherent ideology: some happened to be republicans, while others revered the monarchy. In December 1910 300 delegates from various patriotic societies met in Florence to create the *Associazione nazionalista italiana* (ANI), but republicans and monarchists split almost immediately. Some, like D'Annunzio, were unabashed elitists, while others, such as Giovanni Papini and Corradini, took some interest in the lower classes, claiming imperial territories could be colonized by the poor. Mass emigration, which left a stain on the nation's reputation, could instead be channelled to new Italian lands. While Marinetti and other radicals were initially associated with the new nationalism, by 1913 the ANI had become a thoroughly conservative outfit that could see its way to forging an alliance with the Catholics. In January 1913 *nazionalisti* and Catholics met to consider a common policy platform for forthcoming elections on such key issues as education, law and order, and economic policy, while the ANI's mouthpiece, *L'Idea nazionale*, argued that *nazionalisti* and Catholics should combine to form a strong conservative party. Another source of division within the ANI was the disagreement between those who placed priority on colonial expansion, and those, a sizeable proportion, who argued that the essential goal was to claim unredeemed Italian territories, such as Trieste. Colonialism eventually eclipsed irredentism as the hallmark of the ANI, particularly after Italy's conquest of Libya in 1911 and the Dodecanese Islands in 1912.

The intellectual history of the *nazionalisti* and their fellow-travellers is fraught with confusion and contradiction, but it is useful to remember what this small motley group held in common. They were anti-Socialist, anti-Giolitti and fanatically imperialist – and they relentlessly enunciated these views to the public.

Although no formal nationalist movement existed before 1910, the new nationalists, dominated as they were by journalists, were able to exert an influence disproportionate to their numbers. *Il Regno* was the first of a series of publications that provided a podium for people such as Corradini, Papini, Giuseppe Prezzolini, and Alfredo Rocco, who was perhaps the most coherent thinker of the *nazionalisti*. Other *nazionalisti* publications included *Tricolore*, which appeared in Turin in 1909, *L'Grande Italia* (Milan), *Carroccio* (Rome), and *La Nave* (Naples). More important than these specifically 'nationalist' newspapers, which had limited circulation, were the mainstream publications such as *Corriere della Sera*, *Giornale d'Italia*, *La Stampa* and *La Tribuna*. Some of these papers, including *Corriere della Sera* and *Giornale d'Italia*, were doggedly critical of the Giolittian regime and, in this cause were not averse to enlisting the services of capable, albeit extremist, writers. Thus the press would publish D'Annunzio's diatribes against the Liberal state as well as his poetry. A later leader of the *nazionalisti*, Luigi Federzoni, was to write pieces on Giolittian corruption for the *Giornale d'Italia*. Even though the editors and the readers did not necessarily share their passions and convictions, the basic message of the *nazionalisti*, that the Liberal political order was bankrupt and that the country was in need of some form of regeneration, had wide appeal. Hence why the rather conservative editor of the Milanese *Corriere della Sera* between 1900 and 1921, Luigi Albertini, had few qualms about employing the services of rogues such as D'Annunzio.

Ultra-nationalist writers were expressing sentiments and articulating ideas that were shared by much of bourgeois Italy, and which were to resonate ever more loudly as public tolerance of political ineptitude wore thin. However, it is important not to exaggerate the impact of radical nationalism before the war, as bourgeois Italy was not as yet prepared to throw in its lot with these fanatics, as demonstrated by the fact that the ANI did not produce a mass following. What we have been considering thus far in this chapter has not been the nationalization of the Italian middle classes but the social and ideological beginnings of that process. The experience of a major war would do much more than either the state or the radical Right to bring about that transformation.

War and national consciousness, 1908–18

At the very least, the *nazionalisti* had done enough to disseminate one key idea in the public mind: that the most effective means of nation-building was war. Many 'respectable' bourgeois Italians were convinced of that nexus, and of the notion that Italy's *raison d'être* was to rule an empire – this, of course, had long been an article of faith of the Savoy monarchy and the nation's political elite. Wider social interest in imperialism was also related to international conditions. Europeans generally were certainly anticipating a major continental war in the decade or so approaching 1914, a sense kindled by disputes over colonial territories, the hardening of alliance systems, the growing international arms race, and by a series of major diplomatic crises. For patriotic Italians, however, the decline in inter-state relations did not so much foster a sense of foreboding but a rather well-founded fear that opportunities for making Italy 'great' might be missed. There were recent indications of Liberal Italy's lack of preparedness for the expected challenges. In October 1908, Austria formally annexed Bosnia Herzegovina from the Ottoman Empire, a territory which it had occupied since 1878. Italy too had strong territorial ambitions in that region, and as a nominal Great Power it believed that it was entitled to some form of compensation. None was forthcoming. International disregard of the nation's aspirations, which was tantamount to a denial of its status as a Great Power, provoked clashes between Italian and German students in Vienna and strident condemnation from the Italian press.

After the fallout from the Bosnian Crisis, political leaders were wary of missing the next 'historic moment' when it availed itself. It came in 1911.

Italy's imperial designs had long been focussed on the Ottoman empire, which, like Italy, was a Great Power in name only, and whose territories were slowly being dismembered by rival states. Initial Italian interest had been focussed on Ottoman Tunis, but the French seized it in 1881 – an event perceived as another humiliating 'loss' by Italy's political elites. Imperial interests then shifted to Ottoman Libya. The question was not *if* Libya should be conquered but *when*. In early 1911 supporters of invasion mounted a vociferous campaign, intensified by news that Italian business interests were being harassed by Turkish authorities in Tripoli. Then, in April 1911, came the crisis in Morocco, which brought France and Germany to the brink of war and produced the kind of unstable international climate that the Italians habitually exploited. The chorus for action included highly respectable institutions that had long supported Italian expansionism, such as the *Società Dante Alighieri*, the *Istituto coloniale italiana*, and the leading pro-Giolitti newspapers, *La Stampa* and *La Tribuna*. Journalists did their utmost to drum up enthusiasm for Libya, arguing fancifully that it was an 'Arcadia', a land eminently suitable for colonization. Although personally unmoved by this pro-war public campaign, Giolitti nevertheless committed Italy to a costly struggle which the state simply could not afford.

What influenced Giolitti's decision to invade Libya? Was his hand forced by public pressure? More importantly, was the Libyan war a consequence of the new nationalism? The *nazionalisti* certainly believed that they had impelled the state to act. They claimed credit for Italy's first major colonial conquest, which whetted the appetite for more of the same. The *nazionalisti* were certainly in their element throughout the Libyan affair. A mere three months after establishing the ANI, branches had been opened in the principal Libyan towns of Benghazi and Tripoli, as well as Malta and Tunis, each of which also had sizeable expatriate Italian communities. Throughout 1911 nationalist journalists did their best to mobilize opinion behind Italy's first major colonial adventure. Corradini was moved to proclaim that the proletarian nations were finally launching their bid to claim their rightful share of the earth's surface. *Nazionalisti* also led the calls to expand the theatre of military operations to Asia Minor, the Ottoman heartland, and to go as far as such historic opportunities would allow. Predictably, they were the loudest to criticize the Treaty of Ouchy in October 1912, which ended the war with Turkey in Italy's favour but without satisfying all their territorial demands. As far as the *nazionalisti* were concerned, Italy had gained *only* Libya. (It also gained temporary occupation of the Dodecanese Islands, the legacy of an aborted expedition to Asia Minor.)

Vociferous public lobbying by radical nationalists was not a factor in Giolitti's decision, however, nor did the pressure from economic groups or other interested parties carry much weight. Rather, Giolitti was not being obsequious when he claimed the war was a matter of fate. He was simply following the unquestioned assumption held by his monarch, his predecessors and the post-Risorgimento ruling elite, that Italy should be a Great Power. Imperial expansion was a matter of duty, though Italian statesmen were also wary of the nation's limited power, and could only seize opportunities that involved no direct confrontation with a major European state. Such a moment arose when the Great Powers were at loggerheads over Morocco, and not to have invaded Libya while the door was left momentarily open would have been political suicide for Giolitti. In the short term, victory shored up his political standing at home, and he was acclaimed for presiding over Italy's first major and successful imperial venture. (The horrendous costs and the extremely modest progress of the expeditionary force, which could not move beyond the environs of the coastal towns, were censored.) Vittorio Emanuele III offered Giolitti a dukedom for his efforts.

The same logic governed the decision in May 1915 by the then prime minister, Antonio Salandra, to intervene in the Great War. Italy proclaimed neutrality in the late summer of 1914, watching intently from the sidelines as the anticipated short war deteriorated into a one of stalemate and wanton destruction, yet Italy's political elites continued to assume that neutrality was temporary. To remain a Great Power, Italy had to intervene. The vexed question was when, and on which side. In the meantime, Italian society became deeply divided over the issue, with the great majority of the population opposed to intervention. Catholics, socialists, workers, peasants and business in general saw that no good could come of it, and some, especially the socialists, were prepared to campaign against it. Yet they were drowned out by much more vocal pro-interventionists, an assortment of republicans, disaffected socialists (including Benito Mussolini), conservatives and *nazionalisti*, who dominated the press and the piazzas. As with the pro-war activists of 1911, these self-proclaimed defenders of the national interest would come away believing that the government's decision to intervene was attributable to pressure exerted by them. In reality, Antonio Salandra and his foreign minister, Sidney Sonnino, took the decision to intervene – on the side of the Entente Cordiale rather than the Triple Alliance – without reference to 'public opinion' or even to parliament. Giolitti acted similarly in 1911. The majority of parliamentarians were opposed to Salandra's conduct of the intervention issue, though not to intervention as such. Indeed, they were accustomed to major decisions in politics being taken in such a fashion.

In 1915, therefore, Italy was committed to the most destructive conflict imaginable by a decision made behind closed doors. For Salandra, Italy's war was a nakedly imperialist one, unashamedly justified by the phrase 'sacro egoismo'. And much as the Italian public had little influence over Salandra's decision, the war effort itself was managed with little regard to the needs of Italian society, which was to be subjected to unprecedented privations. Worse still, Italy's performance on the battlefield would be lamentable. One of the consequences of the Liberal regime, which was to emerge mortally wounded from the Great War, was the emergence of mass nationalism that was driven by the desire to install a new political order.

Military success might have preserved the Liberal regime, but Italy's war was typically disastrous. A major offensive was launched along the north-eastern frontier against Austria-Hungary by an ill-prepared, poorly armed and badly led army. The unimaginative commander-in-chief, Luigi Cadorna, sacrificed hundreds of thousands of young conscripts in futile infantry assaults that replicated battles along the Western Front. Unlike their German, British and French counterparts, however, Italian soldiers were not treated to morale-boosting propaganda that tried to give purpose to the war. Rather, these men, the bulk of whom were drawn from the peasantry, were made to feel that they were performing services for their social superiors. Much like Russian soldiers, Italians were bastardized by their superiors, badly fed, and subjected to the most punitive of corporal punishments, including execution by lot. As news from the front filtered back to loved ones, morale and regard for the state plummeted further. In October 1917 the Habsburg army broke through Italian lines at the Battle of Caporetto, leaving much of north-eastern Italy in enemy hands.

As military developments went from bad to worse, the home front teetered on the brink of disintegration. Historians of the Great War normally pay a great deal of attention to the home front, for in terms of state-formation alone the ramifications of this particular conflict were immense. The war's unprecedented demands on national resources required a radical expansion of the powers of government, as did its exorbitant claims on human resources, which also forced a reappraisal of the relationship between state and society. The war hastened a development that began with the French Revolution, whereby the age-old conception of the state as existing to impose law and order, gradually gave way to that of a state supervising the welfare of society. The distribution of welfare, which required greater regulation and therefore control over the citizenry, became increasingly important to the survival of any given political order in an age of rapid modernization.

Total War tested the mettle of all the combatants, and it was a test that the Liberal regime would fail. For most of Italy's war, public morale, food distribution and other matters that British, French and German governments took very seriously were left to voluntary organizations that were never able to perform their tasks adequately. Hunger was perhaps the greatest problem. Food shortages were desperate in urban centres because of the decline in agricultural production and wartime inflation, yet all the while the state did not think it necessary to ration basic foodstuffs. As in Russia, the Italian state preferred to meet the costs of war by printing money rather than raising taxes, which meant that inflation spiralled out of control, made available foodstuffs unaffordable, and allowed the black market to flourish.

When rationing was finally introduced in the latter stages of the war, in some places bread rations were as low as 200 grams per day.

The Italian State did wage 'Total War' in the sense that it intervened directly in the affairs of the domestic economy in order to ensure that production met the exigencies of war. But unlike its German, British and French counterparts, the Italian state was not much interested in gaining the support of unions and meeting some of the basic interests of the workforce in order to guarantee labour discipline. War industries were supervised directly by the military, and strikes and absenteeism were treated in the same way as desertions from the army. Rather than being a society at war, Italy was to be a society at war with itself. Despite state repression, labour unrest was commonplace by 1916, and it had become stridently political and anti-war. Urban discontent was attributable to workplace conditions and appalling pay rates. High production targets meant that factory work could take up most of people's waking hours, yet wages were not enough to meet basic dietary needs. Only after the disaster of Caporetto did the state seek to mobilize the lower orders through more conciliatory means, but by then it was too late. The war did not nationalize the peasants and workers, but it did hasten their politicization. They continued to despise the war and the *signori* that forced it upon them, but, as happened in 1919 and 1920, they were more ready than ever to pursue their class interests through left-wing political movements. Rather than rallying the lower orders behind the state, as the political elite initially assumed the war would do, it merely hardened their anti-state hostility and solidified their class identities.

Meanwhile other Italians were moving in the opposite political direction. The middle classes also suffered greatly from the privations of war, particularly the *petite bourgeoisie*, but their appreciation of its purpose tended to be different. Although not wholly supportive of intervention, much of bourgeois Italy, particularly after the shock of Caporetto, came to identify closely with the war effort. Whereas many poorer Italians hoped the Austrians would complete their victory and punish the local *signori* for having inflicted the war on common folk, the near-collapse of the Italian war effort in late 1917 gave many better-off Italians a new sense of patriotism and commitment. Indeed, through much of the war they set about forming new patriotic associations, including the *Lega nazionale italiana*, the *Comitato d'azione del Fronte interno*, the *Lega antitedesca* (Anti-German League) and the *Fascio nazionale italiano*. Within the parliament, a bloc was formed by the most fervent of patriots, the *Fascio parlamentario*. Their heightened patriotism was also expressed through class antagonism, for they were incensed by the defeatism displayed by the lower orders. They were equally enraged by the increase in Leftist political activism, which not only jeopardized the war effort but sought to induce a revolution in Italy. News of the Bolshevik Revolution in October 1917, which followed very soon after Caporetto, did indeed act as a spur for the Left and convinced the middle classes that both nation and civilization were under threat.

The war experience therefore saw the middle classes rally wholeheartedly to the nation, though crucially not to the Liberal state. If anything, regard for the political order diminished because of its incompetent management of the war effort. State negligence of the home front was resented, but regarded as equally perturbing was the leniency (as they saw it) with which state authorities treated defeatism and anti-war agitators. Some extremist pro-war elements contemplated executing the king and establishing a military junta to ensure the best chance of military victory. Patriotism had become a mass phenomenon, but it was firmly directed against a political order which was deemed to be standing in the way of victory.

Of the war's social ramifications, more will be said in the next chapter, suffice it to say here that the Great War politicized social tensions to the point where, in 1918, the stage was set for an intense period of class conflict. The immediate post-war years were characterized by the challenge posed to the state by the extremes of politics, and, most importantly, by supportive mass movements. In the immediate post-war years, Italy seemed likely to follow Russia down the socialist path, but the Left proved much weaker than it appeared and Italy instead became the first major European nation to succumb to the forces of counter-revolution. Significantly, the Fascist regime that came to replace the Liberal political order attracted mass support *because* it was a nationalist movement, and because Fascist ideas resonated with those middle-class Italians whose vision of a future Italy was informed by the lessons of the war. Fascism's supporters were drawn from the same people who were greatly frustrated by Italian society's lack of cohesion during the war, and who came to believe that Italy could only become strong and socially stable if it was ruled by an authoritarian government.

|7|

Fascist nation: concocting a totalitarian order, 1919–1943

In some European circles, the onset of war in August 1914 was welcomed as a diversion from domestic social and political discord. Some even expected that war would accelerate the 'nationalization of the masses' and therefore complete the triumph of the nation as the ultimate focus of societal loyalty and affection. The war did indeed prove to be a major transformative experience, but not in the ways anticipated. The victorious powers extended the principle of national self-determination to the defunct empires, recasting Europe (save Russia) into a constellation of nations. Budding liberal democracies suddenly appeared where the *ancien régime* had reigned since time immemorial, and a formal international body known as the League of Nations was established for the purpose maintaining interstate security. But the Great War destabilized a great deal more than it put in order. Pre-existing political and social tensions were significantly accentuated and wholly new ones were unleashed. The war empowered socialism and organized labour, and, in Russia, produced the first socialist state. The old empires crumbled, but the liberal democracies created in their wake did not survive the economic crises of the post-war years. The war had so profoundly destabilized political and economic structures that Europe appeared to slip inexorably towards an even more destructive second catastrophe.

A major factor of post-war destabilization was patriotism bred by war, for the Great War did not so much foster the triumph of the nation as that of nationalism, or more specifically, the militant, xenophobic and anti-democratic form of nationalsim that had been hitherto championed by the radical Right. Given the unprecedented extent of societal commitment demanded by Total War, the citizenry more than ever saw themselves as constituting 'the nation', but the new nation-states also understood concepts such as 'the people' and 'the nation' in ethnically exclusive terms.

This meant that minorities were automatically deemed a threat to national security, and inter-state rivalries were more than ever seen as struggles between rival 'peoples' or 'races', all of which flew in the face of the liberal principles on which the post-war settlement was based.

While ethnic nationalism was a major factor in destabilizing international relations in Europe between the wars, in Italy a new acerbic mass nationalism fed directly into pre-existing social tensions. As noted in the previous chapter, right-wing nationalist rhetoric did enjoy some, albeit limited, resonance within Italian bourgeois circles before 1915, but it was the war experience itself and especially the crisis precipitated by the debacle at Caporetto that converted many into fully-fledged nationalists. Especially important in galvanizing mass support for right-wing nationalism were the 'unpatriotically' disruptive activities of the Left and the Liberal regime's failure to keep the home front in order. The regime appeared even less capable of defending the nation in 1919–20, when organized labour activity reached an historical peak and when the Left seemed bent on seizing power. Much of bourgeois Italy was therefore attracted to the nationalist rhetoric of the Fascist movement, which outwardly sought to distinguish itself from a supine Liberal order by conducting a decisive and violent campaign against the Left.

In a limited sense, Italian nationalism did finally emerge from the Great War as a mass phenomenon. When thinking of the post-war crisis in terms of class conflict, it is important to keep in mind that bourgeois Italy remained a highly fragmented and particularistic social formation, and that it is not at all clear what proportion was 'nationalized' by the war experience. What is not in doubt, however, is the fact that mass politics had finally arrived, and that the radical right enjoyed a following that was largely drawn from the disaffected middle-classes. Their support was often contingent on Fascism's ability to meet 'corporate' interests, such as those of business groups that were desperate for the suppression of unions, but it is also clear that the Fascists were capitalizing on sentiments that were now more common in bourgeois Italy, such as the desire for a strong state and the restoration of national pride after yet another disappointing war.

Radical nationalism therefore precipitated Europe's first right-wing 'revolution' after the Great War, and bourgeois Italy would tacitly assent to the Fascist take-over by not opposing Mussolini's dismantling of the Liberal political system, and his establishment of a dictatorship in 1925. It is worth emphasizing that Fascism was principally committed to creating a great nation out of a feeble one, and that nationalism was the fundamental tenet of its credo. The Fascists did not offer a clear political programme, for among their ranks one could find monarchists and republicans, as well as revolutionaries and conservatives, but if anything can be salvaged from their obtuse rhetoric and muddled theoretical formulations, it was the absolute moral primacy of the nation. It was nationalism that bound this

SWITZERLAND

AUSTRIA

formerly South Tyrol

FRANCE

VALLE
D'AOSTA

Aosta

Milan

Turin

LOMBARDY

PIEDMONT

Cremona

R. Po

LIGURIA

Genoa

TRENTINO-
ALTO-
ADIGE

Trent

VENETO

Ferrara

EMILIA ROMAGNA

Bologna

PRIULI-
VENEZIA-
GIULIA

Caporetto

Trieste

Venice

ISTRIA

Rijeka (Fiume)
(to Italy 1924)

DALMATIA

San Marino

Florence

TUSCANY

MARCHE

Ancona

Perugia

UMBRIA

CORSICA
(*France*)

LAZIO

Rome

L'Aquila

ABRUZZI

ADRIATIC SEA

MOLISE

Campobasso

CAMPANIA

Naples

Bari

APULIA

SARDINIA

Potenza

BASILICATA

Cagliari

TYRRHENIAN SEA

CALABRIA

Catanzaro

Palermo

SICILY

Acquisitions by Italy from treaty
settlements 1919-20

Boundary of Italy after 1947

Provincial capitals

0   100   200 km

0   100 miles

MALTA

4 Italy since 1919
After C. Duggan, *A Concise History of Italy* (CUP, 1994)

motley cohort together. For the Fascists, *Italia* demanded precedence over class and religion, even family and monarchy. Their challenge was to transmit that fervent passion for *Italia* to every Italian regardless of class or gender. At the same time, Mussolini sought to impose a definition of *italianità* that took *italianità* and Fascism for one and the same. As Roberto Farinacci, one of the more radical leaders of this early period once asserted, 'In Italy . . .no one can be an anti-Fascist because an anti-Fascist cannot be an Italian.'[1] The Fascists hoped that they would establish their political legitimacy with their exclusionary and rather simple rendition of national culture and identity.

From 1922, therefore, Italy entered the most intensive period of nation construction in its history. The project came under the direction of a regime that endeavoured more earnestly than its predecessors or successors to 'make Italians'. Fascism set itself the task of achieving a national utopian ideal, to forge a truly integrated national community where one barely existed. The ideal nation also had to be a 'great nation' with an empire: Mussolini's Italy was to be a new Roman empire that once again dominated the Mediterranean. Yet in his utterly reckless and deluded attempt to fashion his great nation through a senseless intervention in the Second World War, Mussolini also very nearly destroyed the Italian nation. He certainly diminished the efficacy of nationalist ideology, rhetoric and culture in Italian society, so much so that post-war political leaders quite consciously avoided nationalist rhetoric while endeavouring to reconstruct their deeply traumatized and divided country.

'Mutilated' victory

Why was Italian society more open to the rhetoric of radical nationalism in the inter-war years? Why did the Liberal state lead such a precarious existence in the early post-war years? The rapid success of something as novel as Italian Fascism cannot be explained without the politicizing impact of the Great War and its post-war ramifications for government and society. Most European regimes faced a legitimacy crisis during this period because of international economic instability, which produced mass unemployment and rampant inflation, and which forced governments to retract on promised welfare measures. The crisis was not to abate until the mid-1920s. Moreover, given their sacrifices in wartime, and the now commonly held view that the state was an extension of the people's will, Europeans were more demanding of governments and much more prepared to intervene directly in political life. Popular disillusionment swelled the ranks of the

---

[1] Quoted in Patrizia Dogliani, *L'Italia Fascista, 1922–1940* (Milan, Sansoni, 1999), p. 302.

political extremes, street violence was commonplace, and revolutions and counter-revolutions took place in such places as Hungary and Bavaria. In the latter stages of the war and its immediate aftermath, the political momentum appeared to be carried by the Left. Buoyed by the success of the Bolshevik Revolution in late 1917, organized labour and the pacifist and anti-war Left launched their bid for a share of, or the usurpation of, political power.

In Italy, the Left's forward march was reflected in the election results of November 1919, which saw the PSI attain 32.4 per cent of the popular vote (two million), making it the largest single party in the parliamentary chamber. The Left's ascendancy during this 'Biennio Rosso' (Red Biennium) reached its climax, however, in September 1920, when northern industry was paralysed by strikes and factory occupations. The Italian public sensed that their country might be following in Russia's footsteps, but striking workers and left-wing activists were never in a position to force a revolution, and their movement in any case was soon to lose its momentum. In fact the real political impact of the *Biennio Rosso* was that it intimidated bourgeois Italy and galvanized the forces of reaction. Fascism claimed to be coming to the nation's rescue, and would continue to exploit the myth of a national emergency long after Mussolini had attained power.

Reaction against the Left took a number of forms. It came from associations representing professional and economic interests; thus 1919 witnessed the creation of the General Confederation of Italian Industry, the *Confindustria*, which played a leading role during negotiations with striking workers in September 1920. In the municipal elections of November 1920, bourgeois groups organized themselves into coalitions to fight the socialists, and were victorious in most of Italy's main cities. The most effective reactionary movements, however, consisted of armed gangs that set about destroying socialist and labour organizations through violence and intimidation. During the *Biennio Rosso*, armed gangs of mainly ex-military servicemen took to the streets to engage the national enemy. One such movement, and the chief precursor of the Fascist movement, was founded in Milan in 1919 by the ex- and now anti-socialist Mussolini, who launched the *Fasci di combattimento*. The movement had very little success that year, performing poorly in the November 1919 elections – in Milan it gained a mere 5000 of 275 000 possible votes. Its fortunes changed, however, when the Left seemed at its most threatening. In the latter months of 1920, in the province of Emilia-Romagna, squads of local *fascisti* set about destroying rural socialist leagues in a systematic fashion. Their method was to converge on towns with truckloads of armed men and literally beat up socialist leaders and union organizers, burn their clubhouses and destroy their printing presses.

The success of *squadrismo* proved a turning-point in Italy's general postwar crisis. The defeat of the Left in Emilia-Romagna encouraged the rapid proliferation of Fascist groups all over northern and central Italy, which proceeded to annihilate the Left as a real political force. The propertied classes, impressed by the effective results of *squadrismo*, were often quite willing to subsidize Fascist operations in their own neighbourhoods.

The Italian establishment had found its saviour, but most Fascists did not see themselves as doing the bidding of social elites. In its early incarnation especially, Fascism saw itself as a revolutionary movement that sought to create a completely new Italy. It shared the ANI's idealization of the nation and war, but as with more radical elements such as the Futurists, the Florentine *avant garde*, and the revolutionary syndicalists, Fascism also drew inspiration from socialist and other progressive ideas. In early Fascist rhetoric, one could hear calls for land reform, republicanism and syndicalism, much of which was anathema to conservatives. Compared to its revolutionary counterparts, however, Fascism looked by far the lesser evil. The Liberal political order would try to absorb the Fascists in order to both strengthen the regime as well as to neutralize the Fascists as a potential revolutionary force. At the same time, Mussolini, in his quest to ingratiate himself with the Italian elites, would endeavour to jettison much of Fascism's revolutionary content.

Apart from popularity gained through strike-breaking and terminating the Left's threatened ascent to power, the Fascists grew in strength by tapping the mood of mass disillusionment following Italy's 'mutilated' victory. The Liberal regime's standing was dealt a debilitating blow when its negotiators carried away a mere fraction of promised territorial spoils from the Paris Peace Conferences. The Fascists could claim that the politicians had yet again betrayed the nation and its war dead. Although counted among the victors, the Italians were among those least able to resist the application of the principles of national self-determination, which meant most of their imperial aspirations were denied. Frustratingly, they not could not invoke the treaties on which their intervention had been based (Treaty of London, April 1915 and of St Jean de Maurienne, April 1917), for each had been concluded in secrecy. Those (arguably) ethnically 'Italian' territories within the former Habsburg empire, the Alto-Adige and Istria, were secured, but there was high public expectation of other spoils, such as Dalmatia, Albania and a large share of the Ottoman empire. Italian negotiators returned from the Peace Conferences humiliated: not even the Italian-speaking town of Fiume was attained, and, to make matters worse, Gabriele D'Annunzio and some 2 000 armed followers occupied that town – now part of the Kingdom of Serbs, Croats and Slovenes (soon to become Yugoslavia), from where he taunted the government leadership with insults. For over a year the port city was to remain occupied by this renegade force, partly because the government in Rome did not dare alienate the public further by risking a confrontation with the popular poet. D'Annunzio was not only able to tap a mood of patriotic disquiet, but occupied Fiume also offered a taste of what a radically nationalist polity might look like. Thus his 'legionnaires' wore black shirts, employed the Roman salute and did a great deal of ceremonial marching.

D'Annunzio and his fellow travellers appealed to a disenchanted Italian public that was more responsive than ever to the language of radical right-wing nationalism. The Fascists advocated an authoritarian regime which could fulfil vital national goals, would be more decisive when confronting subversive domestic elements, and would have more spine when dealing with foreign adversaries. The Fascists also believed that for Italy to be a great nation, Italian society would need to be completely transformed. Total War was their principal inspiration. In wartime, society could be persuaded with moral and material inducements to channel all its productive energies towards victory. As such, wartime afforded a perfect model of state–society relations. The Fascists sought to create a society that was in a constant state of mobilization, that relinquished its class differences and thought and acted as a national community. The camaraderie enjoyed at the front set the tone for how the Fascists envisaged inter-class relations in a future Italy. The ideal frontline soldier was also the ideal 'Fascist Man', one who was fearless and yet obedient, and who was eagerly prepared to sacrifice his life for his country. The squads that had been organized to bludgeon the Left were directly influenced by the war: more than half of those who joined the squads were war veterans, while the next largest contingent consisted of middle-class youths who regretted missing their chance to serve.

Whatever their internal ideological differences, the Fascists had enough in common to warrant the ascription of a movement, and radical nationalism was certainly their strongest bond. In November 1921, under the leadership of Mussolini, the National Fascist Party (PNF) was formed. In the meantime, membership of the movement had increased from 800 in early 1919 to close on a quarter of a million. Hitherto the PNF had been composed of independent squads that were dominated by warlords or *ras*, each of whom were in control of specific territories. Thus the flying ace Italo Balbo dominated Ferrara, Roberto Farinacci did the same in Cremona, while Mussolini's own fiefdom had been Milan. It was a rather segmented movement that gradually fused under the leadership of Mussolini, mainly because he was editor of its mouthpiece, *Il Popolo d'Italia*, through which he was able to exercise a great influence over Fascism's political ideals and public image. By 1922, the PNF was cocksure about its prospects of attaining power, particularly after its brutal suppression of a poorly organized general strike in July and August. Once again, a weak-willed Liberal political order was seen to have been upstaged by this decisive upstart, and it now seemed to most contemporaries that it was only a matter of time before the Fascists were in power.

This is not the place to detail the rather curious political revolution that followed, suffice it to say that despite their impudent demands and wild threats to seize power, the Fascists could only realize their goal at the behest of the monarch and the Italian elite generally. By September 1922 Mussolini was quite open about his intention to remove the government by force, and in October the then prime minister, Luigi Facta, hoped the king would invoke emergency powers and order the army to suppress Fascism's highly publicized 'March on Rome'. There was little doubt that the Italian military could have easily crushed the army of 'Black Shirts' which was threatening to descend on the capital, but at that point confidence in the Liberal political order was at its lowest ebb. That the Fascists could be so open about their seditious intentions was indicative of the depth of the crisis. Once Vittorio Emanuele III had been reassured that his own position was safe, Mussolini was handed the job of prime minister. On 28 October 1922 the Fascists nevertheless proceeded to stage their so-called 'March on Rome', if only to sustain their image as resolute activists and revolutionaries. Thus a radical nationalist movement was elevated to a position of power, from which it was eventually able to establish a dictatorship and pursue its vision of *la grande nazione*.

Totalitaria

The making of the dictatorship is also a complicated story that cannot be allocated much space here, but a similar set of circumstances applied. The Liberal political system was still functioning after October 1922. The Fascists were in government but they were forced to comply with political processes which they continued to resent and were determined to dismantle. The revolution in government they sought, however, still required the assent of the country's elites, who in turn needed to be reassured that Fascism, at the very least, did not threaten the social order. Mussolini, who was also determined to shore up his own position within the party, took strides to tame the radicals around him and to demonstrate that Fascism represented the interests of the propertied classes. Yet while outspoken radicals such as Farinacci and Fascist street thuggery continued to embarrass Mussolini, Italy's elites did not impede his quest to destroy the liberal political system.

Demonstrative proof that the PNF enjoyed such tacit permission came in 1924, when Mussolini survived a major scandal involving electoral corruption and the murder of his major parliamentary critic, Giacomo Matteotti. The parliamentary opposition withdrew from the chamber in protest (the so-called Avventine Secession), and as Mussolini had given every indication in the past that he would not be removed from power, it was then expected the king and the army would have to intervene. As it happened, Mussolini, still enjoyed the assent of Italy's elites, and hence there was no attempt to remove him. And as the opposition had removed themselves from the parliamentary chamber, Mussolini was now free to establish a dictatorship. Within a short space of time, Mussolini he had rolled back most of the progressive political reforms that had been put in place since the Risorgimento. There were to be no more free elections. Press criticism of the regime was now forbidden. Real or potential anti-Fascist organizations, such as the Masons, the PSI, PCI and the few remaining moderate opposition groups, such as *Libera Italia*, were suppressed. At the regional level, Italian voters no longer had the right to appoint mayors and local government councillors. Such positions were now filled by state appointees. Moreover, the regime ensured that prefects, the police and the courts each played a very active role in apprehending and confining enemies of the regime. The consolidation of Mussolini's dictatorship was also meant to bring the PNF under full control. When some former politicians were murdered by *squadristi* in full public view during the so-called 'fatti di Firenze' in October 1925, Mussolini seized the chance to abolish *squadrismo* and proceeded to alter the profile of the PNF membership. By the end of the decade, the typical member was no longer a committed Fascist revolutionary but a careerist who equated Fascism with Mussolini.

Although he did not enjoy absolute power – the mere presence of the king in the Quirinale in Rome served as a constant reminder that he did not – Mussolini could now set his sights firmly on completing the Risorgimento by implementing the Fascist vision of *la grande nazione*. Crucial to understanding this vision is to appreciate Fascism's conception of the ideal society and state. We have already noted that the Fascists were far more committed to 'making Italians' than their predecessors. When propagating its rendition of national culture, the Liberal political order had essentially targeted the respectable classes. Its reluctance to socialize the rest of society was largely attributable to fear of mass politicization, though such neglect was as much a reflection of traditional elitism as it was political calculation. Aversion to morale-raising wartime propaganda for the front line and the homefront indicated the elite's indifference to popular welfare. In contrast, the Fascists took as axiomatic that the state was the extension of the will of the people. In wishing to 'bring the masses into the state', Mussolini was following a much more inclusive philosophy, which actually entailed the obliteration of the state–society dichotomy and the consolidation of a single, distinct unit. Where the Great War had greatly increased the state's accountability to the citizenry, the Fascist ideal went further by asserting that state and society were one.

La grande nazione that the Fascists had in mind was therefore predicated on certain indispensable tenets: that class conflict must cease and Italian society form an organic whole; that state and society should no longer function as separate entities but be seen as inseparable; and that only a benevolent dictatorship could dispense the kind of decisive political authority that was required to enforce unity in Italian political and social life. By 1925 the regime had adopted the term 'totalitaria' to encapsulate its vision of the ideal polity. It mattered little to the Fascists that it was initially invented and hurled against them by their political opponents, most notably the liberal critic Giovanni Amendola and the leader of the *Popolari*, Dom Luigi Sturzo. It was a slur that Mussolini gleefully accepted. For the Fascists, Total War and the aftershock of Caporetto especially had seen Italy behave as a real nation for the first time. State and society appeared to function best when they were indistinguishable. In contrast, the more liberal systems that Fascism's critics espoused gave licence to the kinds of social divisions and political infighting that had conspired to keep Italy weak. A great nation needed the organizing capacities of a strong state, whose interests took precedence over individual rights and whose jurisdiction pervaded the private sphere.

The regime's conception of totalitarianism was largely the intellectual labour of its principal philosopher, Giovanni Gentile, who articulated and gave theoretical form to an assortment of authoritarian ideas, many of which were engendered by the war experience. Gentile was among those who believed that Italy's poor military performance during the Great War reflected long-term structural problems in Italian politics and society that could only be remedied by a strong state. He was also one who applauded, and was inspired by, state initiatives to mobilize society in the latter stages of the war. Though a latecomer to the Fascist fold, Gentile's main achievement was to construct a theory of state that articulated the political dispositions of the new Fascist order, which acclaimed the state as an expression of the popular will, yet which nevertheless justified absolute state authority. For Gentile, the state and the individual were inseparable, part of the same being: 'The state is the basis of every living value and every right possessed by the individuals who belong to it.'

> The state is within ourselves; it reigns and lives, and must always live and grow and increase and rise up in dignity. . . The individual develops and so does the state. . .[2]

This Fascist conception of the state, which differed only slightly from Italian nationalist views of the nation, offered nothing less than an ontology or 'philosophy of being', given the state and the individual are seen as a single entity. For Gentile, that entity was a spiritual one. The Italian people and the Fascist state, who together constituted the nation, shared a common will, an inseparable existence. To some extent, Gentile was drawing from the ideas of the great German philosopher Friedrich Hegel, who did not regard the state as merely a means to other ends (i.e. to dispense justice, safeguard private property), but believed it to be the primary moral

---

[2] Quoted in Adrian Lyttelton, *Italian Fascisms: From Gentile to Pareto* (London, Jonathan Cape, 1973), pp. 307, 309.

unit. However, Gentile rendered Hegel's sophisticated formulation into a relatively simple conception of an organic state which negated liberty, in which the individual was totally subordinated to the dictates of the state. For Gentile the individual and state possessed the same will, feelings and thoughts, but these thoughts and feelings were determined by the state. He would have little trouble in equating the state with Mussolini himself, for as he stated in his book, *The Origins and Doctrine of Fascism* (1929), 'the thoughts and wishes of the *Duce* must become the thoughts and wishes of the masses'. Of the dictator as personification of the nation, more will be said below. Overall, Gentile and the totalitarian ideal tried to make *Italia* an all-embracing philosophy of life. Statehood, and, by implication, nation-hood, was everything. As Mussolini famously put it in the *Encyclopaedia italiana* in 1935: 'Everything inside the state, everything for the state, nothing outside the state.'

Totalitaria was the basis of the ultimate nation. Of course totalitarian-ism was also a fantasy that no government, let alone the Italian dictator-ship, was even remotely capable of achieving. But it was a fantasy that Mussolini pursued regardless, and with impertinent zeal. One of the most notable intrusions into the private sphere came in the 1930s in the form of population policy, which was supposed to promote the regeneration of the Italian nation through a vastly accelerated birthrate. Italy needed a popula-tion commensurate in size with its major power status, and had to rapidly replenish its stock of males to ensure sufficient manpower reserves for future wars. One official strategy was to penalize bachelors through the imposition of a progressive tax, as the failure of adult males to procreate was now deemed a dereliction of national duty. Males were treated to a series of positive inducements as well, especially relating to salaries and career promotions, but most state attention was reserved for women, whose bodies held the key to national regeneration. The Fascist state did what it could to repress birth control practices and to promote motherhood, hygiene and domesticity through propaganda and welfare enticements, and by rewarding families with large numbers of children. To qualify for state benefits, state employees had to have seven dependent children, while non-state employees were expected to have at least ten. In 1939 the regime considered controlling the 'quality' of the national progeny by issuing either pre-marital certificates or medical passports that listed medical back-grounds. No secular authority in the past had entertained such a massive intrusion into private life, but pronatalist policy was indicative of the extent to which Italy and many other inter-war powers took seriously the massive extension ascribed to state sovereignty.

The radical expansion of state power was partly attributable to the insta-bility of international relations through the inter-war years, which engen-dered the widespread fatalistic belief that another major war was inevitable. Pronatalists policies conveyed that sense of precariousness. For France, which was one of the few nations to survive the 1930s as a liberal democracy, declining fertility was deemed an infallible sign of national decline. By the same token, nations with better birthrates, such as Germany, were thought to have a promising imperial future. The view that only the fittest of nations could expect to survive in a world governed by ruthless competition and imperialist impulses appeared to justify the all-powerful state, which possessed the means and the will to marshal the nation's resources to meet the challenges of modern war.

States that most nearly achieved the utopian ideal of a 'national community', of an undivided, organic social formation, were expected to have the best chance not merely of surviving but of triumphing in the Darwinian struggle between nations. Apart from offering a philosophy of life, Fascism pursued a series of policies that were meant to give concrete form to the idea of a fully integrated state and society. The chief economic expression of this philosophy was 'productivism'. The Italian people were encouraged to regard their role in the life of the nation as producers, to see their primary function as serving the national economy. Regardless of where one was located on the social scale, whether one was the owner of Fiat or a Fiat factory worker, one was expected to measure self-worth by one's contribution to national wealth.

Creating a nation of producers, which entailed nothing less than the dissemination of a completely novel cultural identity, was part of a broader attempt by the Fascist regime to extend its influence over national economic life. Under the strong influence of Alfredo Rocco, it hoped to tame capitalism as well as labour. The Great War and the post-war economic crises had confirmed the need to manage capitalism during national emergencies, but if Italian society was to remain on a permanent war footing, then state supervision of private enterprise would also need to remain. To be sure, big business was riddled with insecurities throughout the economically volatile inter-war years and yearned for a strong state that could discipline labour, eliminate socialism and uphold the interests of the propertied classes. The creation of the *Confindustria*, whose purpose was to pressure the state in policy formation, reflected a broader belief that liberal democratic institutions could not be relied upon for protection.

In their quest to realize a socially harmonious society, the Fascists saw that their role must be to balance corporate interests, which they could only do by drawing the institutions representing labour and capital into the state. Indeed the regime sought to create a Fascist economy 'to organize', as Rocco put it, 'the producers themselves, under the supreme direction and control of the state'.[3] Relations between corporate interests were to be managed in such a way as to eliminate conflicts that disrupted production. 'Corporatism', which entailed formal regulation of the

---

[3] Lyttelton, op. cit., p. 202.

tripartite relationship between state, capital and labour, was not only expected to enhance the productive capacity of the nation, but also to create and consolidate national harmony. The state now saw its role as maintaining a controlled economic environment, in which labour and capital, and competing capitalist interests, resolved their disputes through conciliation. All major industries, such as insurance, mining and wine production, were organized into corporate bodies that accorded status to all involved, from the highest levels of management to the factory floor. Theoretically, unions, which were now Fascist-controlled, remained the legitimate representatives of workers. Wages and other issues of disputation were to be resolved peacefully through the internal mechanisms of each corporate body.

The Fascists had hoped that corporatism would play a major role in the making of Italians. The Labour Charter of 1927, which heralded the arrival of Corporatism in Italian life, was presented as 'a new way for everyone to be part of the nation'. As producers, Italians were expected to find individual fulfilment and meet national goals at one and the same time. By organizing Italians into corporate bodies, the state could harness the nation's productive capabilities and at the same time create a new basis for national belonging. Thus 1925 saw the creation of the National Fascist Corporation of Intellectual Professions, which included doctors, journalists and lawyers, as well as writers, musicians and other artists whose works could be mobilized by the regime. To give such bodies added status, they were charged with the responsibility of setting the criteria for corporate membership, thus empowering them to control membership of the relevant profession. Of course, corporatism in practice did not sustain Fascism's aspirations to promote class harmony, for while big business endured repeated interference from government ministers and bureaucrats, it nearly always prevailed in disputes with labour. Fascism was very responsive to the needs of capital, which almost always came at the expense of labour. Unprotected by their Fascist-controlled unions, Italian workers saw their working conditions diminish rapidly through the 1930s. The idea that they formed part of a nation of producers could hence have no lasting appeal.

Corporatism in practice failed miserably in its bid to 'make Italians', let alone 'Fascists', but if the regime had very little success through the workplace, it performed slightly better when it came to leisure activities. The most likely memories to evoke nostalgia long after the collapse of Fascism were of the mass activities that were organized through the 'Dopolavoro', which literally translated as 'after work'. Along with the *Balilla*, the regime's youth movement, the *Opera nazionale dopolavoro* (OND) gave many, though not all, ordinary Italians their first positive sense of engagement with the nation. The OND supported many popular sports, including spectator sports, and provided entertainment that ranged from opera to traditional folk festivals. It functioned chiefly through clubhouses where workers could spend their non-working hours.

The OND provided subsidized holiday travel. Though most Italian workers could not afford even the heavily subsidized travel programmes arranged by their local OND or their employers, the organization was yet responsible for the increased volume in domestic travel in the 1930s. The regime was more successful in improving accessibility to the cinema, which otherwise remained expensive. It tried to increase attendance by bargaining with the commercial film industry for cheaper tickets for OND members, by organizing travelling cinemas in localities without theatres, and by designating special days when tickets were particularly cheap, such as the Saturday matinée (*sabato teatrale*). In general, Fascism succeeded in vastly increasing popular access not only to cinema but also to live theatre.

Severe financial restraints meant that, unlike the Nazis, the Fascists could not make tourism and mass media truly popular, but there were mass leisure activities that were not expensive to operate and which the regime could co-opt at relatively little cost. Thus the popular game of *bocce*, a Mediterranean variant of bowling that only required heavy metal balls, was organized and controlled by the regime at regional and national levels. One of the great weaknesses of Italian nationalism had been its refusal to exploit popular cultural traditions. This the OND recognized, and to make up the deficiency promoted local cultural traditions, such as singing competitions in dialect, major festivities associated with local saints, and many festivals that were in danger of disappearing because of urbanization and migration. During the first half of the 1930s, when it was under the direction of Enrico Beretta, the OND was keen on reviving Italian folk culture. It supported 200 dramatic societies that performed works in dialect, and ensured that every provincial council had a folklore section attached to it. For the first time, the proverbial peasant became, to use Ernest Gellner's words, a 'putative representative of the nation'.[4] Through the promotion of folk art exhibitions, festivals, rituals and other practices, the OND sought to project a rustic *Italia* that was finally accorded status within national culture by the Fascist political order. This plurality of Italian cultures now being celebrated, a plurality once deemed the bane of *Italianità*, could henceforth serve to sustain it.

Overall, just under 20 000 OND circles were created by the regime, with about 3 800 000 members by 1939. Hence through the OND a far larger proportion of the population now, in some form or another, enjoyed a sense of involvement in the life of the nation. Fascist youth organizations did much the same: the 'Sons of the She Wolf', the Balilla, the 'Little Italians' and the 'Avanguardisti' sought to shape the more pliable minds of the young.

For the most part, Fascist mass organizations were popular, but did they create Italian patriots? Did they produce fascistized Italians? There is little

---

[4] Ernest Gellner, *Nations and Nationalism* (Oxford, Blackwell, 1983), p. 57.

doubt that members of the OND enjoyed themselves and appreciated the state's intervention in making otherwise costly pastimes accessible. We can only assume that the excursions, sporting competitions and access to radio and cinema did something to promote national consciousness and even national identity. There is little to indicate that organization of the leisure activities, however, created the kind of Italians that the state really wanted. In general, mass leisure activities, save for the more athletic sports, did nothing to promote the Fascist warrior mindset that the regime so dearly sought. As the regime was intent on neutralizing the potential political content of these mass activities, the OND was not well placed to make Fascists. If anything, it made its citizens more relaxed and comfortable. The *Balilla* was a more successful politicizing agency as its express purpose was to prepare children for the physical and mental demands of military training, yet even here, mass participation did not translate well into 'fascistization'. In the late 1930s, at a time when enrolments were climbing, secretaries were reporting that children were not taking their involvement seriously and were frequently absent from meetings and activities. The crisis was deemed so serious that in 1937 the PNF took control over the youth organizations and formed the *Gioventù italiana del littorio*. The new organization placed much greater emphasis on military instruction and physical fitness, but reports continued to complain of the lack of commitment.

The apotheosis of Italy

The state's attempt to absorb the Italian population through the construction of a totalitarian political order was a means to realizing the ideal nation. Yet productivism, corporatism and totalitarianism were hardly the stuff that would stir passion among the masses and thereby create dedicated Fascists. Hence at the same time, Mussolini sought to develop a national culture that engaged directly with the masses, that appealed to their sensibilities and which they might find emotionally uplifting. The new national culture was to be celebrated through new rituals and commemorative practices, through the creation and adoration of new or reinvented symbols and sacred objects. In other words, Fascism sought to establish a new religion that might finally make every Italian love their nation. In most ways, Mussolini's government was demonstrably incompetent, but where it showed considerable ingenuity was in recognizing the importance of culture in politics. Its attempts to solve the problem of mass politics by allowing for cultural instead of political participation was probably Italian Fascism's most distinctive contribution to modern politics.

The treatment of women exemplified the regime's belief that it could disenfranchise, and yet at the same time mobilize, the Italian people. As with its German counterpart, the Italian dictatorship was avowedly anti-feminist. It sought to eliminate women from the labour force and confine them to traditional domestic roles. Yet the regime also sought their active support, especially as bearers of children and as symbolic representations of the Fascist nation. Apart from (largely inadequate) welfare policies designed to promote large families, the regime also extolled the virtues of mother-hood through public celebration and propaganda. Women featured more extensively in Fascist spectacle through the second half of the 1930s, when the quest for empire and economic difficulties demanded greater sacrifices from families. Women had been called upon to submit the wedding rings to help finance the war in Ethiopia, and on 8 May 1935 there were mass cere-monies all over Italy in which women were seen to be offering their gold in ritual sacrifice to the nation. By enlisting women as symbols of nationhood, mainly by extolling existing values such as motherhood, the regime sought to demonstrate that women formed an integral part of the Fascist nation.

Having destroyed Italy's limited democratic institutions, Fascism sought to win mass support by appealing directly to the senses. Both Hitler and Mussolini believed that mass mobilization was achievable while denying mass political representation because ordinary people were far more responsive to myth and ritual than to reason. Each took their cue from a series of pre-war intellectuals who took an interest in mass psychology, such as Georges Sorel and Gustave Le Bon, who believed crowds were governed by instincts and were essentially irrational. To be sure, Liberal Italy had produced public rituals and monuments that celebrated the monarchy and the Risorgimento, but it was not particularly concerned about cultivating popular devotion. The Fascists, on the other hand, were acutely aware of this deficiency and were resolved to make *Italia* the primary object of mass devotion.

Fascism's emphasis on culture drew a great deal of international comment, much of it derisive. Foreign critics referred to Fascist Italy as a propaganda state, of Fascism as lacking substance, and to Mussolini as the 'sawdust dictator'. Yet in practising a very new kind of politics that appealed directly to the irrational and to the base instincts of the masses, Mussolini anticipated that Italy, as a 'proletarian nation', could prevail through sheer will. His insistence that the masses could be made to believe whatever they were told, provided the message was presented to them in a resonant and emotionally uplifting form, was not simply a reference to their gullibility but to their potential spiritual and emotional power. Italy's real handicaps, such as low productivity, lack of natural resources and other factors that limited Italy's military capabilities, could be overcome in the same way that the supernatural can prevail over the natural. Thus the massive propaganda offensive was not simply meant to deify *Italia* but to mobilize the faithful to the extent that they could overcome the nation's material disadvantages.

Italians were bombarded with Fascist propaganda through the radio, to which a growing number of people had access (between 1927 and 1943, radio licences increased from 41 000 to 1.8 million),[5] at the cinema, where documentaries were screened before the feature film, and through printed material such as newspapers and magazines. Even those who could not read and lacked access to radios or cinema houses could encounter Fascist iconography in the form of posters or statues, which in most cases evoked the dynamism, martial spirit and glorious destiny of Fascism. Where the regime paid an exorbitant amount of its attention, however, was in the presentation of staged events in public spaces. Mass rallies were especially important in that they signified the communion between the political order and the general population. Mussolini went to great efforts to address crowds throughout Italy, in a way that previous Italian political leaders had never done. Of course 'Il Duce' would boast the achievements of his regime, but it was the form, rather than the content, of his speeches that suggested the means by which the regime sought to captivate the Italian masses. As was the case with Hitler's speeches, Mussolini played to his crowds in his inimical animated style and distinctively earthy voice, but he expected mass participation through cheers and well-timed chants of 'Du-ce, Du-ce, Du-ce'. Rallies, parades and other rituals requiring mass involvement provided the means of affirming popular consent without elections. All rallies were generously reported in the media as mass events, showing people and regime enjoined in a common performance.

Among the most important rituals in the Fascist calendar was the annual re-enactment of the March on Rome (27–9 October 1922), which began the first year following that heavily mythicized event. In the first year, a whole series of events were planned throughout Italy, but particularly in five cities which had special meaning to the Fascist movement, namely Cremona, Milan, Bologna, Perugia and Rome. In each place, Mussolini or the Fascist movement had experienced defining moments that were now to be celebrated, (e.g. Perugia was the point from where the March on Rome was launched), and which the Fascists expected would become entrenched in national memory as significant historical moments. The culminating event in the festivities took place on 31 October, when Mussolini led the re-enactment of the triumphal entry into Rome, following the route taken by the Black Shirts from the Tomb of the Unknown Warrior to the Palazzo Quirinale.[6]

There is little doubt that those thousands who experienced Fascist spectacle were impressed by its scale and extravagance, but there is little evidence to suggest that Fascism succeeded in sacralizing politics. Despite

[5] David Forgacs, *Italian Culture in the Industrial Age, 1880–1980: Culture Industries, Politics and the Public* (Manchester, Manchester University Press, 1990), p. 63.
[6] Mabel Berezin, *Making the Fascist Self: The Political Culture of Interwar Italy* (Ithaca, NY, Cornell University Press, 1997), p. 84.

their apparent enthusiasm, the crowds were in fact often forced to attend the regime's parades and speeches. When Mussolini visited Turin on 15 May 1939 Fiat workers undermined his performance, and thereby registered their antipathy, by refusing to play the role of the adoring crowd. A confidential report on the incident claimed workers practised their 'hurrahs' and other chants before he arrived, but fell silent when he actually took the podium.[7] Indeed, the Fascists were suspicious of most crowds through the 1930s. Reports suggested that most people who attended rallies and exhibitions were apathetic about their involvement or had simply come for the entertainment. Parades might well have been impressive as spectacles, but in no sense could they be as moving or have the aura of traditional Catholic rituals.

A more successful, but only marginally more effective, agent of fascistization was the cult of Mussolini. As Hitler would demonstrate in Germany, mass mobilization could be achieved through a charismatic leader who managed to personify and render accessible the values of Fascism. The Duce cult extolled all the qualities that he envisaged for his youthful, masculine warrior nation. He cultivated his image of physical fitness, baring his naked chest when the right photo opportunity availed itself, and spreading rumours of his dangerous yet fearless driving and his amazingly prolific extra-marital affairs. To all intents and purposes, Mussolini was Fascism. Representations of the Duce made him the exemplification of virility, of selfless patriotism, masculinity, youthfulness and the triumph of the will. He presented himself as menacing, serious and decisive – qualities which he hoped could be instilled into the nation. His face, his title and the initial 'M' were to be found everywhere, on wall posters and stencils, magazines and newspapers, even clothing. The propaganda offensive ventured frequently into the realm of the absurd. His name was supposed to have been uttered in children's prayers, he was referred to as 'Him' (possessive: 'His'), his title was written in upper case (DUCE), and with the help of slavish acolytes, such as the party secretary Achille Starace, he was virtually deified. In one of the many building proposals designed to glorify the Duce, such as the Casa Littoria, its designer wrote that it would be 'a palace from which the will of the Duce, the force of His convictions, the fascination of His person, will continue to radiate'.[8]

Mussolini tried to present himself as the ultimate Italian. His propaganda apparatus did its best to show him as possessing a superhuman intellect, capable of mastering many ministerial portfolios and of working tirelessly most hours of the day. He could supposedly master the headiest problems of state, and yet at the same time deal with equal attentiveness to

---

[7] Luisa Passerini, *Fascism in Popular Memory: The Cultural Experience of the Turin Working Class* (Cambridge, Cambridge University Press, 1987), p. 189.
[8] Emilio Gentile, *The Sacralization of Politics in Fascist Italy* (Cambridge, MA, Harvard University Press, 1996), p. 127.

minor matters, such as police uniforms. In other words, he resembled the
superman prophesied by Nietzsche and exemplified the totalitarian ideal.
Omnipotent and ever-present, he had the power to solve the nation's problems, and was the only one who could create *la grande nazione*. In becoming the personification of Fascism, he managed to place himself above the
regime, which made the regime, rather than Mussolini, the target of criticisms and disenchantment. Even the Turin workers, recalling Mussolini's
visit in later life, conceded sympathy for Mussolini, to whom they attributed the positive achievements of the regime while maintaining an antipathy for Fascism. In general, it was Mussolini, not the regime, that procured
what popular approval there was, and it was through such approval of the
Duce that Fascism obtained support.

Imperialism, race and war

Small in stature, Mussolini spent an inordinate amount of energy trying to
convince everyone that he was much larger than life. The cult of the Duce
and Fascist culture generally constituted a desperately shrill attempt to
capture hearts and minds in a country where state and society had long
been antithetical, and where nationhood had very little appeal. Fascism
consciously sought to break with earlier political practices so as to correct
Italy's historical maldevelopment, yet at the same time, it could only
succeed if it also presented itself as a product of Italian history. To accord
legitimacy to the culture fashioned by Fascism, the regime saw itself as
inheriting the mantle of the Risorgimento and taking-up where the heroes
of 1860 had left off. The regime was far more interested, however, in drawing a link between Fascism and ancient Rome. As Western civilization's
paradigm of imperial power, Rome had obvious attractions for a regime
bent on national aggrandisement, and for Mussolini especially, *romanità*
was an obsession. On balance, it was *romanità* more than anything else that
guided Fascism's quest to make Italians.

   Romanità was an abundant source of symbolic capital, including the
triumphal arches, columns and mausoleums, and specific symbols such as
the Roman salute, Romulus and Remus, the eagle and the battle standards.
Much greater funding was distributed to archaeologists researching classical antiquity than to those working on any other period; remains from
other periods were often damaged or removed if they obscured Roman
remains. The very word 'fascism' referred to a sacred Roman symbol, the
fasces, a double-edged axe embedded within a bundle of rods and signify-
ing strength through unity. For Alfredo Rocco, Rome's commitment to
unity gave it a distinct advantage over the Greeks, who experimented with
democracy and other systems that addressed the individual. The power of
Rome was not just related to a stable social order but to the unity of the

Italian peoples, as evoked through the Emperor Augustus's celebration of *tota Italia*.

As Galeazzo Ciano noted in his diary on 20 November 1937, what distinguished Italian Fascism from Nazi Germany and other right-wing dictatorships was its Roman imperial legacy. Mussolini's sublime aim was the restoration of the Mediterranean as 'Mare Nostrum', to give to the Italian people an empire which was theirs by right. And by claiming the Roman imperial mantle, the Fascist regime believed it was substantiating its claim to legitimacy. Ancient historians, archaeologists and classicists were sometimes enlisted to provide scholarly credence to the link between Rome and Fascism, as was the case in 1937–8 when the regime celebrated the 2000th anniversary of Augustus' birth, the *bimillenario augusteo*. The occasion was marked by a mass exhibition in Rome called the *Mostra augustea della romanità*, which was opened at the very same time, and in very close proximity to, an exhibition devoted to the Fascist revolution. Most exhibitions in the late 1930s paid homage to the cult of *romanità*, and Italians subscribed to these exhibitions in their thousands.

Classical Rome was construed as a paradigm of power and nationhood, and, as a regime that went far towards confusing image with reality, Fascism did all it could to give the appearance that it was Rome incarnate. For much of the Fascist period, however, *romanità* as an aesthetic style did not monopolize the attention of Mussolini and the Fascist hierarchy. Indeed, through Fascism's first decade in power, Italian artistic movements jockeyed to see which would be able to claim the prestigious epithet of 'Fascist art'. For much of that time, the regime encouraged and patronized several artistic movements, and modern art had particular appeal, given that Fascism also saw itself as a break with the past. Hence its obsession with youth: the regime's anthem was 'Giovenezza' (Youth), and Fascist iconography, regardless of its artistic style, provided recurring representations of young male bodies which stood as allegories to youthful virility and elan. Mussolini himself, the youngest ever Italian prime minister, was exalted for his youthful spirit, referred to in one Fascist youth publication as 'the youngest of us all', whose wonderful youthfulness went 'beyond space and time'.[9]

When Italy declared its imperial destiny with the invasion of Ethiopia in 1935, the regime decided it should focus on *romanità* at the expense of modern aesthetic styles. Whereas major building structures included styles that conveyed the Fascist proclivity for youth and modernity, as reflected by the Casa del Fascio in Como and Foro Italico in Rome, from the mid-1930s major government contracts, sponsorship and other forms of patronage favoured the proponents of *romanità*. Important structures were now

---

[9] Laura Malvano, 'The Myth of Youth in Images: Italian Fascism', in Giovanni Levi and Jean-Claude Schmitt, *A History of Young People*, Vol. 2 (Cambridge, MA, Belknap, 1997), p. 250.

expected to evoke the grandeur of imperial Italy. Monumentalism was the keynote, as exemplified by Macello Piacentini's redevelopment of the University of Rome. Arches and columns conveyed Italy's real destiny, while exponents of modern styles were restricted to designing minor structures.

Empire brought many responsibilities, and as an imperial people, the Italians had to think seriously about their status vis-à-vis their subject peoples. The subjugation of millions of Africans had inevitable implications for *italianità*. For Europe's colonial powers, representations of colonial natives and other 'races' were important, yet barely recognized, means of defining national character with binary contrasts. Blacks, Arabs and Asians were made out to be everything that the British, French and other imperial peoples were not. Yet even the conquest of Libya in 1911 and the continuous and costly involvement in Africa did not really establish an obsession with race in Italian society. Descriptions of Africans in books and depictions in advertising normally referred to rather benign savages on whom the Italians would benevolently bestow civilization.

It was the conquest of Ethiopia, as well as Mussolini's growing attachment to the rising star of Nazi Germany, that signalled Italy's official descent into the mire of racism. 'Razza' had not been a key theme in Fascist or nationalist rhetoric, and of all the inter-war European dictatorships, Mussolini's had been the least concerned with Jews or other 'racial' questions. Yet after the victory in Ethiopia, Mussolini, in one of his most outrageous ventures into the absurd, decided that race was an essential characteristic of *italianità*, and that the integrity of the *razza* required the segregation and legitimized the oppression of inferior peoples. On 15 July 1938, when the regime's manifesto on race, *La difesa della razza*, was issued, *italianità* was officially accorded a biological meaning. Italians were designated Aryans, a superior race, and Italian Jews were now deemed biologically different, and hence not real Italians. Indeed, Jews were now regarded officially as racial enemies, and they were expelled from the PNF, removed from civil service posts, and restricted from professions and from buying property. At much the same time, Mussolini tried to enforce racial segregation in Ethiopia, to instil in Italian colonial personnel a sense of racial superiority as befitted the dominant race. Inter-marriage and sexual relations, indeed any form of social intimacy between 'Aryans' on the one hand, and Jews and Africans on the other, were forbidden.

Of course, cultural exclusivity did feature in Fascist politics before 1935. The regime's motto of 'one nation, one language' did not merely refer to the intention to have standard Italian replace all dialects in everyday life, but to the eradication of non-Italian languages. (Albanian, Serb and Greek dialects were, and continue to be, spoken by small communities located mainly in the south.) In the ethnically Greek Dodecanese islands, the colonial regime first sought to 'Italianize' locals through positive inducements, such as free access to all levels of education in Italian institutions, but from December

1936, when Cesare de Vecchi was appointed governor, Greek schools were shut down and spoken Greek was forbidden in public. Ethnic persecution was sustained throughout the Fascist period in the Trentino/Alto-Adige and Venezia Giulia, where Italians were not the predominant element, and where the Fascists were determined to enforce 'Italianization'. In the port city of Trieste, for example, assimilation took the form of changing the names of streets, and the closure of Slovene and Croatian schools and other non-Italian ethnic institutions.

The Fascist conception of *La grande nazione* mutated into one that was now explicitly defined in racial terms, yet as with everything else propagated by the regime through its twenty years in power, rhetorical discourse did not necessarily translate into social reality. By European standards, anti-Semitism had an unusually weak hold in modern Italian culture, and whereas other dictatorships could depend on shoring up their popularity by playing the anti-Semitic card, in Italy the move fell flat. If anything, Mussolini incurred hostility from those of his followers who believed he was simply ingratiating himself with the Nazis, and who resented the expulsion of committed Fascists who also happened to be Jews. During the latter stages of the Second World War, Fascist and non-Fascist Italians demonstrated their aversion to Mussolini's anti-Semitic turn by actively foiling German attempts to send Jews to death camps. Similar opprobrium was not shown towards the killing of Africans and Slavs, and myths of Italians as being the ultimate non-racist colonizers are found wanting in the light of atrocities committed in Libya and Ethiopia. Yet here too, Fascist attempts to instil an imperial mentality and to segregate the races did not enjoy much success. Authorities could do little, for instance, to stop the widespread practice of 'madamismo', which referred to Italian men cohabiting with Ethiopian women, a practice regarded by the Fascist hierarchy as an affront to Italy's standing as an imperial power.

The failure of cultural policy

Fascism's quest to 'make Italians' was meant to entail nothing less than the reconstitution of identity and everyday life. Even the most basic features of daily custom, such as the common greeting and the handshake, had become matters that the state deemed within its rights to control. Thus the respectful use of the third person 'Lei' when greeting a second person was deemed too deferential to have any place in an organic society, while the handshake was considered too bourgeois and effeminate, and had to be replaced by a vigorous Roman salute. In accordance with the regime's totalitarian pretensions, even facial expressions were not beyond its sphere of influence. Mussolini wanted the world to regard Italians as warriors, as people to be feared and worthy of respect. Hence Italians were expected to adopt a dourer public demeanour so that outsiders could regard them as a serious people, and to free themselves of their supposedly cheerful or comic international image. In propaganda posters and photographs, Mussolini led by example with his piercing stares and threatening postures.

Regulating the appearance of the body was but one strategy through which this extraordinarily creative regime hoped to construct its particular vision of *italianità*. Fascism invested a great deal of its energy into cultural policy because it recognized the importance of culture and the mundane aspects of daily life in nation formation. Parallel developments in Nazi Germany demonstrated the extent to which 'totalitarian' cultural policies could penetrate society and have a profound impact on popular mentalities. German soldiers who committed mass atrocities in the Soviet Union during the Second World War, for example, had been conditioned by years of socialization in racial ideology. In the German case, however, the relative success of Nazi cultural policy was largely attributable to its achievements on many other fronts. It is difficult to imagine the astounding success of Hitler's own hero cult without such amazing feats as having achieved and sustained full employment, and especially without the unrelenting series of stunning foreign policy and military successes to 1942.

In contrast, the Fascist regime's triumphs were very few and its disappointments many, which also meant it was excessively reliant on the socializing and mobilizing power of myth and imagery. By the end of the 1930s the national economy was in steep decline, the living standards of the average Italian had diminished, and Mussolini had waged a series of costly and inglorious military adventures. Another reason why 'Fascistization' had but a superficial impact on Italian cultural identities and mentalities was that the regime did not have the resources to enforce its cultural policies. Thus while it could censor depictions of handshakes in the media and the usage of 'Lei' in films, Italians continued to use both, and in many cases did so to make a political gesture. Indeed, cultural resistance was an important form of subversion, given that the regime was so heavily reliant on cultural policy. While left-wing organizations were smashed, many workers continued to undermine the Fascist project by parodying Fascist rhetoric, while many working-class women were later to reveal that they consciously resisted pronatalist policy because they did not want their children, once fully grown, to be expended in Mussolini's wars. Even popular 'fascistizing' agencies such as the Dopolavoro were almost impossible for the regime to maintain. This largest of the Fascist cultural organizations was never large enough to cater to the needs of all workers. Peasants, for example, were normally beyond the reach of the Dopolavoro, while ordinary women generally never had leisure time to begin with because of work and household duties and the fear of moral opprobrium. In most ways, everyday life in Italy continued to operate much as it had done before the Fascists.

Overall, it is not very clear how many Italians were 'made' by Fascism, but Italian society certainly did not enter the Second World War as a nation of patriots. The propaganda offensive to give Italian culture a homogenized, Fascist form, though aesthetically innovative and at times politically shrewd, appears to have had no more than a superficial success. Some were genuinely enthralled by the myth of the Duce, and many more probably found the draining of the Pontine Marshes, the Battle for Wheat and other heavily publicized national events impressive enough to inspire a sense of national belonging. At the very least, Fascism's wide-ranging propaganda offensives probably had the effect of making *Italia* a more familiar feature in the lives of ordinary people.

The Second World War, however, threatened to obliterate what little the Fascists had achieved. The failures of almost two decades in power had made Mussolini even more determined to realize his *grande nazione* through war. He expected that Italians, indeed Fascist Italians, would be made *through* the restoration of the Roman empire, through the experience of conquest and the attainment of victory. What in fact ensued was the collapse of the Fascist regime and the near destruction of Italy. The next, and final, chapter will consider the ramifications of Fascism's calamitous war for the Italian nation and Italian nationalism.

|8|

Nationhood without nationalism: Italy since 1943

The Second World War was to be the nadir of modern Italian history. Mussolini's foolishly conceived scheme to hasten the realization of *la grande nazione* through war and conquest began with a humiliating near-defeat in Albania. In October 1940 he ordered the invasion of Greece, and, having given the Italian military hardly any time to prepare and having grossly underestimated the enemy, saw his forces driven back into Albania. His fortunes went from bad to worse, culminating in the brutal struggle from mid-1943 over Italy itself between Germany and the Allies. Through the latter years of the war especially, the Italian people suffered dearth, saturated bombing, brutal occupation and civil war. Yet Italy not only survived but was to emerge stronger, especially in material terms. Most startlingly, by 1978 Italy had earned a place among the world's economic elite, the 'Group of Seven' (G7), and in the 1980s would surpass Britain on the world economic league table. As an arbiter of western fashion and cultural consumption, Italy most definitely became, and has remained, a dominant world power. Although persistently tainted by 'Mafia' imagery, 'Italy' is much more readily identifiable nowadays with elegance and style, with sophisticated apparel, expensive automobiles and fine cuisine. To many, contemporary Italy epitomizes chic. Despite their embarrassingly chaotic political system, Italians at the beginning of the twenty-first century no longer have cause to feel the chagrin that comes with national backwardness, poverty and mediocrity.

And yet Italians continue to question whether their nation has substance, as happened most notably in the wake of the demise of the dominant political parties in 1992. In Galli della Loggia's controversial *La morte della Patria* (Death of the Fatherland, 1996), the author claimed that the collapse of the Italian state in September 1943 had exposed the shallowness of Italian identity, a shallowness he also ascribed to the post-war years through to the present. The rise and modest success of the Northern League (*Lega Nord*) in the late 1980s and 1990s had many local and foreign commentators prophesying the nation's break-up. Its rambunctious leader, Umberto Bossi, won notoriety for advocating a new, separate nation in the north called *Padania*, the news of which was grist to the mill for those critics who considered Italy to be a superficial nation. Yet by the beginning of the 1990s the *Lega* had modified its talk of separatism, and during the 1994 elections, most voters in the *Lega*'s constituencies responded to the call of Forza Italia ('Go Italy'), the neo-liberal party built around the media magnate Silvio Berlusconi. For the great majority of Italians, the break-up of their nation was never a real issue. *Italia* may not have been sacralized by earlier regimes, but for the great majority of the population, it was, and remains, a given.

What continues to intrigue observers of Italy is the near absence of a strong nationalist culture. The patriotic exhilaration witnessed throughout the country after the World Cup soccer triumph in Madrid in 1982, and the tears shed after the *'azzuri'* lost the 1994 finals in Los Angeles, were aberrant demonstrations of nationalist culture that otherwise does not feature prominently in Italian life. Although ascribed a readily recognizable identity by outsiders and by much of the diaspora, Italy remains substantially a collection of 'Italies', of people whose 'patria' is likely to be their locality rather than their nation. Fascism clearly failed in its attempts to create a nation of nationalists, let alone fervently radical ones, but Italy's development as a nation continued regardless. This final chapter discusses some of the reasons for the failure of nationalism by looking at the demise of the Fascist regime and at the reconstruction of Italy after the war. It then proceeds to identify, albeit rather schematically, the great transformations in social, cultural and economic life during the second half of the twentieth century, changes that have made the nation a real source of identification for ordinary Italians. A widespread sense of nationhood was consolidated in this period, though it appears that nationalism played at best a very minor role in that achievement.

Nationhood reappraised

Italy's Second World War amounted to one military humiliation after another. Following the debacle along the Greek-Albanian border, the East African empire, which had taken generations to construct, fell almost instantly and effortlessly into British hands. Libya was not as effortlessly conceded, but German-led Italian forces were gradually driven out of North Africa by the early summer of 1943. Perhaps the most poignant indication that the Italian masses had not been sufficiently 'nationalized', and of the woeful inadequacies of national leadership, was the pathetic dissolution of the Italian army when the Armistice was finally announced in September. Moreover, the government made no provision to resist the anticipated German occupation that followed. Mussolini had needlessly thrown in his lot with a reckless ally bent on an all-or-nothing course of creating a new racial world order, but when the tide turned against the Axis it was the Italian homeland that was first exposed to Allied invasion. From July 1943 to May 1945, Italy was a battleground for foreign armies bent on total victory, bringing wanton destruction and leaving Italian society deeply traumatized. Aerial bombing killed about 64 000 civilians, while German occupying forces struck terror into the hearts of the civilian population, particularly Italian Jews, who quickly became victims of genocide. Meanwhile, anti-Fascist partisans fought desperate battles against the German occupiers and the new the Fascist government installed in the north (the so-called Republic of Salò), effectively producing a conflict that was both a war of resistance and a civil war. The struggle inevitably enveloped thousands of village communities, many of which experienced massacre and were put to the torch. Much of the countryside was plunged into lawlessness. Individuals and political groups took the opportunity to settle personal scores, and homicide rates skyrocketed. German-occupied Italy was a world turned upside down.

Though the war was a shattering experience for Italians, one significant consolation was the end of Fascism as a major political force (although quasi- or neo-fascist parties would continue to find their niche in national political life). If Italy was to be 're-made' after 1945, or if the nation was to survive at all, the reconstructed version would require a wholly new source of legitimation. Ever since national unity had been first established under the Savoyard dynasty, the prevailing assumption had been that Italy's *raison d'être* was that it should be a major imperial power. For the Liberal political order and the Fascist regime, matters of high politics, principally foreign affairs, held precedence over all other state matters. Yet the protracted pursuit of an ambitious foreign policy by a nation so lacking in economic and military resources was a contradiction that neither the Savoyards nor their ministers, from Cavour to Mussolini, were ever able to overcome. Whereas statesmen such as Giolitti had few illusions about the limits of the nation's imperial prospects, and did their best to build an empire without committing the country to ruinous war, Mussolini was more than willing to throw caution to the wind. Either way, the quest for imperial Italy was to be inevitably paid for with the blood of ordinary Italians, who by 1945 would no longer brook the subordination of society to an irresponsible state. As with the British people, who dumped the wartime hero prime minister Winston Churchill in favour of a Labour Party promising a welfare state, so their Italian counterparts wanted their 'people's war' to be followed by a 'people's peace'. They sought a fundamental reorientation of the priorities of the state, which had hitherto subordinated the interests of society to the exigencies of High Politics. No sooner had Mussolini been dismissed than anti-Fascist elements were drawing blueprints for a new Italy based on a completely different state–society relationship.

Visions of a new Italy had been formulated during the nation's darkest hour in the summer of 1943, when anti-Fascist movements appeared both within the German-occupied north and centre, and in the Allied-controlled south. Behind German lines a brutal struggle was waged between the Resistance, which consisted of a variety of political groups, and German forces and supporting militias that had been enlisted by Mussolini's restored Fascist regime. The campaign that saw Italy liberated by 1 May 1945 was essentially an Anglo-American effort, but the anti-Fascist Resistance made a respectable contribution. For much of the time partisans had tied up about 25 per cent of Axis forces, and one of their great achievements was the liberation of major northern cities, including Milan and Turin, in May 1945. Partisan casualty rates were extremely high, but their ranks were replenished by a constant stream of new recruits.

For many Italians, the partisans did much to restore patriotic pride, while the Allies, namely the United States and Britain, had little choice but to allow the Resistance a substantial role in national reconstruction. To be sure, Italians did not become a nation of resisters – most civilians sought to remain out of harm's way by not committing themselves to either side. But, considered in its European context, Italy was not unique in this regard. As in other occupied zones, there were sections of the population that made extraordinary sacrifices in the face of great peril: workers in the industrialized north, for example. Prior to the Allied invasion of Sicily, northern working-class communities were already waging industrial protest campaigns of a kind not seen since the *Biennio Rosso*. But it was after the summer of 1943, faced by utterly ruthless German authorities and under the threat of mass deportation to slave labour camps, that northern workers demonstrated extraordinary courage. Not only did worker protests increase in scale but they had become overtly anti-war and anti-Fascist. During the first few days of March 1944, much of northern Italy was engulfed by waves of strikes that involved hundreds of thousands of workers, and in April 1945, during the dying days of the Third Reich, Italian workers and partisans chose not to wait for the advancing Allies and fought desperate street battles against the German occupiers.

The only real impetus for Italian renewal during the war therefore came 'from below', from the Resistance and from northern workers, who in turn insisted upon overseeing the reconstruction of *Italia*. Although diverse political groups were involved in the Resistance, including Liberals, Catholics and Communists, they all agreed on enough substantial points to make their alliance workable. Above all, they agreed that Fascism had to be extinguished and its legacies eradicated from national political culture. This anti-Fascist alliance was aware that Italy now had a unique opportunity to make a complete break from its authoritarian past and to finally bridge the gap between state and society. The new Italy therefore was to be a liberal democracy, and ideally one no longer burdened by a monarchy.

As the cornerstone of the pre-Fascist political order and the core symbol of the pre-Fascist vision of Italian nationhood, the Savoy monarchy had also played a key role in maintaining Italy's state–society divide. Whereas the British monarchy from the mid-nineteenth century had acclimatized itself to the heady world of mass politics by cultivating mass consent and thereby transforming itself into a popular institution, the Savoyards persisted in regarding Italy as their patrimony. It was clear that for the House of Savoy dynastic interests always took precedence over national interests. Vittorio Emanuele III, who had been responsible for elevating Mussolini to power and who stood by as the Fascist regime brought the country to the edge of ruin, demonstrated that quite plainly in the summer of 1943. It was only when the Allies had landed in Sicily in July and an invasion of the mainland was imminent, that the monarchy, in an effort to distance itself from the Fascist regime, decided to sack Mussolini. Yet rather than quickly throw in his lot with the Allies, which required unconditional surrender and the possible dissolution of the monarchy, Vittorio Emanuele insisted on negotiating the terms of Italy's capitulation. He was determined to attain guarantees for his monarchy and held out for forty-five days, all the while leaving the country dangerously exposed to German reprisals. (In the meantime, the new government headed by Marshal Pietro Badoglio was following a disingenuous and foolhardy scheme of reassuring the Germans that their alliance remained intact, all the while making next to no defence preparations for the time when Germany should get wind of their treachery.) The king finally agreed to the Allies' demand for an unconditional armistice on 3 September, but through sheer incompetence his government failed to organize with the Allies to secure Rome, while Italian forces had no instructions regarding how to deal with German troops. When the armistice was publicly announced by the Allies on 8 September, the king and his government, having made no provisions for the defence of the capital, abandoned it. Locally stationed Italian forces fell apart in the face of numerically inferior German troops.

The king's flight from the capital, which was widely regarded as a cowardly and unpatriotic act, dealt a fatal blow to the monarchy's reputation. The Allies reluctantly reinstalled Vittorio Emanuele in the so-called 'Kingdom of the South', but the local patriotic formation known as the 'Committee for National Security', which contained representatives of all anti-Fascists groups, refused to recognize the king or his new government. Many committee members were not simply incensed by the king's appalling behaviour in recent months but also by the kind of authoritarian regime he sought to restore behind Allied lines. An indication of what the

Mezzogiorno could expect was demonstrated during the so-called 'Forty-Five Days' following Mussolini's dismissal, when the king and the Badoglio government were evidently much more concerned about suppressing social discontent, even patriotic demonstration, than they were in preparing for war against their former Axis partners. The government did everything possible to discourage celebrations that followed the fall of Fascism, if only because it feared the excited masses might pose a threat to the new government. Later anti-war demonstrations in Bari, Milan and Turin were brutally suppressed, indicating in the starkest possible terms the new government's authoritarian disposition. When Italians were later given a chance to decide on the fate of the monarchy on 2 June 1946, the overwhelming majority of those who had been abandoned to German occupying forces in September 1943 voted for an end to it.

That same day, voters took a further step towards a new Italy when they elected the first Constituent Assembly since the advent of the Fascist dictatorship. Anti-Fascist parties that had done most to develop a mass support base polled well, while those that had not, such as the Liberals, did poorly. The most successful were the Christian Democrats (DC), who had been busy developing as broad a social support base as possible, appealing to peasants as well as big business. The Communists (PCI), the party that contributed most towards the Resistance, came in second. Needless to say, in rejecting the monarchy voters also determined that Italy was to be a republic, and that a new constitution had to be written. This 'statuto' was more or less completed in mid- 1947, and came into force on 1 January 1948, enshrining the powers of the president while banning Vittorio Emanuele III and all his male descendants from Italian soil. The constitution reflected the anti-Fascist spirit of inclusiveness by advocating the principle of egalitarianism, as well as such progressive ideas as the right to employment and the right of workers to organize. Moreover, even minor interest groups could manage to send a representative to the Constituent Assembly through the creation of an electoral system based on proportional representation. Such a system promised a parliament that might serve the diverse interests of this most complex of societies.

Another important development that had implications for the reconstruction of Italy and its future as a sovereign nation-state was the strong interest in European integration. National rivalries during the inter-war years and the damage subsequently wrought by the Axis powers fostered much enthusiastic talk throughout the continent about the necessity of a federated Europe, and Italians were among its most active proponents. The Ventotene Manifesto, widely regarded as the first detailed blueprint for a united Europe, was formulated in a Fascist gaol in June 1941. Significantly, its ideas were widely adopted among the anti-Fascist parties during the war, and it was Italian activists who organized the first major conference on the issue in Geneva in July 1944. Commitment to Europe was even more apparent in the post-war years, as Italy sought to redeem itself in the eyes of the international community. (The hope of procuring significant European assistance for economic reconstruction also played a part.) The anti-Fascist parties were for the most part willing to sacrifice a share of Italian national sovereignty for the sake of continental integration, and of Europe's post-war leaders, Italy's Alcide De Gasperi was among the most assiduous proponents of integration along military, economic and political lines.

It is not surprising that European integration enjoyed such widespread support in a country where nationalism, despite Mussolini's strident attempts at mass cultural engineering, and because of Italy's abjectly disastrous war experience, enjoyed comparatively little resonance. Italy's commitment to European co-operative schemes, its determination to be among the founding signatories of significant international organizations, such as the European Coal and Steel Community, received due recognition when Rome was chosen to launch the European Economic Community in 1957. Since then, Italian political parties generally have lived quite comfortably with the prospect of further integration and loss of sovereignty, but as will be shown below, another important influence on their outlook has been a lack of faith in the competence and integrity of their national political order.

State and civil society, 1947–92

Memories of the Resistance proved to be very useful to the parties that dominated national politics in the post-war years. Christian Democrat, Communist and Socialist politicians were able to draw on personal wartime records to underscore their political credibility. With Fascism having been completely tainted, the Resistance and the myths arising from it provided the values on which the new Italian nationalism was to be based. Schoolchildren could now be taught that the Italian people were a nation of resisters, that the test of war and occupation revealed the true Italian character. Being Italian now meant one was a lover of liberty and democracy, and therefore an anti-Fascist. The *partigiani* were seen as evoking the true spirit of Garibaldi, and as holding the same ideals and passions as the democratic heroes of the Risorgimento. In many ways the so-called 'Wind from the North' provided for a form of 'constitutional patriotism' in that it extolled a national identity based on devotion to liberal democratic values and the institutions that sustain a civil society. It demanded adherence to the constitution of 1948 and the complete rejection of the recent Fascist past.

The anti-Fascist reading of the Second World War remained virtually uncontested in the post-war period, as the dominant political parties used their common struggle against Mussolini and the Nazis as a source of their political legitimacy. However, anti-Fascism could not provide the basis for a truly hegemonic national ideology. There were too many elements within Italian society to whom the Resistance meant something else, or nothing at all. The latter was particularly true for much of the Mezzogiorno, where there had been no resistance activity. Here the monarchy actually received overwhelming support in the 1946 referendum, a sobering reminder that the 'Wind from the North' did not blow south of Rome. Even in German-occupied areas, support for the Resistance had not been overwhelming, while at the same time, the Republic of Salò, although remembered by anti-Fascists as a heinous collaborationist regime and therefore more execrable than any foreign adversary, did in fact have a genuine support base. Mussolini's puppet regime managed to attract just under half a million soldiers, many of whom believed that fighting against the Allies was a patriotic duty and that the Resistance was the vanguard of the Bolshevik menace, set to destroy Italy.

Perhaps more important than the limited resonance of the Resistance was the failure of the post-war state to establish its own hegemony in Italian society. Far from procuring a new political order that was fundamentally committed to liberal democratic values and societal welfare, the Italian people found the new establishment to be not much different to the old. Outwardly, post-war Italy appeared to have had experienced a political revolution, but neither the introduction of the republic and democratic practices, nor the elimination of Fascism and the Savoy monarchy, were enough to substantially affect the manner in which power had long been distributed and exercised in Italy. As had been the case during the Liberal and Fascist periods, the state would continue functioning in an authoritarian mode, reacting, for example, with comparable ruthlessness to social movements and political dissent. More importantly, when it came to matters of government administrative efficiency, social equity, political and social reform and general regard for the public interest, the post-war political order was almost as malevolently negligent and apathetic as the Liberal regime. With the revival of clientelism, the plundering of public resources by the mainstream political parties, and the stranglehold on government offices by the conservative politicians determined to keep civil society at bay, no fundamental change in Italian political culture could be effected from above. More to the point, the post-war political order, which persisted until 1992, possessed neither the political will nor the moral credibility to 'make Italians' on whatever basis.

It is worthwhile detailing some of the main developments in post-war politics and their impact on Italian culture, mainly because public disenchantment also reflected more widespread and much deeper concern for the condition of the nation, and hence in the meaning and future of *Italia*. Admittedly, some of the more extreme responses included regional secessionism, as initially threatened by groups in Sicily in the early post-war period, and much later by the *Lega Lombarda* in the mid 1980s. Since the

Second World War, however, Italian society has demonstrated an interest in making the nation work *despite* the state, and most substantial political, legal and social reforms up to the early 1990s have been the result of pressure 'from below'.

From the early years of the Republic, Italian society quickly assumed the well-founded belief that they were being governed by the same masters. The sense that the power structure had not been changed was evoked in one of the landmark books of Italian literature, *Il Gattopardo* (The Leopard), by Giuseppe Tomasi di Lampedusa, which was published in 1958. Although set in the Risorgimento period, the book's inspiration was the political transition of the 1940s, when, despite profound formal political reform, roughly the same people controlled the levers of power. Things did change, to paraphrase Lampedusa, but only so that things could remain the same. Naturally most of the politicians after 1945 were new, but the personnel of most state agencies remained much the same as under Fascism, despite great expectations of a purge. Judges, police officers and bureaucrats tended not to lose their jobs, or only did so temporarily. In the immediate aftermath of the war, a great deal of bloodletting occurred as the more notorious agents of Fascist oppression were targeted for revenge. The Fascist leadership proved easy targets – Mussolini was executed and his carcass was strung upside down in the Piazza Loreto in Milan – but punishing all who were thought to have collaborated with Fascism presented more difficulties than could be solved. A real concern was the consequences for government administration, as it was feared that certain ministries could lose half their experienced personnel. All political parties, including the PCI leadership, agreed that national reconstruction might be jeopardized if the purges were too thorough. Moreover, as often happens after a prolonged war, exhaustion and the desire to move forward meant that Italian society's preparedness to come to terms with its recent past and bring Fascism's collaborators to justice was limited.

The most important reason for the restoration of an authoritarian political order, however, can be attributed to the Cold War. Many notorious and indictable ex-Fascists and collaborators remained not only at large but in positions of authority because of their solid, anti-Communist credentials. Worse still, many retained positions from which they could continue to persecute the Left. Thus former agents of the Fascist secret police, the OVRA, became top officials of the Republic's Interior Ministry, while judges closely associated with the former regime were actually allowed to preside over cases dealing with Fascist crimes. At the same time, former left-wing partisans found they were being barred or removed for state employment, while from 1947 left-wing parties, namely the Communists and the Socialists, were excluded from government coalitions that were always dominated by the Christian Democrats (see p. 161). Needless to say, the progressive values associated with the Resistance, and that informed the making of the Republic and the new constitution, had no application when it came to government practice.

Moreover, the Cold War provided the Christian Democrats with the perfect pretext for maintaining a paternalistic political order. Communism, they urged, had to be kept at bay, and labour too had to be contained. Although the DC-dominated governments led by that political stalwart de Gasperi pushed through some significant social reforms, namely the agrarian reforms of 1950 that finally forced substantial land redistribution among the rural poor, they were normally as uninterested in questions of social amelioration and equity as were earlier regimes. Being the party of big business, the DC were nevertheless always ready to curb labour activism and circumscribe workers' rights, which promoted enduring antipathy between the state and a vastly expanding Italian working class. The DC's constructive relationship with capital certainly fostered an economic revolution that saw Italy emerge as one of the world's leading economies, but during its early stages especially, the boom was based on the refusal to raise wages or improve workers' conditions. The PCI and PSI maintained a presence in parliament, but labour organizations as such did not have much legal standing and the bludgeoning of labour protesters was reminiscent of earlier times. Thus on 9 January 1950 six workers were killed and 50 injured during a factory occupation in Modena. Overall, it is estimated that 75 workers were killed and over 5000 injured in labour protests between 1948 and 1954. In the meantime, the state continued to demonstrate malign neglect in the face of unprecedented social change and greater demand for social services. Mass migration to industrial urban centres from throughout rural Italy, and particularly from the Mezzogiorno, saw the greatest demographic shift in the nation's history, swelling the ranks of the working class. Needless to say, rampant urbanization exacerbated existing social problems whilst creating new ones. Apart from low wages and a highly regimented and dispiriting workplace, workers had to suffer poor housing and the absence of welfare facilities.

Apart from a brief spell between 1960 and 1963, capital and the state kept labour in check, but it could not be long before outmoded paternalistic approaches to social problems would be met by organized responses from within civil society. As the middle and lower classes gradually claimed their share in national economic growth and enjoyed a marked increase in living standards through the 1960s, and as social and demographic change inevitably unleashed a whole range of political challenges, the state's relationship with civil society became ever more strained. Finding that the state was not responsive to society's pressing needs, such as providing adequate medical care, many social and extra-parliamentary political movements took matters into their own hands. Many European centres erupted in social turmoil in May 1968, when a variety of youth and labour grievances on the one hand, and over-zealous responses from the police on the other, produced the most intense series of mass protests since the Second World War. In Italy the tremors of May 1968 were felt long after they had subsided elsewhere. The Red Brigades and other violent organizations, for example, were to wage terror campaigns against politicians and business leaders. For the most part, however, the decade following 1968 was one in which extra parliamentary groups managed to procure important progressive reforms from an otherwise immobile state. This was the period when divorce was finally legalized, when the Charter of Workers' Rights was introduced, and when referenda could be held provided each was supported by 500 000 signatories. The 1970s saw the belated introduction of a range of welfare measures that were essential to this rapidly modernizing society, as was the long-delayed establishment of regional government. Indeed, it was the inadequacies and widespread distrust of the centralized system that put questions of devolution back on the political agenda.

The essential problem of the post-war Italian polity, however, of an unresponsive state on the one hand, and a rapidly modernizing society on the other, was not solved by the decade of social conflict and reform that followed 1968. The key source of *immobilismo*, of political and bureaucratic incapacity to respond effectively to pressing and everyday problems, was the persistence of corrupt and wasteful political practices. The establishment of the Republic did not preclude the revival of clientelism and the pursuit of private interests at the public's expense, as politics quickly reverted to something reminiscent of the Liberal era. The most distinguishing feature of Italian political system in the latter half of the twentieth century was the phenomenon of *partitocrazia*, which in its most negative and widely understood form referred to routine plunder and distribution of public resources and jobs among the mainstream political parties and their supporters. The electoral system of proportional representation determined that no party could govern in its own right, and of the two major parties, the DC and PCI, only the DC could forge a coalition from among the smaller parties and form government. In effect, the DC were able to remain in power until the political crisis of 1992, yet at the same time, DC dependence on coalitions meant that governments were unstable and short-lived. The creation and maintenance of government coalitions required Giolitti-style manoeuvres, in that forming government demanded a similar kind of political guile, a comparable volume of favour exchanges, and, inevitably, analogous forms of corruption. For example, one of Italy's longest-serving prime ministers, the PSI's Bettino Craxi, operated in the typical mode, distributing patronage, enjoying massive kickbacks and doing his best to deflect public scrutiny.

During the 1980s, however, the decade dominated by Craxi-led government coalitions, there were also signs that public tolerance of *partitocrazia* and other comfortable political arrangements was wearing thin. Although ranked among the world's economic elites in that period, Italy was also wilting under burgeoning public debt and declining public services, problems that were widely attributed to political corruption and *immobilismo*. By 1992 Italy's mainstream political parties were crumbling. This general crisis had a variety of sources, but among the more telling was the collapse of Communism in Europe, which not only resulted in mass desertion of the PCI but now allowed those who had grudgingly voted DC just to keep the Left out, to vote against it. Another major cause were the judicial investigations from February 1992, which finally managed to expose and deal with the incredibly high level of political corruption. By September 2600 people, including 325 parliamentarians, were under judicial investigation. Meanwhile, parallel inquiries into organized crime confirmed enduring links between Mafia bosses and the highest echelons of politics, including the long time DC leader and former Prime Minister, Giulio Andreotti.

In the wake of the collapse of the post-war party system, Italians were uncertain as to whether the country would experience real political change or whether Lampedusa's fatalistic dictum would continue to apply. Some new political parties were in fact old wine in new bottles, but Italians were determined to use their vote to protest against *partitocrazia*, *immobilismo* and the post-war system generally. Political conditions were also perfect for parties on the far Right to exploit public disquiet and push their own agendas. As happened during earlier crises of political legitimacy in modern Italian history, nationalism again reared its head as an anti-state ideology, but the similarities between the Liberal period and the age of *partitocrazia* were not strong. Fascistic movements lingered on the fringes of Italian politics long after the execution of Mussolini, and by the mid-1990s they were ready to re-enter the mainstream. The *Movimento italiana sociale*, led by Gianfranco Fini, which along with other right-wing groups had re-formed as the *Alleanza nazionale* (AN), grabbed 13.4 per cent of votes in the national elections of April 1994. The AN became a junior member of a coalition government dominated by Silvio Berlusconi's *Forza Italia*. Initially, members of the far Right, such as the Duce's own granddaughter, Alessandra Mussolini, celebrated the memory of Fascism and exposed a lingering nostalgia that was all too pervasive among sections of Italian society. Fini also made public his admiration for Mussolini, but Fini's AN gradually distanced itself from Fascism in its quest to appear more respectable and appealing to contemporary conservative voters. Thus Fini limited his admiration to the Mussolini of pre-1938, before he was tainted by anti-Semitism and the Nazi link. In retaliation to claims likening the AN to the party of the Austrian politician and Hitler sympathiser, Joerg Haider, Fini reaffirmed his party's declared commitment to democracy and its rejection of totalitarianism, racism and nationalism.[1] Clearly, nationalism was

---

[1] *Secolo d'Italia*, 3 February 2000.

understood here in its pejorative or 'Balkan' sense, as something associated with chauvinism, xenophobia and militancy.

The modest role played by nationalism in the revival of the far Right was indicative of its limited currency in Italian political culture. It also under-scored the British historian Eric Hobsbawm's claim that nationalism was no longer a major vector of historical change in Europe after the Second World War.[2] Nationalism was simply not the mobilizing force that it had once been. In Italy's case, Mussolini's Fascists had so discredited nationalism by 1945 that Italians remained suspicious of leaders who tried to appeal to patriotic sentimentality. The national interest nevertheless figured strongly in the rhetoric of the new parties. The name of the major liberal–conserva-tive party, *Forza Italia*, bespoke of a national revival, while the fight against *partitocrazia*, organized crime and other national embarrassments would require Italians to rally to the nation. The mainstream parties therefore did seek to tap into a basically civic form of Italian patriotism.

The progress of the *Lega Nord* also raised specifically 'national' questions. The *Alleanza nazionale* found their main support base was in the south, where resentment of Fascism was weakest, where the Resistance was irrele-vant, and, most importantly, where the break-up of the nation, as threatened by the *Lega Nord*, caused the most consternation. (More affronting, perhaps, was the barrage of racist slurs directed against southern Italians by *Lega* supporters.) The AN presented itself as the champion of national unity and integrity, which could take the form of waging border disputes with Slovenia and posing as the bulwark against northern secessionism.

The *Lega Nord* was formed in 1991 from a number of northern regional movements that included the *Lega Lombarda*, *Piemont Autonomista*, the *Liga Veneta*, the *Alleanza Toscana*, the *Lega Emilia-Romagnola* and the *Unione Ligure*. Led by Umberto Bossi, by the mid-1990s it had become the nation's fourth largest party. In 1996 the *Lega* stood unequivocally for secession. Its calls for an independent state in the north, to include all terri-tories north of Umbria and the Marches inclusive, have perhaps done most to direct the spotlight on the substance of Italian nationhood since unifica-tion. The party's unexpected electoral successes in the 1990s have been interpreted by many as a revelation of the shallowness or the fraudulence of *italianità*, and as an indication that the break-up of Italy is only a matter of time. Given the *Lega*'s large following – it remains the largest party in the far north, particularly in Friuli, the inland provinces of the Veneto, much of Lombardy and western parts of Piedmont – its threats to Italian unity are difficult to ignore. As with the *Alleanza nazionale*, the *Lega Nord*'s ascent has been rapid, as it too was part of the Berlusconi coalition that won the national elections of 1994. However, it is equally difficult to

---

[2] Eric Hobsbawm, *Nations and Nationalism since 1780*, 2nd edn (Cambridge, Cambridge University Press, 1992), p. 162.

measure the extent to which the *Lega* supporters have seriously entertained the break-up of Italy. Have its voters merely tolerated Bossi's threats to undo the Risorgimento and essentially used their vote as means of protesting against the state?

Certainly the autonomy leagues that emerged in the 1980s were not so much driven by the desire for independence as aimed against the political and bureaucratic system centred in Rome, and against high taxes. Their chief concern was ingrained state maladministration, especially *partitocrazia*, and their common assumption was that the prosperous and productive northern half of the country was subsidizing the corrupt and culturally backward southern half. In order to enhance its electoral prospects during the politically and economically turbulent early 1990s, the *Lega Nord* modified its stance on federalism. Bossi advocated the reformation of Italy into three autonomous regions, arguing further that political and economic devolution was in harmony with the broader quest to integrate Italy into the European Union. The party certainly did expand its electoral base in the north and secured substantial successes in national and local elections between 1992 and 1994, but then the momentum slowed. Originally an implacable critic of the state, the *Lega* was now part of the state. Although it proved to be a highly disruptive coalition partner, which in January 1995 succeeded in bringing down the Berlusconi government, the *Lega* languished in an identity crisis that was reflected in a drop in support. Its electoral stocks improved in the April 1996 elections, however, seemingly because it had revived its calls for secession. The *Lega* stood for an independent state called *Padania*, to be created through a peaceful parting of ways or 'velvet' revolution. But how many of the 10 per cent of Italians who cast their vote for the *Lega* actually voted for *Padania*? When on 15 September mass demonstrations were held along the Po Valley and in Venice to proclaim Padania, the event attracted less than 300 000 people, hardly amounting to a popular endorsement.[3]

The short history of the *Lega Nord* does not, therefore, provide a useful measure of the success or failure of Italian nation formation. Ordinary Italians have traditionally demonstrated a strong interest in national affairs: by European standards, Italy has enjoyed high voter turn-outs. But through most of the late twentieth century, Italians have voted with the assumption that their chances of effecting political change are remote. They have often listened to, and even joined, anti-state movements such as the *nazionalisti*, the Fascists and the *Lega Nord* to effect real change. Certainly the *Lega*'s electoral successes have been more than mere protest votes against the

---

[3] Ilvo Diamanti, 'The Lega Nord: From Federalism to Secession', in Roberto Alimonte and David Nelken (eds), *Italian Politics: The Centre–Left in Power* (Boulder, CO, Westview, 1997), p. 78.

system, but thus far it seems likely that *Padania* is an eccentricity or its advocacy is a tactical manoeuvre that supporters are prepared to tolerate so long as it promotes the *Lega*'s more substantive issues.

Italy as a nation

In spite of *partitocrazia, tangentopoli* ('kick-back city'), low public esteem for state institutions and personnel, the northern secessionist phenomenon and the limited appeal of 'flag-waving', jingoist patriotic culture, there are good reasons for thinking of Italy as a real nation. It is pointless to specu-late on how many citizens feel self-consciously 'Italian' and how much importance is ascribed by each individual to their Italian-ness as opposed to their other identities. Particularist, as opposed to national, loyalties appear to retain greater emotional weight among Italians than they do among many other European nations, yet for all the talk of regional devolution and for all the enthusiasm for European integration, the political crisis of the 1990s revealed that Italians do recognize their nation as the essential polit-ical unit. This commonplace disposition was confirmed by the declining popularity of federalism and greater interest shown in 'national' solutions. (The very name Forza Italia – Come On, or Go Italy – was meant to be a rallying cry for a national revival.) There is also ample evidence that *ital-ianità* has popular cache, that it is not just communities in the diaspora that value a specifically Italian cultural identity. For while there are numerous Italies, there is also a synthesized, negotiated and ever-changing national culture that is recognized as being distinctively 'Italian' and not say French, Yugoslav or anything else. Scholars (including those dealing with Italy) are only beginning to unravel the many ways in which the nation is collectively imagined, its cultural characteristics and binary contrasts, the manner in which it is produced and reproduced, and the agencies that inform its permutations. Suffice it to say here that there are more than enough indi-cations to suggest that Italy is a nation, sufficiently so at least to counter prognostications of its likely demise.

The Italian nation's survival after the collapse of the post-war political system in the early 1990s can be attributed to stable economic foundations that were laid in the 1950s, and which are likely to sustain Italy long into the twenty-first century. The revival of capitalism in Western Europe after the Second World War and the social distribution of national wealth through the welfare state, allowed for the consolidation and preservation of social stability and basic liberal democratic institutions. But Italian society was largely denied the benefits of welfare-state capitalism that were being enjoyed among its northern and north-western neighbours during the 1950s and 1960s, because in Italy's case the economic boom had initially been based on the suppression of wages and a lack of improvement in workers' conditions. But Italy's economic 'miracle' did succeed in fundamentally modernizing its social structure and cultural mores, and significant improvements in living standards did belatedly follow. Italy's transformation into one of the wealthiest national communities by the 1980s was inevitably accompanied by a more positive international image, in which elegance and style replaced poverty and backwardness. And the substantial increase in public and private wealth also provided more conducive conditions for the making of Italians.

Italy followed the general pattern among rapidly modernizing societies in using education, that most important mechanism for 'nationalizing' the citizenry, more extensively and effectively than in earlier times. National governments took a keener interest in the quality and outcomes of education after the Second World War, particularly at the primary and secondary level. Vastly increased and sustained public investment saw to great improvements in teacher training and schooling facilities. In 1962 schooling became compulsory for Italian children up to the age of fourteen, and retention rates at all schooling levels conformed to general European patterns.

The growth of mass literacy and the fluency in Italian, as well as rising living standards, also meant that ordinary Italians could finally participate in, or at least feel part of, national cultural experiences through such media as cinema, television, magazines or radio. Italians in the post-war years were not great consumers of newspapers, mainly because journalists for a long time persisted with a rather stodgy style that was designed to appeal to a literary rather than a mass readership. However, the reading public did subscribe heavily to publications that were more accessible and gave more emphasis to entertainment, such as national sports magazines (e.g. *Il Corriere dello Sport* and *La Gazzetta dello Sport*), weekly lifetsyle magazines and comics. Initially it was the cinema that served as the chief source of mass entertainment. Audiences grew from 417 million in 1946 to 819 million in 1955, sinking back to 632 million by 1966, suggesting that for most people cinema-going had become a special event rather than a regular pastime. Audiences were initially saturated with American films dubbed over in Italian, but Italian films managed to claw back a respectable share of the market by the early 1960s. As film audiences began to drop off, the cinema was replaced as a purveyor of cultural ideas by television. Between 1954 and 1966, the number of television licenses issued increased from 90 000 to 6.85 million, and by the 1970s the television had become a normal household item. Only in the case of television did government seek to manufacture opinion in the fashion of Mussolini. Until television ownership was deregulated in 1975, it was a government monopoly, which also meant it was easily censored. The programming for the national broadcaster RAI (*Radio Audizione Italiana*) placed much emphasis on education and high culture, thus it offered documentaries, school programmes and serialized Italian novels. A second national station, RAI-2 was established in 1961 to break the DC monopoly, but the deregulation of ownership in 1975 meant that television decreased its commitment to educating, and began to pander to, or manufacture, mass tastes in popular culture.

Unexceptional as Italy's post-war transformation might seem in its western European context, it does appear revolutionary in the light of the nation's history since unification. At the beginning of this period most Italians still lived in traditional village communities, a world that was deeply Catholic and where *italianità* hardly resonated at all. By 1970 Italy had become a largely urban society, dominated by large industrial and service sectors, in which the rhythms of everyday life bore the hallmarks of modernity: industrial discipline, secularism and consumerism. The economic miracle induced a social revolution, particularly after 1958 when an export-driven economic boom fostered a massive demographic shift from rural regions and the Mezzogiorno to the cities, particularly those of the industrial north-west. Between 1955 and 1971, the peasantry, hitherto the largest section of the population, began to vanish. Over 9 million Italians moved out of their respective localities, their own particular 'Italies', into much more culturally integrated urban spaces. Most cities across the country experienced a mass influx of 'immigrants', though Rome and the cities of the industrial triangle received the most substantial numbers. At the height of the economic 'miracolo' (1958–62), the annual number of immigrants streaming into Milan was 55 860, 59 856, 66 930, 87 000 and 105 448.

The cultural implications of this demographic revolution are obvious. Immigrants from given regions tended to settle in the same neighbourhoods, but the necessity of interacting socially in the workplace and in the wider public sphere forced most immigrants to make significant cultural adjustments. More than ever, standard Italian became a necessity in urban environments that now contained a whole range of Italian peoples. Original inhabitants of industrial cities and towns receiving large numbers of immigrants were themselves adapting to their changing environment, particularly parents within smaller communities, who were finding it increasingly difficult to justify teaching the local dialect to their children. Integration inevitably entailed some cultural attrition, though immigrants faced their challenges as family units and found much emotional sustenance in their cultural legacies. Thus a poll conducted in 1974 concluded that something like three-quarters of Italians continued to speak dialect for everyday purposes, and 23 per cent spoke dialect exclusively. Another poll in 1991 showed that those speaking exclusively in Italian had only risen to 35 per cent. At the same time, the Italian language today has been influenced by the many cultures which have adopted it, thus there are many different working versions of spoken Italian, a situation that enrages the purists, who occasionally warn of the demise of the language. On the contrary, the mere existence of these new vernaculars is indicative of the value of the dominant language in most people's lives.

In more recent times, migration movements have given salience to national identity in another, albeit more negative, way. Although a significant economic power nowadays, Italy is also positioned on the frontier between Europe and the developing world, from which it has received waves of legal and illegal migrants, as well as refugees. Most have come from parts of the northern half of Africa, the Middle East, South Asia, Latin America and East Asia. Eastern Europeans, especially Albanians, have also streamed to Italy in search of work and a better life. As a country that now receives, rather than exports, vast numbers of people, who inevitably demand a share of employment opportunities and welfare services, Italy also has a racial problem. With so many cultural groups within the country, locals have tended to resort to familiar blanket categories such as *marocchini* (Morrocans) and *zingari* (gypsies), which are normally meant to be insulting, while right-wing politicians such as Bossi and Fini have played on popular fears of an uncontrolled influx of foreigners overrunning the country. In cultural terms, xenophobia produces boundaries that bar unwanted foreigners through the making or affirmation of an exclusive conception of national identity. Much as constructions of the backward southerner were employed after unification to define, by contrast, the ideal modern Italian, so now the presence of peoples from the developing world draws attention to the Italian (and equally European) self or 'us' as opposed to the racially distinctive other, or 'them'.

Definitions of national identity and culture have been the focus of constant debate and revision in Italy every since Fascism's attempt to enforce its own eccentrically militant and exclusionary vision. In the early post-war years, for example, when Italy was flooded by American commodities, fashions and ideas, groups contending for moral leadership within Italian society, such as the Catholic Church or the PCI, were galvanized into offering their own visions of *italianità*. Representations of women in American film and advertising, for instance, motivated local attempts to retaliate with 'Italian' ideals of feminine beauty. *Italianità* was, and continues to be, subtly deliberated upon and negotiated within the various branches of the arts, especially in literature. Historiography has always afforded blunter discussion. Italy is no different to other nation-states in having sought to fashion useful national pasts in order to underscore desired national identities, and in finding such identities constantly being questioned, revised and overhauled through historical debate. During the early 1990s the end of the 'First Republic' saw intellectuals and journalists focus a great deal of attention on the extent to which the legacies of Fascism and the Resistance had contributed to the present political crisis. At the heart of these discussions was the substance of Italian nationhood, whether Italians were sufficiently dedicated to their nation, and the extent to which the partitocratic 'First Republic' had failed to make Italians. Some bemoaned the abolition of the Savoyard monarchy and traditional nationalist culture, and its replacement by a divisive anti-Fascist nationalism that was too exclusionary. Much discussion centred on why Italians are not sufficiently nationalized in comparison with other Europeans, and what kind of nationalism or patriotism Italians were thought to have been missing.

The apparent lack of patriotism in Italian society troubled many prominent intellectuals, yet it was condition in keeping with the broader cultural European trends. That Italians tend to wear their nationalism very lightly can nowadays be viewed as a progressive trait. Indeed, among the comparatively stable and prosperous nations of Western Europe after the Second World War, militant nationalism of the kind desired by some Italian critics can now only be found at Europe's less affluent margins, e.g. in Greece or Spain, or within the marginal groups in western European political scene. Significantly, Europeans nowadays associate the term nationalism with political extremism and backwardness – with adolescent-filled football stadiums, illegal neo-Nazi organizations, or the blood-soaked fields of *fin-de-siècle* Bosnia and Kosovo. 'Ethno-nationalism', with its emphasis on blood-ties, ancient hatreds and dubious historic claims, is normally ascribed to places deemed insufficiently European, such as the Balkans and the former Soviet Union. At the same time, western Europeans tend to assume that they have retained a civilized, rational and temperate form of constitutional patriotism which, unlike nationalism, denotes identification with institutions and ideals rather than ethnicity and blood-ties. However dubious these assumptions might be, the term 'nationalism' is nowadays a stigma, an embarrassing legacy from a violent, forgettable past.

Nationalism nevertheless continues to be practised in the West. There are the formally controlled and modest displays of nationalist sentiment on designated holidays, when important historic moments in the nation's history (e.g. American Independence Day, Bastille Day) are annually celebrated, or special events such as the successful Risorgimento centenary celebrations between 1959 and 1961. Acceptable also is the exuberance often expressed in the aftermath of a sporting triumph – one of the unforgettable sights of the World Cup victory in 1982 was the animated delight of Italy's unusually popular octogenarian president, Sandro Pertini. More importantly, citizens are also reminded of their nationality on a daily basis. In Italy, as elsewhere, people are exposed to rarely noticed inscriptions on packaging (*Prodotto in Italia*), to sightings of quintessentially Italian products such as Fiat or Alfa Romeo automobiles, to newspaper stories that refer to matters that hold national implications, or to television weather services that describe national climatic conditions. In a whole series of unremarkable ways, citizens experience nationhood as an intrinsic part of their everyday lives. In an age of mass communications and consumer culture, nationhood is constantly 'flagged' while people carry on with their mundane habits, which in turn ensures that the nation remains entrenched in mass consciousness.[4] Italy shares with other Western nations a kind of banal nationalism, whereby nationhood is affirmed constantly by national referents that at the same time do not demand self-conscious reflection. So much of what is received through television, newspapers, streetscape signs, political rhetoric and commercial advertising implies the existence and the importance of the national culture, national community or the national interest.

At the beginning of the twenty-first century, the Italian nation is in better shape than ever before. For most observers, however, the outlook for Italy and every other nation is gloomy, for along with the state, it already appears at the mercy of global forces. Where once nations appeared as the building blocks of global capital, nowadays the destinies of national communities are shaped by decisions taken by major corporations, by international organizations such as the IMF, NATO and the EU, or by the flow of international finance. Whereas the revival of capitalism was worked out from within nation-states after the Second World War, capitalism today insists on functioning without concern for the nation-state or the national interest. Indeed, the extent to which nation-states will be able to claim sovereignty in the future is something much debated. Nevertheless there is good reason to think the nation will actually assume growing importance in the face of so-called globalization, especially as international capital is not entirely autonomous and international organizations are linked to major nation-states, notably in Western Europe and the United States. In these circumstances, in which globalization deepens inequalities within and between nation-states, national identity continues to have a powerful and even growing resonance among many peoples. Given that market forces ride roughshod over social welfare and national cultures, the nation-state, with its institutional structures, cultural capital, and political legitimacy, will probably constitute the principal unit of resistance. Although Italy was only really 'made' within the last fifty years, it probably now has the where-withal to survive in this new global environment.

---

[4] Michael Billig, *Banal Nationalism* (London, Sage, 1995).

Selected bibliography

The selection is restricted to English language publications.

On the nation, nationalism and the state

Anderson, Benedict, *Imagined Communities: Reflections on the Origin and Spread of Nationalism*, 2nd edition (London, Verso, 1991)

Billig, Michael, *Banal Nationalism* (London, Sage, 1995)

Calhoun, Craig, *Nationalism* (Buckingham, Open University Press, 1997)

Creveld, Martin van, *The Rise and Decline of the State* (Cambridge, Cambridge University Press, 1999)

Davis, John A., 'Remapping Italy's Path to the Twentieth Century', *Journal of Modern History*, 66 (1994)

Eley, Geoff, 'Nations, Publics, and Political Cultures: Placing Habermas in the Nineteenth Century', in C. Calhoun, ed., *Habermas and the Public Sphere* (Cambridge, MA, MIT Press, 1996)

Eley, Geoff and Suny, Ronald, eds, *Becoming National: A Reader* (New York, Oxford University Press, 1996)

Gellner, Ernest, *Nations and Nationalism* (Oxford, Blackwell, 1983)

Hobsbawm, Eric, *Nations and Nationalism since 1780: Programme, Myth, Reality* (Cambridge, Cambridge University Press, 1992)

Hroch, Miroslav, *Social Preconditions of National Revival in Europe: A Comparative Analysis of the Social Composition of Patriotic Groups among the Smaller European Nations* (Cambridge, Cambridge University Press, 1985)

Hroch, Miroslav, 'From National Movement to Fully-formed Nation', *New Left Review*, 198 (1993)

Mosse, George L., *The Nationalization of the Masses: Political Symbolism and Mass Movements in Germany from the Napoleonic Wars through the Third Reich* (Ithaca, NY, Cornell University Press, 1975)

Spruyt, Hendrik, *The Sovereign State and its Competitors* (Princeton, NJ, Princeton University Press, 1994)

Weber, Eugen, *Peasants into Frenchmen: The Modernization of Rural France, 1870–1914* (Stanford, CA, Stanford University Press, 1976)

On Italian history: General

Absalom, Roger, *Italy since 1800: A Nation in the Balance?* (London, Longman, 1995)

Bosworth, R.J.B., *Italy and the Wider World, 1860–1960* (London and New York, Routledge, 1996)

Clark, Martin, *Modern Italy, 1871–1995*, 2nd edition (London, Longman,1996)

Cunsolo, Ronald, *Italian Nationalism* (Malabar, FL, R.E. Krieger, 1990)

Duggan, Christopher, *A Concise History of Italy* (Cambridge, Cambridge University Press, 1994)

Forgacs, David, *Italian Culture in the Industrial Era, 1880–1980* (Manchester, Manchester University Press, 1990)

Gabaccia, Donna R., *Italy's Many Diasporas* (London, UCL Press, 2000)

Levy, Carl, ed., *Italian Regionalism: History, Identity and Politics* (Oxford, Berg, 1996).

Woolf, Stuart, *A History of Italy, 1700–1860: The Social Constraints of Political Change* (London, Methuen, 1979)

Italy, 1795–1815

Furet, F. and Ozouf, M. eds, *The French Revolution and the Creation of Modern Political Culture*, Vol. III: *The Transformation of Culture, 1789–1848* (Oxford, Pergamon, 1989)

Broers, Michael, 'Italy and the Modern State: The Experience of Napoleonic Rule', in F. Furet and M. Ozouf, eds, *The French Revolution and the Creation of Modern Political Culture*, Vol. III: *The Transformation of Culture, 1789–1848* (Oxford, Pergamon, 1989)

Broers, Michael, 'Revolution and Risorgimento: The Heritage of the French Revolution in Nineteenth-Century Italy', in H.T. Mason and W. Doyle, eds, *The Impact of the French Revolution on European Consciousness* (Gloucester, Sutton, 1989)

Broers, Michael, *Europe after Napoleon: Revolution, Reaction and Romanticism, 1814–1848* (Manchester, Manchester University Press, 1996)

Broers, Michael, 'The Police and the *Padroni*: Italian *Notabili*, French Gendarmes and the Origins of the Centralized State in Napoleonic Italy', *European History Quarterly*, 26 (1996)

Grab, Alexander, 'Army, State and Society: Conscription and Desertion in Napoleonic Italy (1802–1814)', *Journal of Modern History*, 67 (1995)

Grab, Alexander, 'State Power, Brigandage and Rural Resistance in Napoleonic Italy', *European History Quarterly*, 25 (1995)

Meriggi, Marco, 'Italy', in Otto Dann and John Dinwiddy, eds, *Nationalism in the Age of the French Revolution* (London, Hambledon, 1988)

Noether, Emiliana Pasca, *Seeds of Italian Nationalism, 1700–1815* (New York, AMS, 1951)

Woolf, Stuart, *A History of Italy, 1700–1860: The Social Constraints of Political Change* (London, Methuen, 1979)

Risorgimento Italy

Clark, Martin, *The Italian Risorgimento* (London, Longman, 1998)

Davis, John A., *Conflict and Control: Law and Order in Nineteenth-Century Italy* (London, Macmillan, 1988)

Davis, John A. and Ginsborg, Paul, eds, *Society and Politics in the Age of Risorgimento: Essays in Honour of Denis Mack Smith* (Cambridge, Cambridge University Press, 1991)

Haddock, Bruce, 'Political Union without Social Revolution: Vincenzo Gioberti's *Primato*', *The Historical Journal*, 41, (1998)

Hearder, Harry, *Italy in the Age of Risorgimento, 1790–1870* (London, Longman, 1983)

Hughes, Steven C., *Crime, Disorder, and the Risorgimento: The Politics of Policing in Bologna* (Cambridge, Cambridge University Press, 1994)

Grew, Raymond, *A Sterner Plan for Italian Unity: The Italian National Society in the Risorgimento* (Princeton, NJ, Princeton University Press, 1963)

Grew, Raymond, 'The Paradoxes of Italy's Nineteenth-Century Political Culture', in Isser Woloch, ed., *Revolution and the Meanings of Freedom in the Nineteenth Century* (Stanford, CA, Stanford University Press, 1996)

Lyttelton, Adrian, 'The National Question in Italy', in Mikulás Teich and Roy Porter, eds, *The National Question in Europe in Historical Context* (Cambridge , Cambridge University Press, 1993)

Mack Smith, Denis, *Mazzini* (New Haven, CT, Yale University Press, 1994)

Mack Smith, Denis, *Cavour* (New York, Knopf, 1985)

Mack Smith, Denis, *Victor Emmanuel, Cavour and the Risorgimento* (London, Oxford University Press, 1971)

Mack Smith, Denis, ed., *The Making of Italy, 1796–1870* (New York, Harper & Row, 1968)

Patriarca, Silvana, *Numbers and Nationhood: Writing Statistics in Nineteenth-Century Italy* (Cambridge, Cambridge University Press, 1996)

Riall, Lucy, *The Italian Risorgimento* (London, Routledge, 1994)

Riall, Lucy, 'Liberal Policy and the Control of Public Order in Western Sicily 1860–1862', *The Historical Journal*, 35 (1992)

Riall, Lucy, 'Elite Resistance to State Formation: The Case of Italy', in M. Fulbrook, ed., *National Histories and European History* (London, UCL Press, 1993)

Schneider, Jane, ed., *Italy's Southern Question: Orientalism in One Country* (Oxford, Berg, 1998)

Thom, Martin, 'Unity and Confederation in the Italian Risorgimento: The Case of Carlo Cattaneo', in S. Berger, M. Donovan and K. Passmore, eds, *Writing National Histories: Western Europe since 1800* (London and New York, Routledge, 1999)

Woolf, Stuart, *A History of Italy, 1700–1860: The Social Constraints of Political Change* (London, Methuen, 1979)

Liberal Italy

Adamson, Walter, 'The Language of Opposition in Early Twentieth-Century Italy: Rhetorical Continuities between Prewar Florentine Avant-gardism and Mussolini's Fascism', *Journal of Modern History*, 64 (1992)

Bellamy, Richard, *Modern Italian Social Theory* (Cambridge, Polity, 1987)

Bosworth, R.J.B., *Italy, the Least of the Great Powers: Italian Foreign Policy before the First World War* (Cambridge, Cambridge University Press, 1979)

Bosworth, R.J.B., 'The *Touring Club Italiano* and the Nationalisation of the Italian Bourgeoisie', *European History Quarterly*, 27 (1997)

Corner, Paul and Procacci, Giovanna, 'The Italian Experience of "Total" Mobilization, 1915–1920', in John Horne, ed., *State, Society and Mobilization in Europe during the First World War* (Cambridge, Cambridge University Press, 1997)

Davis, John A., 'Socialism and the Working Classes of Italy before 1914', in Dick Geary, ed., *Labour and Socialist Movements in Europe before 1914* (Oxford, Berg, 1989)

De Grand, Alexander, *The Italian Nationalist Association and the Rise of Fascism in Italy* (Lincoln, NE, University of Nebraska Press, 1978)

Dickie, John, 'A World at War: The Italian Army and Brigandage, 1860–1870', *History Workshop Journal*, 33 (1992)

Dickie, John, 'La macchina da scrivere: The Victor Emmanuel monument in Rome and Italian nationalism', *The Italianist*, 14 (1994)

Drake, Richard, *Byzantium and Rome: The Politics of Nostalgia in Umbertian Italy, 1878–1900* (Chapel Hill, NC, University of North Carolina Press, 1980)

Duggan, Christopher, 'Francesco Crispi, "Political Education" and the Problem of Italian National Consciousness, 1860–1896', *Journal of Modern Italian Studies*, 2 (1997)

Fava, Andrea, 'War, "National Education" and the Italian Primary School, 1915–1918', in John Horne, ed., *State, Society and Mobilization in Europe during the First World War* (Cambridge, Cambridge University Press, 1997)

Gooch, John, 'Nationalism and the Italian Army, 1850–1914', in C. Bjorn, A. Grant and K. J. Stringer, eds, *Nations, Nationalism and Patriotism in the European Past* (Copenhagen, Academic Press, 1994)

Grew, Raymond, 'Catholicism and *Risorgimento*', in Frank J. Coppa, ed., *Studies in Modern Italian History: From Risorgimento to the Republic* (New York, Peter Lang, 1986).

Grew, Raymond, 'The Paradoxes of Italy's Nineteenth-Century Political Culture', in Isser Woloch, ed., *Revolution and the Meanings of Freedom in the Nineteenth Century* (Stanford, CA, Stanford University Press, 1996)

Lumley, Robert and Morris, Jonathan, eds, *The New History of the Italian South: The Mezzogiorno Revisited* (Exeter, University of Exeter Press, 1997)

Malatesta, Maria, ed., *Society and the Professions in Italy, 1860–1914* (Cambridge, Cambridge University Press, 1995)

Meriggi, Marco, 'The Italian Borghesia', in J. Kocka and A. Mitchell, eds, *Bourgeois Society in Nineteenth Century Europe* (Oxford, Berg, 1993)

Moretti, Mauro, 'The Search for "National" History: Italian Historiographical Trends Following Unification', in S. Berger, M. Donovan and K. Passmore, eds, *Writing National Histories: Western Europe since 1800* (London and New York, Routledge, 1999)

Patriarca, Silvana, *Numbers and Nationhood: Writing Statistics in Nineteenth-Century Italy* (Cambridge, Cambridge University Press, 1996)

Pick, Daniel, *Faces of Degeneration: A European Disorder, c. 1848–c.1918* (Cambridge, Cambridge University Press, 1989)

Procacci, Giovanna, 'A "Latecomer" in War: The Case of Italy', in F. Coetzee and M. Shevin-Coetzee, eds, *Authority, Identity and the Social History of the Great War* (Providence, RI, Berghahn, 1995)

Whittam, John, *The Politics of the Italian Army, 1861–1918* (London, Croom Helm, 1977)

Fascist Italy

Berezin, Mabel, *Making the Fascist Self: The Political Culture of Interwar Italy* (Ithaca, NY, Cornell University Press, 1997)

Berezin, Mabel, 'Political Belonging: Emotion, Nation, and Identity in Fascist Italy', in George Steinmetz, ed., *State/Culture: State-Formation after the Cultural Turn* (Ithaca, NY, Cornell University Press, 1999)

Bosworth, R.J.B., *Explaining Auschwitz and Hiroshima: History Writing and the Second World War, 1945–1990* (London and New York, Routledge, 1993)

Bosworth, R.J.B., 'Tourist Planning in Fascist Italy and the Limits of Totalitarian Culture', *Contemporary European History*, 6 (1997)

Bosworth, R.J.B., *The Italian Dictatorship: Problems and Perspectives in the Interpretation on Mussolini and Fascism* (London, Arnold, 1998)

Grazia, Victoria De, *The Culture of Consent: Mass Organisation of Leisure in Fascist Italy* (Cambridge, Cambridge University Press, 1981)

Grazia, Victoria De, *How Fascism Ruled Women: Italy, 1922–1945* (Berkeley, CA, University of California Press, 1992)

Falasca-Zamponi, Simonetta, *Fascist Spectacle: The Aesthetics of Power in Mussolini's Italy* (Berkeley, CA, University of California Press, 1997)

Gentile, Emilio, 'Fascism as Political Religion', *Journal of Contemporary History*, 25 (1990)

Gentile, Emilio, *The Sacralization of Politics in Fascist Italy* (Cambridge, MA, Harvard University Press, 1996)

Ghirardo, Diane, '*Città fascista*: Surveillance and Spectacle', *Journal of Contemporary History*, 31 (1996)

Koon, Tracey, *Believe, Obey, Fight: Political Socialization of Youth in Fascist Italy, 1922–1943* (Chapel Hill, NC, University of North Carolina Press, 1985)

Stone, Marla, 'Staging Fascism: The Exhibition of the Fascist Revolution', *Journal of Contemporary History*, 28 (1993)

Stone, Marla, 'A Flexible Rome: Fascism and the Cult of *romanità*', in Catherine Edwards, ed., *Roman Presences: Receptions of Rome in European Culture, 1789–1945* (Cambridge, Cambridge University Press, 1999)

Visser, Romke, 'Fascist Doctrine and the Cult of *romanità*', *Journal of Contemporary History*, 27 (1992)

Willson, Perry R., *The Clockwork Factory: Women and Work in Fascist Italy* (Oxford, Oxford University Press, 1993)

Italy after Fascism

Allen, Beverly and Russo, Mary, eds, *Revisioning Italy: National Identity and Global Culture* (Minneapolis, University of Minnesota Press, 1997)

Dogliani, Patrizia, 'Constructing Memory and Anti-Memory: The Monumental Representation of Fascism and its Denial in Republican Italy', in R.J.B. Bosworth and P. Dogliani, eds, *Italian Fascism: History, Memory and Representation* (London, Macmillan, 1999)

Forgacs, David, *Italian Culture in the Industrial Era, 1880–1980* (Manchester, Manchester University Press, 1990)

Ginsborg, Paul, *A History of Contemporary Italy: Society and Politics, 1943–1988* (London, Penguin, 1990)

Gundle, Stephen, 'Feminine Beauty, National Identity and Political Conflict in Postwar Italy, 1945–1954', *Contemporary European History*, 8 (1999)

Gundle, Stephen and Parker, Simon, eds, *The New Italian Republic: From the Fall of the Berlin Wall to Berlusconi* (London and New York, Routledge, 1996)

Levy, Carl, 'From Fascism to "Post-Fascists": Italian Roads to Modernity', in Richard Bessel, ed., *Fascist Italy and Nazi Germany: Comparisons and Contrasts* (Cambridge, Cambridge University Press, 1996)

Levy, Carl, 'Historians of the First Republic', in S. Berger, M. Donovan and K. Passmore, (eds), *Writing National Histories: Western Europe since 1800* (London and New York, Routledge, 1999)

Lumley, Robert, *States of Emergency: Cultures of Revolt in Italy, 1968 to 1978* (London, Verso, 1990)

Forgacs, David and Lumley, Robert, eds, *Italian Popular Culture: An Introduction* (New York, Oxford University Press, 1996)

Neri Serneri, Simone, 'A Past to be Thrown Away? Politics and History in the Italian Resistance', *Contemporary European History*, 4 (1995)

Index